The Integrity of the Servant Leader

The impact of the global financial crisis is still being felt today and the deeply unethical behaviour of the top level leaders at those economic and financial organisations, that were at the heart of the crisis, has served to highlight the importance of integrity, and in particular the need for servant leadership, if we are to avoid another major catastrophe in the management of both commercial and non-profit organisations. Servant leadership has many features in common with transformational leadership but is primarily focused on caring about employees and their personal development.

Ethical behaviour is one of the most important components of successful leadership yet this remains insufficiently investigated, especially from an interdisciplinary perspective. With the help of theory, empirical analysis and the relevant methodological apparatus, the authors fill the gap in the analysis of integrity and its impact on leadership and locate the significant factors which affect integrity in general.

They develop and assess the forces that impact the servant leadership style, as well as the ability to engender trust. As a starting point they make two assumptions: an important element in leading is the ethical dimension of leadership and the ratio of factors that affect leading and the servant leadership style is complex, but the integrity of leaders is the most important among them.

The authors examine four integrated scientific areas: ethics and business ethics, human resource management and psychology and focus on the analysis of the process of leadership and the factors within that process of leading that influence its success and its ethical dimension.

Robert Šumi, PhD, is head of the Research and Social Skills Centre in the Slovenian Police.

Dana Mesner-Andolšek, PhD, is Professor of Sociology at the Faculty of Social Sciences, as well as a researcher at the Institute of Social Sciences, University of Ljubljana (Slovenia).

The Integrity of the
Servant Leader

**Robert Šumi and
Dana Mesner-Andolšek**

Routledge
Taylor & Francis Group

LONDON AND NEW YORK

First published 2017
by Routledge

2 Park Square, Milton Park, Abingdon, Oxfordshire OX14 4RN
52 Vanderbilt Avenue, New York, NY 10017

Routledge is an imprint of the Taylor & Francis Group, an informa business

First issued in paperback 2020

British Library Cataloguing in Publication Data
A catalogue record for this book is available from the British Library

Library of Congress Cataloging in Publication Data
A catalog record for this book has been requested

ISBN: 978-1-138-21292-3 (hbk)
ISBN: 978-0-367-59606-4 (pbk)

Typeset in Times New Roman
by Sunrise Setting Ltd., Brixham, UK

Contents

Figures

5.2	The differences in mean values of the variables in the questionnaire on leader integrity in for-profit organisations and the non-profit organisation	144
5.3	Factor analysis of the variables in the questionnaire on integrity	147
5.4	Factors affecting the first dimension of servant leadership (conceptual skills)	148
5.5	Factors affecting the second dimension of servant leadership (empowerment)	149
5.6	Factors affecting the third dimension of servant leadership (helping employees with personal growth)	150
5.7	Factors affecting the fourth dimension of servant leadership (putting the employees first)	151
5.8	Factors affecting the fifth dimension of servant leadership (on ethical behaviour and conduct)	152
5.9	Factors affecting the sixth dimension of servant leadership (emotional support)	153
5.10	Factors affecting the seventh dimension of servant leadership (caring for the community)	155
5.11	Factors affecting the integrity of the leader	156
5.12	The influence of integrity on the servant leadership style: the final model	168

Tables

Preface

Vida and Albina have by their own example inspired both authors to write the essential content of this book, which to this day remains our mission and guiding light in our work environment. The writing of this book and the work involved has been both a challenging and pleasurable task. We would like to express our deepest gratitude to both our families for helping us cope and overcome difficult moments. The first author thanks Tina for caring for the family and her steadfast support, as well as Marija, Lea and other family members for lending their support. The lead author especially thanks Črt and Aljaž for their selfless assistance, and Stane for his infinite emotional support and advice.

We would also like to thank everyone who has helped us with our research and exploration of philosophical premises, and who helped us through long and short conversations to shed light on and to understand the studied concepts.

Special thanks also goes to our co-mentor Branko, who consulted us on designing the book, as well as to Heather for proofreading, Murray for copy-editing and Tom for final editing.

We dedicate this book to daughters Ema and Lana, and sons Črt and Aljaž, and wish that the book's fundamental message will also be their guiding light in life.

Abbreviations

B	Beta coefficient
BI	The BI measurement instrument (behavioural integrity)
(Crombach α)	Coefficient of internal consistency
CRS	Corporate social responsibility
ESLS	Executive servant leadership scale
F	F statistics
GLOBE	Global leadership and organisational behaviour effectiveness
LMX	Leader member exchange
M	Mean value
p	Level of significance
PLIS	The PLIS questionnaire (perceived leader integrity scale)
r	Correlation coefficient
R^2	R square
SD	Standard deviation
SLBS	Servant leadership behaviour scale
SLM	Servant leadership measure
SLS	Servant leadership survey
SPSS	Statistical package for the social sciences

Introduction

These days, much attention is paid to ethics, morality, virtues and the desired management of society and, as shown by Greenleaf (1998), we live in a period when the above mentioned are once again being intensively discussed. Sadly, it appears that this is mostly happening through the prism of negative consequences, which occur due to the gap between the declarative and actual actions and behaviours of the subjects involved. Musek (1993: 124) discussed this matter 20 years ago and realised that it can be rightly said that we are living in a period of a crisis of values, which he considers as 'value emptiness, value confusion (related to value conflicts), particularly the inconsistency between the existing values on the one hand and actual behaviour on the other'. This finding is certainly not merely a reflection of today's society, it was already present 'at the death of Socrates, when Plato finally saw, that he lives in a world where values are falling apart' (Kocijančič 2002: 519). This means that the debate on the crisis of values is constant; here we also agree with Musek (1993), when, on one side, he rejected the idea that humanity has not advanced morally while, on the other side, the problem lies with the fact that people only rarely behave in accordance with the standards and values that we defend. In our estimate, this only confirms the fact that moral behaviour, conduct and leadership are not easy jobs while being simultaneously of the utmost importance; proof of this is the fact that in the area of today's Europe, Socrates, Plato, Aristotle and others have already discussed the topic. Hence the development of virtue ethics stretches back to antiquity, while today we can observe that virtue ethics is a subject of research by various authors once more (Bass and Steidlmeier 1999, Carroll and Buchholtz 2000, Koehn 2005b, Northouse 2010). In a narrow sense, and in the context of business ethics, virtue ethics are focused on the moral character, conduct and virtues of leaders. The latter include the *personal integrity of leaders*, which is one of the two cornerstones of the study and research in our task. Its important role in managing is stressed by different theories of management (Bass 1990, Kirkpatrick and Locke 1991, Bass and Steidlmeier 1999, Burns 2010) as well as empirical findings (Craig and Gustafson 1998, Parry and Proctor-Thomson 2002, Palanski and Yammarino 2007, 2011). The various authors and researchers emphasise the need for further study and research on the impact of integrity on management (Craig and Gustafson 1998, Palanski and Yammarino 2007, 2009, Carroll 2009, Northouse 2010).

For the other cornerstone of our research, we chose *servant leadership*, which falls within the framework of ethical leadership (Schermerhorn et al. 2008, Reed et al. 2011, Dion 2012). Whetstone (2001) noted that of all the approaches to leadership, the most balanced is the tripartite approach to leadership based on ethical principles and virtues and a deontological and teleological principle. Like virtue ethics and personal integrity, the start of servant leadership dates back to antiquity (Nandram and Vos 2010, Trompenaars and Voerman 2009, Searle and Barbuto 2011). The modern model of servant leadership was designed in the 1970s by Robert Greenleaf, although the boom period of its theoretical studies (Bass 1997, Covey 2002b, Russell and Stone 2002) and empirical research (Ehrhart 2004, Barbuto and Wheeler 2006, Liden et al. 2008) has unfolded in our millennium.

In addition, both personal integrity and servant leadership are relevant in terms of the social responsibility of organisations and the social responsibility of leaders (Greenleaf 2002a, Carroll 2009, Burns 2010), which have been more and more in the centre attention in the last decade. This is especially true for individual social responsibility, which is closely related to personal integrity and ethical conduct.

This led us to decide on a subject of the book, thus resulting in a combination of two themes, namely personal integrity as a virtue and servant leadership. The decision on this topic is also linked to a personal conviction that the higher the integrity of the individual, the better the leader and, in addition, that both the personal integrity of leaders, as well as their caring for others, are the foundations of good governance. Caring for others, on one hand, reflects altruism, and on the other, surpasses egoism and solely satisfying one's own benefit. In our book, we will try to provide an answer to the following question: Why is caring for others such an important factor of leadership and why does servant leadership particularly emphasise it? Before we do that, we will try to address and explain the role and importance of personal integrity and highlight all of its benefits.

Given that both personal integrity and servant leadership are of interest to us, we will thus also shed some light on the impact of the personal integrity of leaders and how this influences their leadership. At the same time, we will highlight all other factors that have either an impact on personal integrity or servant leadership and leadership in general. Parallel to this, we will try to answer the question of how to reconcile the desire to be the best in our performance and behaviour based on high levels of integrity. This is especially a challenge in practice, where it is necessary to simultaneously achieve good and above-average results, while at the same time worrying about development (personal growth), motivation and employee satisfaction.

To this end, we will describe the concept of integrity, ethics as the postulate of integrity, the distinction between ethics and morality, business ethics as a sub-genre of ethics, relevant ethical theories, virtue ethics and virtue *per se*, justice in relation to integrity, integrity as a virtue, personal integrity and its relationship to character, moral development and organisational integrity. We will also present our findings of the research of integrity.

In the following chapters, we will define leadership, delimit it from management and present different conceptions of personal integrity in relation to leadership. This is followed by a brief review of the studies of leadership and the development of management styles, where we will focus on ethical leadership. In that context, we will discuss transformational, authentic, spiritual and servant leadership that, together with personal integrity, occupy the centre of our interest. In doing so, we will focus in particular on the relationship between servant and transformational leadership.

Dealing with servant leadership, we will not only deal with the concept and its development, but also its meaning, characteristics and its relationship with other leadership models. With the help of other authors (Page and Wong 2000, Sendjaya and Sarros 2002, Sendjaya et al. 2008, Lewis 2008), we will delimit the concept from its negative connotation that could be associated with its description. We will also emphasise the social aspect of integrity and servant leadership.

For the purpose of studying the above mentioned in as much detail as possible and thus arriving at the most competent findings and conclusions, we will study the available literature from antiquity to the present. Such an approach is advocated by Griffin (2002), who believed that awareness and understanding of important historical milestones are important for our modern leaders because these strengthen the sense of heritage and allows learning from the mistakes of others. Unfortunately, developments in practice indicate that such leaders are more of an exception than the rule, and that each generation again repeats the mistakes of the former or, worse, makes even bigger mistakes. This is clearly presented by Schermerhorn (2008), who states that it is wise to know the historical roots of today's modern ideas, and at the same time, admits that it is still hard to turn these ideas into a reality today. We will attempt to justify our findings with the thoughts and works of different historical authorities such as Socrates, Plato, Aristotle, Descartes, Spinoza, Kant, Rousseau and modern authors such as Moore, MacIntyre, Comte-Sponville, Kohlberg, Burns, Greenleaf, Bass, Drucker, Avolio, Adair, Carroll and many others. However, we will try to keep in mind Rousseau's assertion that

> the most useful but the least developed of all human knowledge, it seems to me, is the knowledge about Man, and I dare to say, that the very inscription on the Delphic temple[1] contains more important and heavier commandments than all the thick books of moralists together.
>
> (Rousseau 1993: 21)

With the desire for a deeper understanding of the topic, we will then proceed to study ethics, morality, virtue ethics and virtue, justice and personal integrity as a virtue, management and leadership, the scientific study of leadership, ethical leadership and, in part, also the social importance of personal integrity and servant leadership. Regarding personal integrity, we will try to emphasise its importance through the use of analogy. This means, for example, that for integrity as a virtue all the general characteristics of a virtue apply to it, such that 'the same causes from which it arises, the same causes also strengthen it and (if such causes change) it also disintegrates' (Aristotle 2002: 80) or 'virtue depends on us, as is with wickedness' (Aristotle 2002: 106). At the same time, this means that a person is not born with integrity; on the contrary, people strengthen this virtue throughout their entire lives (Crane and Matten 2004).

We will tackle leadership similarly; we will try to answer the question: what is leadership and what does good leadership look like? (Ciulla 2004). The reason for our distinguishing of leadership from management is that we want to adequately place it in a broader context, likewise we will deal with integrity and the broader context of virtue ethics even more widely in the context of ethics and morals. For us, the division between ethics and morality is also important as the latter constitutes a practical aspect of ethics, which comes to the fore when behaving in line with a high level of integrity. Such behaviour also includes the very important factor of leading by example (Comte-Sponville 2002, Audi 2008, Brown et al. 2005).

In the second part of the book, after discussing the relativity and universality of the topic, we will present the results of the research. This was done in one large national non-profit organisation in the field of safety and 16 small and medium-sized profit organisations in the field of development in engineering and tourism. The main reason for the choice of organisations is that we wanted to obtain data from both non-profit and for-profit types of organisations. The selection was based on the typology of formal organisations made by Blau and Scott (2003) and the findings of Drucker (2001, 2004, 2005). Given that we found differences between non-profit and for-profit organisations, among other things, we have tried to explain these differences in a final debate.

In the conclusion we will discuss the results and present our own views and positions in light of the observed impacts. We will also present the final model that we believe is of an applied nature. It was designed based on the theoretical and empirical findings of domestic and foreign authors, as well as our own findings. The empirical part will be completed with a presentation of the limitations of our research coupled with conclusions.

The formal aim of our work is to contribute to raising awareness of the importance of personal integrity, which has a positive impact on any activity performed by humans, as well as to raising awareness of the importance of the need to care for each other, which is the cornerstone of servant leadership.

The entanglement of two fields, namely, ethics and management, places this book among interdisciplinary fields. In the context of business ethics, we will be studying the personal integrity of leaders, whereas we will study servant leadership in the context of management. The research also touches on the field of psychology, where we will include findings we deem appropriate; further, we will want certain contents thereof to be examined in more detail where clarification is required.

The purpose of this book is to provide an in-depth theoretical and empirical attempt at researching the significance and role of personal integrity in the process of leadership and the importance of the philosophy along with it and the effects of servant leadership. The objective goal is to determine whether the personal integrity of leaders impacts on servant leadership.

When choosing methods, we proceeded from the view that 'there is no gap between theoretical and practical sciences, but rather, that they are very strongly interlinked: whoever wants to be a good practitioner must first obtain the best possible, thorough and broadest theoretical knowledge' (Gantar 2002: 19). We thus decided to employ both theoretical and empirical research methods.

By applying the above-mentioned methods, we want to examine the question of integrity and leadership in all of its complexity. To this end, we will at first study this topic from the ancient Greek philosophy, touching on certain philosophical authorities that have marked the various historical periods. Our research question will focus on how the integrity of a leader impacts servant leadership.[2] We will try to ascertain the latter via the empirical approach.[3]

In conjunction with the study of ethical conduct, Northouse (2010) notes that it should be focused on what leaders do and who the leaders are – the conduct and the character of leaders. The study of moral conduct and the consequences of the behaviour of leaders is divided by the author into three segments, namely (Northouse 2010: 378–80):

1 Ethical egoism (creating the greatest benefit for oneself).
2 Utilitarianism (creating the biggest benefit for the largest possible number of people).
3 Altruism (the main purpose here is caring for others).

The division is also shown in Table I.1.

The altruistic aspect occupies the centre of our study; it is highlighted because caring for the needs of others makes up the core of the servant leadership model and it is an important segment of individual social responsibility. Conversely, personal integrity, which along with servant leadership represents the heart of our research, is in the category of the most important virtues that should be developed and strengthened by every leader. In fact, as we stated at the outset, we believe that the higher the integrity of a leader, the better the leader. Moreover, if the fundamental concern of a leader is caring for others, we believe that, at the same time, this is a direct manifestation of servant leadership. If the goal of business ethics is to achieve high levels of integrity in practice, then we strongly agree with the idea of Tavčar (2000) and Možina et al. (2002) that the latter therefore represents the implementation of philosophy or practical philosophy.

Table I.1. Examining the consequences of the moral behaviour of leaders

Taking care of one's own interests	High	Ethical egoism		
	Middle		Utilitarian	
	Low			Altruism FF
		Low	Middle	High
		Taking care of others' interests		

Source: Northouse (2010: 380).

The increased interest in the study and exploration of servant leadership is characteristic of recent years and the new millennium in general, especially with the outbreak of corporate scandals and the economic crisis itself in recent years. The drive of organisations to achieve short-term economic goals and to reach these goals by all means necessary is having adverse consequences on society and affects a multitude of stakeholders within society as a whole. Already in the 1980s, Greenleaf (2002a) found that personal integrity, which is also a fundamental component of servant leadership, is a key factor of social exchange. In addition to the latter, another essential component of servant leadership is altruism (Vidaver-Cohen et al. 2010, Reed et al. 2011), both of which, social exchange and altruism, are extremely important in the context of social responsibility of organisations. It follows that a genuine servant leader is undoubtedly one who is socially responsible (Northouse 2010), which among other things reflects in the way he/she cares for both the haves and have-nots, who he/she treats as equal stakeholders. It also should be noted that the present-day concept of an organisation's social responsibility still ignores the individual's responsibility as a bearer of his/her own role.

1   Servant leaders, in addition to caring for their employees' development and the achievement of the organisation's objectives, are also receptive to the needs of other stakeholders, including those within the broader social environment.
2   Servant leaders encourage their colleagues to apply moral assessment and are committed to their needs and interests, which is the very essence of the moral dimension of leadership. According to Trompenaars and Voerman (2009), this is particularly effective today, due to the constant pressure within society to do more for less money and in the shortest possible time.
3   Trompenaars (2009) notes that in addition to the abovementioned, servant leadership is also useful in times of crisis (e.g. the economic downturn) and within the context of crisis management, as care for employees does not preclude the making of difficult decisions. On the other hand, Searle and Barbuto (2011) note that servant leadership can be very effective in working environments with a history of unethical behaviour, for this type of leadership encourages moral behaviour among the employees.

A good leader used to be defined by the criteria of effectiveness and efficiency, while today it is excellence and ethical conduct that are expected of leaders. The modern manager or leader can therefore no longer be focused only on the objectives and welfare of his/her organisation, but also on stakeholders and the quality of services (Bowie 1991). Waddock et al. (2002) claim that it is from the pressures of primary and secondary stakeholders and social and institutional pressures that we can extract those basic expectations of integrity, respect, standards, transparency and accountability. Yet what all of them have in common is that they demand integrity and it is the integrity of an organisation that should provide the maximum level of responsible management (Waddock et al. 2002). At the same time,

Shahin and Zairi (2007) believe that social responsibility requires the unconditional implementation of these so-called 'social contracts' between organisations
and society. In doing so, organisations must be responsible for the needs and
demands of their environment, strive for optimising positive impacts and mini-
mising the negative consequences they might have on society. According to the
authors, this can only be achieved when leaders start changing the way they think
and act (Shahin and Zairi 2007).

Notes

1 Delphic (or Socratic) call to 'know thyself!' (Bahovec 1993: 109).
2 The scientific development of the theory of business ethics and the servant leadership
  style began in the 1980s.
3 We shall confine ourselves to the European and American authors and study the ethical aspects of leadership from Socrates onwards. The reason for this lies in the fact
  that the philosophy of ancient Greece greatly influenced European currents of thought
  (Andolšek 1996).

1   Integrity

The origin and the meaning of integrity

The first part of the book is divided into two parts. Based on the relevant and accessible literature, we will first define integrity, ethics as the postulate of integrity, virtue ethics, integrity as a virtue, personal integrity and organisational integrity and present the empirical research of integrity. In the second part, we will use the relevant and accessible literature to identify leadership, delimit it from management, deal with personal integrity in relation to leadership and conduct a brief review of the scientific studies of governance and the development of the leadership styles. We will then focus on ethical and servant leadership and the empirical research into ethical and servant leadership. At the end of the theoretical part, we will highlight the social importance of integrity and servant leadership.

The etymology or source of the word 'integrity' comes from the Latin word, *integritas, integer*, meaning comprehensiveness, consistency and purity (Petrick and Quinn 2000, Worden 2003, Paine 2005, Audi and Murphy 2006); it also originates from the French and Latin words, *intact, integrate, entirety*, meaning that everything works connected, unharmed and incorruptibly (Cloud 2009).

Audi and Murphy (2006) discovered that the wider understanding of integrity is connected with two similar concepts: *integral* and *integration*, which are also Latin in origin. The concept of *integral* means wholesome or undivided. In conjunction with man, we can talk about the integrity of his personality characteristics and, in conjunction with his behaviour, we can talk about the completeness of his actions. The concept of *integration* is understood as an amalgamation of completeness and wholeness, and can be understood in our context as the integration of human personality traits (key characteristics).

We can also identify one of the possible sources of the meaning of integrity through Aristotle's philosophy, that a good man is 'always of the same opinion with himself and tends with his wholeness of soul toward the same goals' (Aristotle 2002: 278), while 'words are convincing only if they coincide with the actions' (2002: 300). However, if this is not so, then 'they provoke contempt and the denial even of what is true in them' (2002: 300). Aristotle also thought that within a bad man there is a disagreement between what he must do and what he does; while on the other hand, a good man does what he must do. For reason always decides what is best for him, and a good man obeys reason.

(2002: 287–8)

The concept of integrity somewhat varies over time; integrity, more or less, used to mean completeness or wholeness, and yet today, some of its conception is intertwined with honesty, trust and so on (Palanski and Yammarino 2007).

Petrick and Quinn (2000) showed that integrity is defined in philosophical and psychological literature as a moral conscience, moral judgement, moral reasoning, public responsibility, moral commitment, moral character, moral consistency or authenticity. The authors note that integrity as a construct, which can be individual or collective, is focused on four fundamental factors: (i) the process (moral awareness, moral deliberation, moral character – strengthening the virtues, moral behaviour); (ii) understanding and prudence (a balanced application of basic ethical theories – teleological, deontological, developmentally systematic, virtues – with the aim of the right conduct and achieving the right destination); (iii) development (cognitive development of the pre-conventional and post-conventional phase after Kohlberg); and (iv) the system (implementation of organisational rules that encourage the development of an ethical environment) (Petrick and Quinn 2000).

Paine noted that, despite the different denominations, integrity contains or is defined by one or more related characteristics such as moral conscientiousness, moral responsibility, moral obligation and moral consistency (Paine 2005: 247–9). Moral conscientiousness is reflected in the desire to do what is right, moral responsibility (including accountability) means taking responsibility for yourself and for your own conduct, the moral imperative (including commitment) is reflected in loyalty and effort concerning the implementation of certain principles, moral consistency (moral coherence) is reflected in different ways such as the consistency between belief and expression as well as between words and deeds (Figure 1.1).

Given that our task entails focusing on personal integrity and integrity in relation to leadership, the remaining concepts of integrity explained below are mainly for information purposes. The only exception is organisational integrity, which is presented at the end of the chapter on integrity.

For a general example of a practical application of integrity, we may use the integrity of the hull, which would mean that it is 'water-resistant' and waterproof (Palanski and Yammarino 2007), while mathematical integrity would be represented as an integer (Fitsimmons 2008).

The meaning of integrity depends primarily on the activities in which it is understood or interpreted or on the activities for which it is implied. Thus, the concept of integrity can be traced in medicine (the integrity of the patient), philosophy (the integrity of the soul), religion (the integrity of faith), industry (the integrity of surface materials, constructions, reproductions), computer science (data integrity), management (personal integrity, organisational integrity), politics (state integrity,

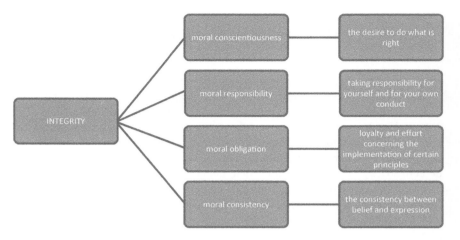

Figure 1.1 Integrity.

Source: Paine (2005).

integrity of a proceeding), the army (integrity of the military leader), the police and so on.

The importance and use of the concept of integrity can also be understood as a relationship between the foundation and the attributes in a sense that a single, indivisible thought is given, which translates into countless idioms.

Definition of integrity

There is no universal definition of integrity (Yukl 2002, Audi and Murphy 2006, Palanski and Yammarino 2007, 2009). It is always defined differently by various researchers and authors. Comprising the centre of our study, personal integrity is most commonly understood as consistency between words and deeds (Kirkpatrick and Locke 1991, Simons 1999, 2002, Paine 2005, Brown 2006) and in conjunction with moral behaviour or the absence of unethical behaviour (Craig and Gustafson 1998, Posner 2001, Parry and Proctor-Thomson 2002, Palanski and Yammarino 2007, 2009).

Those already mentioned and other conceptions of personal integrity will be discussed in detail in the following sections. Before that, we found the following definitions of integrity in different dictionaries:

In dictionaries, integrity is defined as perfection (Oxford 1989b, Webster's 1996, Cambridge 2003), wholeness (Oxford 1989a, 1989b, 2004, 2009, Webster's 1996, Dictionary of the Slovenian Language 2001, Cambridge 2003), compliance (Dictionary of the Slovenian Language 2001), undivided (Oxford 1989a, 1989b, 2009), unreduced (Webster's 1996), a thing of chastity and purity, something unspoiled (Oxford 1989b) and the original perfect condition or state where any part or element is not lacking (Oxford 1989b).

It is also defined as fairness (Oxford 1989a, 1989b, 2009, Webster's 1996, Cambridge 2003), justice (Oxford 1989b), authenticity (Oxford 1989b), moral principles and uprightness (Oxford 1989b, 2009, Webster's 1996), firmness with moral virtues (Oxford 1989b, 2004, Cambridge 2003), dedication to moral and ethical principles (Webster's 1996), untouched moral status (Oxford 1989b), internal consistency (Oxford 2004) and uncorrupted (Oxford 1989b).

The Oxford Dictionary of Philosophy divides the concept of integrity into two parts, first, in the simplest sense of the word, it is defined as a synonym for honesty (Blackburn 2008). Often, however, it refers to a more complex understanding of integrity or the harmony of the individual who perceives himself as someone whose life without integrity would have lost harmony or that it might be tarnished because of doing different things (Blackburn 2008).

Ethics as the postulate of integrity

Given that integrity as a virtue falls within the framework of ethics and that ethics is its baseline, we firstly identified ethics and morality, and the difference between them through the findings, thoughts and ideas of historical authorities and contemporary researchers. Starting from their role in relation to integrity and its 2,000-year-old development, we want to emphasise their importance and at the same time narrow down and limit the number of authors given the enormous amount of literature. In the following, we looked at business ethics as a kind of practical and applied ethics because our empirical study focused on the integrity of leaders and leadership in non-profit and for-profit organisations. We continued with the definition of our relevant ethical theories and pointed out virtue ethics. We also defined the concept and importance of virtue, which is similar to ethics, only more focused on the foundation of personal integrity, which is in the core of our interest. In addition, we emphasised justice in relation to integrity, which Aristotle considered as the highest and most perfect virtue (Aristotle 2002).

Ethics and morality

In dictionaries, ethics is defined as a science of morality (Oxford 1989b), a study of ethical principles (Oxford 1989b), addressing moral issues (Oxford 1989b) and studying what is morally correct and what is not (Cambridge 2003), while ethic is understood as accepted beliefs or a set of moral principles that control, manage or influence behaviour (Cambridge 2003, Oxford 2004) (Figure 1.2).

In Merriam-Webster's Encyclopedia (2000), ethics is defined as the branch of philosophy that examines the nature of the fundamental values and norms by which human actions can be judged as correct or incorrect. In the dictionary of modern use of the English language (Fowler 2009), it is defined as the science of morality that studies and discusses the principles that define the human duty to others. The Oxford Dictionary of Philosophy (Blackburn 2008) defines ethics as the study of the concepts involved in practical understanding or interpretation,

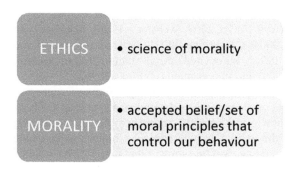

Figure 1.2 The difference between ethics and morality.

Source: Authors.

such as good, right, obligation, virtue and so on. In the case of morals, it is essentially 'the same thing' as in ethics, taking different approaches mutually differ (e.g. Kant had moved to the obligations, commitments and principles of conduct, Aristotle on practical reasoning through the prism of virtues – virtue ethics) (Blackburn 2008). According to the Oxford Dictionary (1989b, 2004), moral should relate to the character or the situation taking good or bad into account and the difference between right and wrong. Moral sense is the ability to detect the difference between right and wrong (Oxford 1989b, 2004). It means the standards of good behaviour in which each individual believes or it means the manner of conduct by most people regarded as correct and fair (Cambridge 2003). Moral is defined as a feeling of a person or a group of people at a given time (Oxford 2004).

Etymologically speaking, the term ethics comes from 'the old Greek word ethos, which means custom, or tradition, character, while the term morals derives from the Latin mos, which means a similar custom, proper handling and morality' (Strahovnik 2010, 5).

Philosophical debates about ethics in Europe began in ancient Greece in the fourth century BC (Palmer 2007), whereby the ancient Greek philosophy was divided into three degrees, namely logic, physics and ethics – manner science (Kant 2005). As noted by MacIntyre (1993: 151), throughout history there have appeared three different understandings of moral rules, as a form of human life in which we strive for good (Plato, Aristotle), as the commandments of God (Christianity) and as an indicator of which actions bring more of the desired (sophists and Hobbes). The first concept refers to functional well, the other concepts refer to rewards and punishments and the third to our wishes and the means to achieve the objective (MacIntyre 1993). At the end of the last century, Badiou (1996: 7) realised that the word ethics, 'in which so clearly shows the trail of Greek philosophy or teaching that evokes the memory of Aristotle', is again in the spotlight. In Greek, it means 'finding good ways to stay or wisdom of the operation', while for the Stoics in ancient times it meant the heart of philosophical wisdom (Badiou 1996). As he says, it is known 'that the Stoics philosophy is usually compared with an egg: the logic is the eggshell, white is physics, and ethics is the yolk' (Badiou 1996), or as Strahovnik says, 'the Stoics' logic is compared with a terrace fence, physics with a tree growing in the garden and, finally, ethics with the fruits of the tree of philosophy' (Strahovnik 2010: 4).

The foundation of ethics as a science was laid by Socrates (Sovre 2003) in dialogue with the sophists (Jerman 1992: 202) when he was posing ethical questions about how a man should live (Raeper and Smith 1995: 10). 'In his typical teachings all of the virtues are actually manners ... and also from the moral-intellectual virtues he realized that all human happiness depends on that' (Kocijančič 2002: 571). Kunzmann et al. (1997) concluded that it was in the heart of the philosophy of Socrates' question about good and virtue (*areté*), whereby the quest for philosophical insight into the essence of virtue was understood as a concern for the human soul.

Later, Plato, who was dealing with ethical issues taken up by his teacher Socrates defined an internal ethical criterion, the concept of conscience. According to Plato, a man must behave ethically towards himself, others and the gods, while the truth of his morality (ethos) is ethical and political virtue (*areté*) (Kocijančič 2004: 1102). Plato, in his most important work 'The Republic', in the debate on *dikaiosyne*, covered most of what the word morals means, where the concept of *dikaiosyne* is translated as righteousness, which is narrower than the Greek conception (MacIntyre 1993, Palmer 2007: 287). At the same time, there is a difference between ancient Greece and contemporary Europe (modern English) in the way of social life (MacIntyre 1993). The author also believes that justice is not an appropriate translation of what is also true for other translations because the word *dikaiosyne* has 'completely unique importance and in this way combines fairness in small things with personal integrity that cannot be captured by any English word' (MacIntyre 1993: 23). For an allegory of what it means to act morally, Plato wrote Socrates' comparison of the human soul with the state and the division thereof into three classes or sections (rulers – the mind; soldiers or keepers – whip; the working class – desires). Each component of the soul has its own virtue, namely the intellect – wisdom, zeal – courage and desire – moderation. If all three components of the soul

> act according to the law of reason, justice (dikaiosyne) is the result and anyone whose soul is governed it would be clear why it should or should act fairly (i.e. the moral). Why is it so? As is the opposite of justice, injustice, chaos ... which is incompatible with virtue.
>
> (Palmer 2007: 295)

This means that 'man is moral, when he grasps this sensible principle, draw his heart to follow and heart should temper the passion' (Palmer, 2007: 296), at which 'as in Plato there is later in Kant's philosophy more than a sagacious implication that the mind should overcome the desire'.

Aristotle, Plato's pupil, established eudaimonic ethics, the main sense of the moral principles and values of human bliss and happiness (Jerman 1992, Barnes 1999, Solomon 2004). For Aristotle, eudaimonia or happiness means the result of a life of virtue (Grant 2011), due to which he put 'doing well' at the centre of ethical concepts (Solomon 2004).

Aristotle thus put ethics among practical philosophy as its purpose was not only to provide the truth but also to stimulate action (Barnes 1999: 91). His ethics had to be subject to 'the area of human practices of function which is based on the decision and thus differs from the theoretical philosophy, which is adjusted to a constant, eternal' (Kunzmann et al. 1997: 51). He focused on that which is actually 'good' for man because an ordinary man with 'good in itself' cannot do much to help himself (Jerman 1992: 41). Solomon (1992: 334) notes that Aristotle had understood the word 'should' in a practical sense, while the later Judeo-Christian approach transferred it to the domain of God and from individual morality to universal morality. According to Rowe and Kellam (2011), Aristotle was the first man in the West to develop a clear (explicit) theory of moral responsibility, viewing human life, like Solomon (2004), comprehensively and not in isolation of the perspective of various social roles (e.g. private and professional life).

Unlike Aristotle's approach, the ethics of both Socrates and Plato was intellectualistic, as was their emphasis on knowledge and wisdom of good, 'good in itself' (Solomon 2004: 41). As noted by Musek (1993) and Palmer (2007), the opinion of Socrates and Plato that mere knowledge of good is sufficient for good behaviour backfired because, even if someone knows what is good or moral, it is not necessary that he will act the same way. Nietzsche (1988) regarded Plato's idea of good in itself as the most prolonged and even the worst mistake of all time. In order to demonstrate this, there are more than a few cases where highly educated managers and leaders, despite their knowledge in the field of business ethics, committed offences and triggered the collapse of organisations and companies. Conversely, Šter (1994) noted that the problem of immorality is associated with ignorance and that Socrates was right in asserting that knowledge is the key to morality, while Palmer (2007) believed that moral theory can really help or promote moral thinking or behaviour, but it cannot create it alone. Musek consequently agreed with Aristotle that it is important to have good ethics management, although he also sees a problem,

> even if we are aware of the moral responsibility and if a behaviour is clearly recognised as the only proper and necessary way in a moral sense (and thus we fulfilled the conditions set by Immanuel Kant), it eventually happens that we will not be doing so.
>
> (Musek 1993: 132)

At the same time, he considers that humans' 'old and perhaps eternal problem is how to reconcile the values of our actions' (1993: 132). This was all after the onset of sophistry for the Greek philosophy the central question of ethics in how man must live (Kocijančič 2002). 'The answer was to be happy and to be happy only if it is good – that is, if he has *arete*, due to which the entire Greek ethics was 'just as eudaimonic as ethics were *arete*' (Kocijančič 2002: 571). Descartes showed the role of ethics and morality, understood as the foundation of everything that man does, by way of the metaphor of a tree:

> That all philosophy is as a tree: the root is metaphysics, physics is the trunk, and the branches, which run from this trunk, are all other sciences. These are reduced to three main categories – named medicine, mechanics and morals. Under the morals, I see the highest and most complete science of ethics, which is the highest level of wisdom, whereas it assumes complete knowledge of all the other sciences.

(Descartes 1957: 302)

Descartes wrote the moral rules or maxims in the 'Debate on the method' when developing the principles of scientific research. He understood the moral rules as (Descartes 1957: 51–5):

1 The conduct of the laws and customs of someone's own country (countries), religion and the most moderate opinions of the most judicious people;
2 the strength, endurance and perseverance in someone's own actions; and
3 the control of oneself and the customisation of one's own desires, because man, with the exception of thought, has nothing in power.

Spinoza (2004) was convinced that people without moral virtues should rightly be considered inhumane, while he recognised virtue as belonging only to man or his nature, with the assumption that it is in his power. Ethics is considered intellectually because he believes that confused ideas are devastating for man on the basis of which affects or passions occur. The more a man deepens on them, the more he controls them, whereas the ethical path is pointed by intellect (Jerman 1992: 72). Voltaire understood ethics or the doctrine of morality as the only true religion (Jerman 1992: 80).

Kant tries to justify universal morality, 'which does not apply to anyone, if they do not apply to all, irrespective of the spatio-temporal conditions, i.e. rational beings in general' (Riha 2005: 35). His attempt was not based on reinventing new moral principles but on finding a formula that would define morality in an appropriate manner (Riha 2005). According to Kant, morality had no doctrine on how to become happy but 'how we must become people worthy of happiness' (Kant 2003: 150). He said that 'the moral law directly determines will', which is the essence of all morality (2003: 85), while the 'highest good is urgently the highest aim of a morally determined will' (2003: 134). He was convinced that the most important subject of philosophy is ethics (Raeper and Smith 1995: 155) and had morals and its theory – ethics placed in the area of human free will or the autonomy of the human will, independent of other factors – including reason (Jerman 1992: 89). As a result of his efforts, he formulated a categorical imperative that states: 'Operate in such a way that the maxim of your will can apply at the same time as the general principle of the laws' (Kant 2003: 37) and should be unconditional. This means that everyone should judge his actions through the prism of what would happen if everyone acted like he or she (Raeper and Smith 1995: 157). He wrote the Categorical Imperative, which he named an imperative of morals morality, in yet another way 'do only that which you could want to become universal law' (Kant 2005: 37) or 'work by such that the maxim of your operation becomes through your will a universal law of nature' (2005: 38), and 'work the way you would humanity both in your person as in the person of anyone else ever used simultaneously as an aim, never merely as a means' (2005: 45). As stated, it is necessary that 'we want the maxim of our actions to become universal law: it is a canon of its moral judgement in general' (2005: 40). Kant wrote that

> the concept of duty requires of the acts, objectively, that it is consistent with the law and of the maxim to act, subjectively, in a way that respects the law as the only way of determining the will of the law.
>
> (Kant 2003: 95)

He said that the moral imperative is binding because it means our duty, and that 'every action reasoned by it should be recorded as a duty rather than as a way of handling that we like or could become likeable by itself' (Kant 2003: 96). MacIntyre (1993) notes that contrary to Kant's categorical imperative is the hypothetical imperative. The categorical imperative is not limited to any condition like the hypothetical imperative is and puts man as the moral sovereignty. The author says that 'the version of Kant's categorical imperative is undoubtedly acting in the ordinary moral statements in our society: "You must do this and that." "Why?" "There is no reason. You just have to"' (MacIntyre 1993: 195).

Kant attributed man a great role because of his mental abilities, namely on the basis of facts, 'because man belongs to the world of morality, which applies the principle that a man is never a means to achieve goals, but always just an "aim in itself"' (Jerman 1992: 90). At the same time, Kant refused to be focused solely on the behaviour of people from the slopes (taste preferences), and he defended the thesis that morality has very close ties with the duties. He said that man is truly moral when he follows the rules because they impose a moral obligation and he also understands it the same way (Raeper and Smith 1995: 156). He was convinced that

> the moral law is given, so to speak as a factor of pure reason, which is *a priori* aware and which is indisputably certain, even if we take that in experience a case cannot be found in which it was executed perfectly adequate.
>
> (Kant 2003: 56)

Dion (2012), when taking Kant into account, considers that ethical principles are the categorical imperative that must be universally understood and should apply to all people.

Agamben, commenting on Kant, says that the wealth of his ethics 'is in the fact that the form of the law is left as an empty principle' (2004: 63). He adds that

> this force is irrelevant in the ethical sphere and it corresponds to the transcendental object in the sphere of knowledge, which is not a real object, but just the idea of a pure relationship, which expresses only being in the relation between thinking and the absolute indefinite thought.
>
> (2004: 63)

Rousseau understood the fundamental principle of morals in the way 'that man is inherently good, that he loves righteousness and order, that in the human heart there is no original perversion and that the first moves of nature are always correct' (Bahovec 1993: 116). The moral being is defined as an intelligent being, free and considered in his relations with other beings (Rousseau 1993: 23). At the same time, regarding the human in his natural state, he said that given the fact that he had no moral duty and relations to other people, he could neither have been good nor evil (Rousseau 1993: 47).

Moore (2000) connects ethics with a discussion of human behaviour where proper handling is connected with good and improper behaviour is regarded as a fault. As he says,

> the speciality of ethics is not that it examines the statements on human behaviour, but in examining the statements of those properties of things, which are often described as "good", and her other qualities, which are often described as "bad".
>
> (Moore 2000: 101)

The author simultaneously notes that, although it is unable to provide a complete list of duties, ethics has a practical benefit. He considers that

> although we cannot hope for the discovery of the best of all possible options under the circumstances, it is certainly possible to show which of the alternatives that are likely to be available to anyone, will produce the maximum amount of good. This task is the most ethics can carry out.
>
> (2000: 220)

Moore also believes that 'the law of ethics does not have the character of a scientific law, it is more similar to a scientific projection: the latter is still at such a high probability still only plausible' (2000: 226).

MacIntyre understands the natural morality of man, which is largely defined as aggressive and horny, as 'a necessary compromise between the natural desire of people to attack others and the natural fear of people to get attacked by others and leaving fatal consequences' (1993: 29). The author notes that 'morality does not really withstand any external justification; if we do not do the right thing for its own sake, whether it be in our interest or not, then we do not do what is right' (1993: 92).

According to Pribac, 'the zone of morality should stop where the range of voluntary decisions stops and where the area of necessity starts, i.e. the action that cannot be changed by the moral subject' (Pribac 2001: 149). Yet Gantar believes that the aim of ethics is the definition and implementation of the highest good, which is sought by both human and society. The highest good represents happiness, not in the form of a hedonistic life but life that is consistent with the virtues (Gantar 2002: 20). Strahovnik (2010) understands ethics as the foundation of human relationships to themselves and to their surroundings and concludes that ethics, given that it is a human skill for its existence, requires human cooperation.

> Respect for ethical norms means respect for man and the creation of his welfare. Ethics or morality should represent the values and integrity of man as an individual (entity), of the company in relation to itself, to others and to the social environment.
>
> (Strahovnik 2010: 8)

Carroll (2009) thinks that being only familiar with the ethical principles is one thing and significantly easier than acting in accordance with them, or even more – also motivating others to do so. As he says, people are motivated for ethical behaviour by internal or external stimuli, wherein the first impact (internal) is made by people who set an example and the second one (external) is triggered by benefits and penalties.

Lennick and Kiel (2009, 2011) discovered that morality is the product of a combination of our nature, education and experience. They believe that almost all men have the innate capacity to be moral, which is not enough (Lennick and Kiel 2009), wherein they normally perceive moral competence as a moral life in harmony between the individual's moral principles and values, goals and behaviour, including thoughts and feelings (Lennick and Kiel 2011: 11). After Greenleaf (2002a), a moral individual is one who with proper handling contributes to moral greatness in society. Kunzmann et al. consider that

> the fundamental questions of ethics are concerning the Good which determines human behaviour and conduct. Its aim is to methodically secure a way to show the basis for a fair, reasonable and sensible behaviour and a (communal) life. The principles and justification of ethics should be without reference to external authority and conventions universally applicable and mentally apparent, hence deeming ethics a superior, critical view of the currently valid morality.
>
> Kunzmann et al. (1997: 13)

Griffin (2002), Robbins and Langton (2003) and Northouse (2010) understand ethics as the study of moral values, virtues, principles and motives that influence people's behaviour, namely, in terms of right and wrong, desired and undesired and acceptable and unacceptable behaviour. Robbins and Langton (2003), in this regard, think that the study does not produce black-and-white answers.

Tavčar (2008) defines ethics as the theory of morality and as its cornerstone the concept of good and achieving the highest good for the individual and society. Šter (1994) understands moral functioning as an intentional, conscious doing on the ground of moral values or human obligations, not arising from the expectations of rewards or benefits. He understands it as a kind of social relationship. Morally, he feels 'much more happiness and pleasure; it is much more exalted than the selfish satisfaction and benefits. What is worth is significantly associated with the duty rather than the usefulness' (1994: 63), wherein he argues that 'morality is no supermarket' (1994: 63) and that 'moral values cannot be exchanged, but only given' (1994: 112). At the same time, the author notes that it is the moral development of humans from heterogamous morality to autonomous morality, where

> morality in the full sense of the word is only autonomous morality because a full of moral action is only where we are clearly aware of the needs and consequences, and we do it out of conviction on the moral value of acts, in other words, it is an autonomous decision whose purpose and result we understand.
>
> (1994: 90)

This infers that the 'responsibility applies only to the conscious situation' (1994: 170).

Palanski and Yammarino (2007) noted that the word ethics used to be connected with human nature, but that today it deals with the issue of conduct. Hartman (2008) also believes that to be ethical means above all to have a good character, including mutually compatible virtues, emotions and practical handling.

Batson et al. (1999) concluded that moral people often behave immorally. Research studies (Batson et al. 2006) show that motive is linked to opportunity when a person can pretend to act fairly, but, in fact, does not. Batson et al. (1999) associate the above stated with moral hypocrisy, which represents the interests of individuals, where he is recognised as a moral person, however, whenever possible, avoids the 'costs' that require a moral attitude. Such a man outwardly looks like he has integrity and is complying with the principles of morality, but he is in fact only interested in his own benefits. The same applies to the pursuit of a transaction when moral hypocrisy allows someone to gain trust by carrying out a specific obligation, while still steadfastly pursuing their own personal gain or interest (Batson and et al. 2006). The authors conclude that moral hypocrisy is nowadays recognised as a pragmatic value, particularly in the business world and is increasingly present. It is believed that the reason for this is because getting the maximum benefits in this way is 'allowed', which otherwise, with respect for moral principles, they would not be able to obtain (Batson and et al. 2006). At this point, various current issues are raised as to which this book offers direct or indirect answers, namely the role and importance today of personal integrity and ethical servant leadership when, on one hand, we can find increasingly expressed the need for the individual genuine social responsibility of leaders, while, on the other hand, the reality of capitalism and neoliberalism ruling over the principles of socialism, solidarity (Lech Walesa), care for the little man and so on (Figure 1.3).

ETHICS

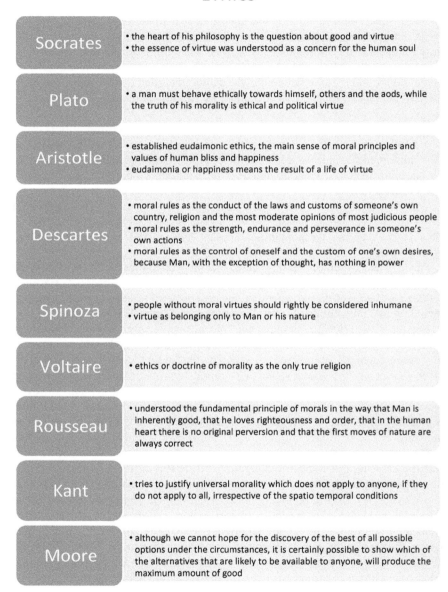

Figure 1.3 Ethics through history.

Source: Authors.

Distinction between ethics and morality

As mentioned, when seen from the etymological point of view, the concept of ethics derives from Ancient Greece, whereas the concept of moral derives from Latin (Šter 1994, Možina et al. 2002, Fowler 2009, Strahovnik 2010). At times, the two concepts are synonymous, although today we can observe a fundamental difference: *ethic* is understood as a *science* of morality, whereas morality is understood as an ethical practice. In other words, from the theoretical standpoint we are talking about *ethics*; from the practical standpoint and personal actions, we are talking about *morality* (Jerman 1992, Šter 1994, Carroll and Buchholtz 2000, Ciulla 2004, Crane and Matten 2004, Fowler 2009).[1] Berlogar (2000), Tavčar (2000), Ciulla (2004) and Fowler (2009) further agree that in today's use, the two terms are often employed interchangeably wherein, according to Fowler (2009), an unwarranted impression is present in the sense that ethics is more independent of religion, while morality is not.

Some authors distinguish between the two concepts. For example, Ciulla (2004) notes that some associate ethics with social values, while morality is associated with personal values. As a result, we shall present a few examples of such differentiations from the perspectives of various authors. Jelovac sees ethics as a philosophical science of morality, and not as a morality in itself because it deals

> with the theoretical clarification and critical evaluation of the phenomenon of morality, the exploration of the origin of human morality, the criteria of moral valuation, understanding of the aims, purposes, goals, the meaning of moral character, conduct, functioning, self-awareness of individuals as well as the broader social community.
>
> (Jelovac 1997: 14)

Tavčar (2000) sees the difference in the sense that ethics is applied philosophy or as a philosophy of morality that operates with the principles of good and bad, whereas morality deals with the rules for decision-making and compliance with ethics. Crane and Matten (2004) understand ethics as a study of morality and the study of ethical rules and principles, while morality is understood as a practice dealing with values, rules or beliefs present in concrete social processes and determine what is right or wrong for an individual or society as a whole. Carrol and Buchholtz (2000) see ethics as a discipline that deals with the study of moral duties or principles and what is good and bad, whereas morality is regarded as a science about specific correct and/or incorrect moral behaviour. Schermerhorn (2008) understood ethics as a code of moral principles that define the standard behaviour of an individual or group in relation to what is good or right, contrary to what is bad or wrong. Jerman (1992) understands that ethics should be considered as a theory of 'right', which explores moral phenomena in the broadest sense, while morality is seen as the individual's ability to act accordingly with the understanding and identification of good and bad. Možina et al. (2002) note that at the present time, ethical behaviour is increasingly understood as decision-making consistent with the values of human moral behaviour, whereas morality is understood as behaviour consistent with those decisions.

Conversely, Berlogar (2000) noted that the point of a clear distinction between the two concepts is *rarity*; he believed ethics to be wisdom about the life of the community, which understands morality as its own object of study and interpretation, meaning that ethics is the overarching concept. Ethics sets the reasons for the morality a certain society advocates, while morality defines how the individual should behave in order to comply with social norms. For ethics, morality acts as the main object of research because it is a 'human phenomenon par excellence, because only a human being can establish and maintain a critical attitude towards the behaviour and actions of other people, their character and finally to himself, from the perspective of good and bad' (Jelovac 1997: 14).

Business ethics as subcategory of ethics

Given that, in addition to integrity, we are studying leadership, this section specifically discusses applied and business ethics (business or professional ethics), which is closely associated with leadership and based on the personal integrity of leaders and other leadership virtues. In addition to its development and meaning, we will deal with altruism and the golden rule.

The Oxford Dictionary of Philosophy defines 'applied' or 'useful' (practical) ethics as ethics that focuses on the practical problems[2] of business ethics as a branch of ethics that deals with the analysis of the problems and dilemmas in business practice[3] (Blackburn 2008).

Applied ethics denotes a narrower field of ethics that focuses on the study of the application of moral principles in particular occupations or professions; the connection of theory and practice in applied ethics separates it from ethics as a philosophical discipline (Pagon 2000). Carroll and Buchholtz (2000) understand the distinction between ethics and business ethics in the sense that ethics deals with the questions of what is right, wrong, fair and unfair, whereas business ethics deals with these ethical issues in connection with the performance of an action. The authors also assert that to understand business ethics, it is necessary to consider the relationship between ethics and morality and the relationship between good and right through the prism of fairness, justice and equality in a specific case. At the same time, in their opinion, it is necessary to realise that the ethical behaviour of leaders is influenced by external/social values, as well as by internal/internal organisational values and that the moral tone in the organisation is always provided by the top management, which inspires the other managers and employees.

Business ethics can be seen as 'useful' or 'applied' ethics because it 'primarily motivates people to deal with ethics, while also focusing on the final and practical goal of the said endeavour – to make human life better and more equitable' (Miščević 1993: 294). In connection with this, Dienhart (2005) considers that, given that moral thinking is present in all life circumstances and thus also in the course of business, there is no question about whether ethics is present, but *how* it is present and what is its role.

In the context of the debate on business ethics, Solomon (1992, 2004) developed his own theoretical approach and called it 'Aristotle's approach to business and business ethics', believing that the first business ethicist was Aristotle (Solomon 2004). Aristotle's approach to business ethics is focused on the individual's role and responsibility in a specific organisation or community that has shared goals and missions, while putting human beings before profit. At the same time, the author believes that almost all of Aristotle's virtues are directly applicable to today's business practices, and that the personal integrity of employees determines organisational integrity and vice versa (Solomon 1992: 335–8). Aristotle's approach to (business) ethics stresses the importance of individual virtue and integrity, which a successful organisation promotes and reinforces (Solomon 2004). In this regard, Mintz (1996) found that interest in using Aristotle's virtues in modern business ethics was growing towards the end of last century.

According to Solomon (1992), business ethics can be understood as a component of the business environment (the world) with a keen sense of social values and virtues, where a large number of virtues are relevant to doing business (Figure 1.4). The author identified six dimensions of ethics in business: virtue of the community (the individual in relation to the community), virtue of excellence (denoting virtue in itself, as *areté*, in the context of exceeding standards and mediocrity), virtue of

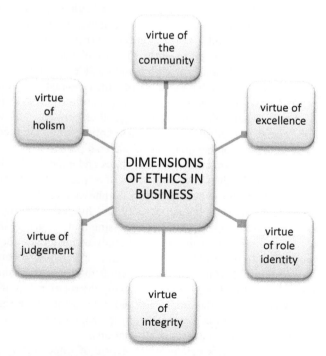

Figure 1.4 Dimensions of ethics in business.

Source: Solomon (1992).

role identity (man in different social roles in their lives, including the organisation), virtue of integrity, virtue of judgement and virtue of holism (integration or coordination of social roles). The author also notes that business ethics is often seen as a set of obligations and constraints that hinder the performance of the business, instead of being seen as a motivating factor for the desired behaviour. In this context, Solomon (2004: 1025) notes that altruism cannot be understood as self-sacrifice but as a perception of oneself that is in close liaison with the community, friends and family, and which can have more meaning to an individual than an individual to himself. MacIntyre (2006) understands altruism as the opposite of egoism and asserts that it is necessary to be able to distinguish between altruism and generosity. He states that we can talk about altruism

> only on the assumption that there are two types of tendencies in the human nature: some are to one's own benefit, others are to the benefit of other people. Altruists are thus those, with which the second group of tendencies at least sometimes prevails over the first group.
>
> (MacIntyre 2006: 169)

Crane and Matten (2004) understand business ethics as the study of business situations, activities and decisions in the light of morally correct or morally wrong behaviour, which is influenced by the internal organisational culture and external social and cultural context. With this, a '*good life*' in business, in the context of ethics, is understood in a much broader sense than mere profit as it represents only one segment of good business. Consequently, *the way* of obtaining profits, employee satisfaction and good relationships within and outside the organisation are also important. Ciulla (2004) notes that the study of ethics and history of ideas help to understand two intertwining issues which form part of most research on leadership, namely, what is 'leadership' and what is 'good leadership'. The first question deals with the essence of leadership and is descriptive, while the second question is normative and focuses on the qualities of leadership.

Brenner and Molander (1977) found that business ethics and ethical behaviour in business, in addition to moral values and obligations of a specified profession, includes existing social values and expectations. As Strahovnik (2010) shows, it is related to the individual areas of human activity and his influence on the surrounding area (for example, business, media, advertising and so on). Možina et al. (2002) believe that the essence of the object of study of business ethics is how organisations comply with the prevailing social values in relation to human beings and other organisations. Griffin (2002) understands the focus of business ethics and leadership ethics within three segments, namely the relationship of the organisation towards its employees, the employees' attitude to the organisation and the relationship of the organisation to all others involved, where leaders and managers must take care of the ethical aspect in all relations.

Johnson (2007) believes that ethics belong in the centre of leadership as this effectively prevents harmful and deviant behaviour that harms the organisation. On the other hand, ethics encourages many positive effects on the employee side (strengthening of personal integrity, loyalty, employee satisfaction and so on) as well as on the organisation's side (greater confidence in the organisation, reputation in the community, stronger desire for cooperation and so on). One way of promoting the moral development of the organisation entails leaders assisting employees in anticipating and reacting to ethical dilemmas.

According to Ferrell et al. (2011), business ethics consists of principles, values (e.g. integrity) and rules that guide behaviour in the business environment. In this regard, Audi and Murphy (2006) hold the view that integrity in business ethics plays an important role as it presents itself as an ideal, a virtue or a desired or missing factor. The authors then understand the purest example of integrity as honesty, which they understand as the exceeding of any possible coherence between beliefs and statements or words and deeds. Paine (2005) notes, however, that business ethics sees integrity as a characteristic of moral self-control.

Carroll (2009) states that the ethical behaviour of leaders in different types of organisations (for-profit, non-profit, educational, government) is not only useful but also just. Ethical behaviour of leaders is in fact the basis of a fair and just society, while unethical behaviour has destructive effects on people, relationships, organisations and society. Carroll (Figure 1.5) divides ethics into two periods since 2000: first, the period from 2001 to 2008, understood as the Enron era, and the second period, from 2008 onwards, as the era of Wall Street financial scandals. The author then shows that, before Enron, the majority thought of business ethics is intended only for workers and lower to mid-level leaders and managers, while a number of ethical dilemmas (such as sexual harassment in the workplace) in the relationship between the organisation and the social environment were occurring in the final decade of last century (Carroll and Buchholtz 2000). With the emergence of Enron, the focus shifted to the top management and the highest decision-making bodies of organisations. The recent period has brought even more sophisticated forms of financial scandals that, in contrast to the period up to 2008, were taken on a legal but unethical basis, leading to a complete lack of trust in the financial system. Accordingly, Carroll (2009) defined four factors that lead to unethical behaviour of organisations, namely weak or incompetent leaders who do not promote ethical behaviour, excessive pressure to generate profits, the presence of a code of silence among employees and fake concern for the community or organisation with the purpose of covering up harmful practices. Brown et al. (2005) see the unethical business scandals in the first decade of the twenty-first century as a reason to again reflect on the role of leadership in the management of ethical behaviour in organisations, while Carroll and Buchholtz (2000) found that a number of economic, legal, social and ethical issues in the relationship between the private sector and society only became a subject of public discussion at the turn of the millennium. The reason lies in the fact that the public scandals involving executives that have been published in the media, books and films trigger real disappointment in people (Yukl 2002). Huberts et al. (2008) also note that more and more attention, even on the global level, is nowadays being devoted to ethics and integrity in the spheres of for-profit organisations, public administration, politics and society in general.

Figure 1.5 Periods of business ethics.

Source: Carroll (2009).

Notwithstanding the above, Carroll and Buchholtz (2000) believed it is not true that all organisations make use of unethical practices, but that those organisations that do behave unethically cast negative attention and generalise unethical behaviour across all other related organisations.

Carroll (2009) thought that business ethics can be taught in three different ways, namely by means of indoctrination, by defining values and with the cognitive development model through which we develop ethical analysis and reflections through the prism of ethical principles (for example, justice, utility, the golden rule and so on) (Figure 1.6). The golden rule 'do unto others as you would have them do to you' constitutes a universal moral principle that is a very simple and effective ethical principle that embodies business relationships and delivers reciprocity to mutual relations (Carroll and Buchholtz 2000: 139, Carroll 2009: 142). Tavčar considers this form of the golden rule to be positive, whereas he understands its negative counterpart as 'do *not do* unto others what you do not want others to do unto you' (Tavčar 2008: 128). Maxwell (2007) understands the golden rule as an effective leading principle of integrity in every situation. By this, he highlights four main reasons that people should always act in accordance with it, namely, it is acceptable for most people, it is simple and understandable, it follows the philosophy of the win-win situation and it serves as a signpost when we need help with decision-making (Figure 1.6).

Ciulla (2004) considers that the golden rule is a fundamental moral principle in most culture as it advocates redirecting or moving beyond the concerns of self-interest towards interest in caring for others. In other words, the golden rule illustrates a bridge between selfishness and altruism. At the same time, the author notes that Plato and many others after him already found that the greatest ethical challenge for humans regarding leadership relates to the temptation of power. Leaders are

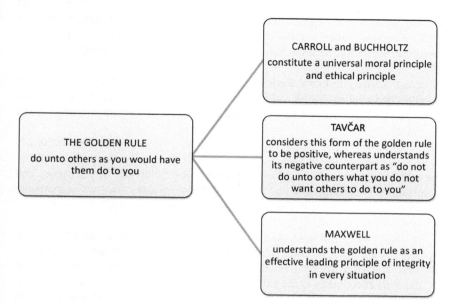

Figure 1.6 The golden rule.

Source: Authors.

those who have the primary role in creating an ethical climate in the organisation and in generating organisational values. Ethics plays the central role in leadership as it is particularly important regarding the possibility of leaders influencing their associates and employees (Northouse 2010). Badaracco and Ellsworth (1992) also consider that the ethical standards that form the cornerstone of a healthy organisation are personal in nature because they reflect the behaviour, opinions, experiences and values of employees, especially leaders. Therefore, they are convinced that the key factor in leadership is exactly the existing ethical standards.

Možina et al. (2002) believe that both ethical and moral conduct are necessary conditions for the success and existence of organisations and their leaders. Brown (2006) therefore hopes that business ethics will one day become social ethics and that improving and strengthening integrity in organisations will grow in the social context.

Berlogar (2000) prefers to use the term 'organisational ethics' instead of business ethics as it seems more appropriate as ethical irregularities occur in different organisations and not only in business. At the same time, the same as Greenleaf (2002a), Berlogar notes that business and organisational ethics have been a subject of research over the past two millennia,[4] wherein all the way to the nineteenth century, and beginning of the Industrial Revolution, being an entrepreneur was seen as not honourable. At the same time, social responsibility was much more pronounced, which grew in proportion to their power and influence in society. With the advent of the Industrial Revolution, the social responsibility of companies and growing corporations began to weaken, and the interest in the maximisation of profit, economic power and the emergence of power elites began to strengthen. Therefore, the author believes that to understand organisational ethics,

> it is necessary to know the historical development of business as a specific form of social exchange, values and philosophies of holders of trade and the context of the wider society in which this type of exchange always takes place.
>
> (Berlogar 2000: 28)

The call for business ethics and socially responsible behaviour of companies and organisations is nothing new, and the belief of leaders that ethics and responsible behaviour are an obstacle in the way of making profit is wrong.

> If those, who lead companies, possessed more knowledge about the past, they would see and understand, that economic and commercial operations were always a strictly regulated instrument of social development and that the market economy is the exception rather than the rule.
>
> (Berlogar 2000: 27)

Jelovac (1997) believes that accurate knowledge of philosophy is a prerequisite for understanding ethics and business ethics, which falls within its scope. Morality in this context represents a subject of autonomous will, whereas

> business morality is a voluntarily chosen obedience to good business practices, which, together with the traditional socio-cultural environment, act as a perfect way of understanding and a valid standard of assessing things, proceedings, procedures, character and behaviour in the field of management.
>
> (Jelovac 1997: 76)

Consequently, the sanction for violating business ethics is only a bad conscience or a sense of shame, while any punishment falls within the scope of law.

Tavčar (2000) believes that business ethics and management ethics form part of general ethics, which is within the category of useful or applied philosophy. He deals with the decisions of leaders and managers in accordance with their values and the values prevailing in the organisational environment. Acting that establishes values and is in line with ethical decisions is moral, while a leader who acts in such a way is understood by the author as a moral leader. At the same time, the author notes that business ethics extends to three levels, namely the level of the individual, the level of the organisation and the external environment and the level of interpersonal relationships within those levels.

Painter-Morland (2008) states that it is assumed that business ethics deals with business in the same way as it does with ethics, while the people who are professionally engaged in this field frequently receive complaints that their research does not pay enough attention to the overall complexity and dynamism of modern business and the organisational world. Therefore, the author argues that ethics must reflect everyday business practices and not only in a declarative sense in various regulations and policies. If that is the case, then ethics represents only the minimum requirement or a compromise for the implementation of activities, thus losing its legitimacy and effectiveness.

Business ethics is also an integral part of the system of value orientations of employees (in addition to the organisational culture, overall social ethics and so on), which 'always exist in the combination with specific situations and concrete problems faced by the actors' (Mesner-Andolšek 1995b: 172).[5] In contrast, Peterson (2004) notes that most theoretical and empirical findings indicate that situational factors influence unethical behaviour and they are associated with the operation of the organisation and the characteristics of individuals (employees) or a combination of both factors (Figure 1.7). In relation to situational influences, Jelovac (1997) notes that the true value of leaders and managers can only be evaluated on the basis of their behaviour in crises.

With regard to business ethics, Avolio and Bass (2002) recognise that many people understand it as an oxymoron as they believe they cannot be pursued simultaneously in practice. The authors reject this view and consider that, for example,

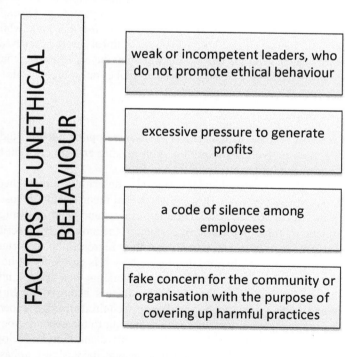

Figure 1.7 Factors of unethical behaviour.
Source: Becker (1998).

an authentic transformational leader leads his colleagues by example, acting in a moral, fair, equitable and transparent way. The difference lies only in the fact of whether the leader primarily leads by the ethical principles of justice, fairness and the principle of utility or by the principles of the expected consequences of their own decisions – for instance, usefulness for everyone present.

Notwithstanding the above, Maxwell notes that

> there is no such thing as "business ethics" – there is only one ethics. People otherwise try to stick to one of the ethics in relation to their profession, the other in relation to their spiritual life, and again a third in relation to their families, but precisely this is in fact the problem. Ethics is ethics. If one wants to be ethical, then one should choose only one criterion and keep it with oneself always and everywhere.
>
> (Maxwell 2007: 7)

De George (2001) considers the same, namely that the same ethical principles apply to all roles in which man finds himself on a daily basis, where his moral conduct is based on his personal integrity.

However, along with all of that Waddock (2006) sees, in addition to various education and training programmes, that professional journals in this field play an important role in the development of business ethics in a company (e.g. *Business Ethics Quarterly, The Journal of Business Ethics, Business and Society*), while Rowe and Kellam (2011) believe that nobody can become ethical purely on the basis of reading literature dealing with the ethical. Instead, they understand that acting responsibly every day and taking responsible decisions makes one more ethical.

Relevant ethical theories

A brief presentation now follows of ethical theories that are important to our study as they are related to an individual's moral decision-making and are relevant to both personal integrity and leadership.

Crane and Matten (2004) divide ethical theories into 'descriptive ethical theories' and 'normative ethical theories'. Descriptive ethical theories have focused on the study of how ethical decisions are made in business and what influences the process and results of those decisions. According to the authors, by describing why and what people in business actually do, they represent an important contribution to normative ethical theories, exploring how it is necessary or how things should be done. Influences on ethical decision-making are divided into individual and situational,[6] wherein the individual factors acquired by birth (gender, age) belong to the first group, and factors acquired through experience and socialisation (education, way of conduct) belong to the second group. Individual factors also include personal integrity, cognitive and moral development.[7] Regarding integrity, the authors assert that despite increasing emphasis on integrity itself, there is still much uncertainty about how and why integrity impacts ethical decision-making processes. However, the authors consider it, in addition to cognitive moral development, as a major factor of influence on individual moral decisions. Situational influences include factors related to the work environment (organisational culture, rules, systems of rewarding and sanctioning) (Mesner-Andolšek 1995a) and to the direct work practice (ethical and moral aspect), wherein the authors believe that behaviour and decisions in business cannot be adequately explained only by individual influences and the characteristics of the parties involved (Crane and Matten 2004: 111–38).

Regarding the normative ethical theories, the authors note that most of the traditional ethical theories advocated an absolutist approach (universal rules and principles that can be applied in any situation), while the contemporary ethical theories adopt an increasingly relativistic perspective. Traditional ethical theories are divided into consequentialist or teleological theories, where the goal and the result are the most important parts of the moral practice. The second group of traditional ethical theories is the non-consequentialist or deontological theories where duty and motivation are the most important parts of the moral practice. The first group of traditional ethical theories, which is consequentialist, includes the egoistic and utilitarian perspectives. The second group, which is non-consequentialist, includes the ethics of duty/Kantianism and the theory of rights and justice. The egoistic aspect considers pursuing desires and one's own interests as the highest principle of morally correct behaviour. Utilitarianism considers activities that bring the greatest good for the greatest number of people as the highest principle of morally correct behaviour (comfort-hedonistic aspect; happiness-eudaimonistic aspect; friendship and love – intrinsically valuable human goods). Founded by Kant and belonging to the non-consequentialist (second) group, the ethics of duty is based on the fact that the morality of a decision does not depend on the individual situation or the consequences of behaviour. The ethics of duty presents its own theoretical framework for decision-making known as the *categorical imperative*, which is valid in all circumstances for everyone at all times. Conversely, the ethical theory of rights and justice has its own focus on protection of the absolute natural rights (life, liberty, property) and respect for justice (procedural and distributive justice).

Among the contemporary ethical theories, the authors include those that were placed in the foreground or developed in the field of business ethics in the final decade of last century. These are *virtue ethics*, which will be examined in the next chapter, feminist ethics, discursive ethics and postmodern ethics. Feminist ethics stresses empathy, healthy interpersonal relationships and mutual concern. Discursive ethics focuses on resolving ethical dilemmas through rational reflection on practical examples, while postmodern ethics emphasises tracing their own sense of morality and inner belief in the decision-making process (Crane and Matten 2004: 79–109).

Ferrell et al. (2011) note that the difference between deontological/teleological and virtue ethics is that the first two theories solve problems with the deductive method, while virtue ethics uses the inductive method. Žalec (2006) considers that the essential difference between virtue ethics and deontological and utilitarian ethics is that the former is focused on answering the question what kind of person we should be, while the latter two focus on answering the question of which ethical principle is the right one. Palanski and Vogelgesang (2011) note, however, that up until recently, most research in the field of applied business ethics concentrated on the deontological approach, based on respecting existing rules, and on the utilitarian approach that focuses on achieving benefits. Yet, in the recent period, research has become increasingly directed to virtue ethics, which deals with the question of how and what an individual should be. The authors note that the deontological and utilitarian approaches strive for the optimal decision in a specific situation, while virtue ethics focuses on the definition of good character and positive patterns of behaviour over time and different situations.

In connection with this, Northouse (2010) notes that the ethical theories related to leadership are mainly concentrated on the character and behaviour of leaders. The character of the leaders falls within the framework of virtue ethics, that is, examining the leader as a human being. Deontological theories focus on dealing with the rules that govern the behaviour of leaders, while teleological theories look mainly at the consequences of behaviour. The study of consequences, as mentioned in the introduction, constitutes three parts: ethical egoism, utilitarianism and altruism.

Virtue ethics

The beginning of virtue ethics dates back to ancient Greece, with Aristotle being understood as its founder (Carroll and Buchholtz 2000, Crane and Matten 2004, Flynn 2008, Carroll 2009). Unlike Socrates and Plato, he emphasised that it is not only *possessing* virtues but *acting* in life in accordance with virtues that is a source of happiness. Virtues are understood as ideals of a good life, to which all human activities are directed.

In recent years, virtue ethics has been growing in importance in the context of business ethics. Strahovnik (2004) understands that the resurgence of virtue ethics started somewhere in the final quarter of the last century. Its core represents the virtues of leaders, the moral character of leaders and leader conduct. Regarding character, Flynn (2008) understands virtue ethics as the ethics of character, which deals with the strengthening of integrity and excellence. However, Laabs (2011) notes that a good character, as was advocated by Aristotle, forms through virtuous behaviour and finding a balance between the extremes in conscious rational decision-making.

Schumann (2001) understands virtue ethics as moral conduct via which exclusively moral virtues are reflected. Virtue ethics considers what a morally correct or 'right' act is and what a person with virtuous characteristics does. Virtues are a prerequisite for moral behaviour (Crane and Matten 2004). Virtue ethics is focused on the moral character of an individual who makes certain decisions and not on the consequences of actions. Virtues represent a set of desired characteristics of a person's character and, as such, enable a good life. The authors divide virtues into intellectual virtues (for example wisdom) and moral virtues (courage, honesty, loyalty, humility and so on), whereby a man is not born in possession of them but acquires them through learning and practice. Because of this, virtuous behaviour and the tendency towards a good life lie at the heart of virtue ethics. Aristotle also connects a good life with the feeling of happiness and not with hedonism (Crane and Matten 2004: 79–109).

Ferrel et al. (2011) believe that the subject of virtue ethics is not just judging what is moral in a particular situation in terms of general social morality. They believe that it is also about what a mature person with a good moral character deems important. At the same time, they recognise that a pluralism of virtues enables a person to have a good character with integrity and that moral conduct, which society demands in certain situations, merely represents a minimum and the basis for virtue ethics.

In the context of virtue ethics, Whetstone (2001) advocates a balanced tripartite approach to leadership based on the deontological theories and teleological theories along with ethical principles and virtue ethics. Goethals et al. (2004) note that virtue ethics, in comparison to utilitarianism and the Kantian approach, attributes leadership with a spectrum of moral width, wherein none of these three approaches is perfect. Thus, according to the authors, the Kantian approach is based too much on rules and not enough on people, while utilitarianism focuses too much on benefits and, as such, also not enough on people. With virtue ethics, which deals with the analysis of character behaviour, we have the problem of leaders overestimating their own roles and their relations with employees. In this connection, Whetstone (2001) believes that a perfect virtuous leader is in reality an unattainable ideal, which serves as a good model for leaders, who then try to achieve it in practice.

Carroll thinks that the essential goal of virtue ethics is the human heart, which is the ethics principles opposite to the ethics of duty which deals with how a leader should act. It follows from this that virtue ethics focuses on *being*, while the ethics of duty focuses on *doing* (Carroll 2009: 107).[8] Virtue ethics is not solely focused on the character of the leader but also on personal qualities such as courage, honesty, fairness, truthfulness, faithfulness, kindness and so on. It deals with the question of what a person should become or will be, which is different from other approaches to the study of ethics (for example, utilitarianism, the principle of fairness, legality and so on), which focus on the question of *how* to act (Figure 1.8).

Virtue ethics is directly linked to the human character. This is confirmed by various training programmes from the virtue ethics field that are associated with the development of human character. In addition to the virtues of honesty, fairness, loyalty, fulfilling promises and so on, Carroll and Buchholtz (2000) include another virtue in the set, namely *personal integrity*.

Definition of virtue

In the Oxford Dictionary (1989b, 2004), a virtue[9] is defined as the characteristic that is understood as morally good and desired and it is associated with an appropriate way of life and behaviour according to high moral principles, voluntarily abiding by moral rules and standards, an absence of immoral conduct, personified moral quality and the effectiveness of moral principles. The Cambridge Dictionary

VIRTUE ETHICS

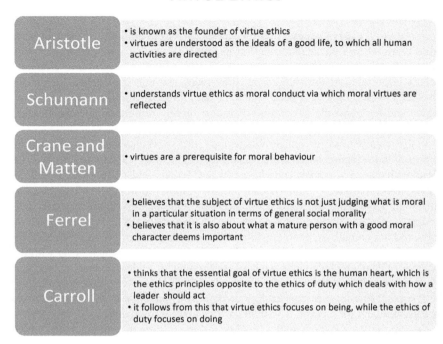

Aristotle	• is known as the founder of virtue ethics • virtues are understood as the ideals of a good life, to which all human activities are directed
Schumann	• understands virtue ethics as moral conduct via which moral virtues are reflected
Crane and Matten	• virtues are a prerequisite for moral behaviour
Ferrel	• believes that the subject of virtue ethics is not just judging what is moral in a particular situation in terms of general social morality • believes that it is also about what a mature person with a good moral character deems important
Carroll	• thinks that the essential goal of virtue ethics is the human heart, which is the ethics principles opposite to the ethics of duty which deals with how a leader should act • it follows from this that virtue ethics focuses on being, while the ethics of duty focuses on doing

Figure 1.8 Virtue ethics.

Source: Authors.

(2003) defines virtue as a good and moral quality (property, quality) of a single person or as a general quality and excellence in humans. The opposite of a virtue is represented by a moral flaw or weakness in the character of the individual (for example, unfairness), and immoral or illegal acts (Cambridge 2003).

Virtue (gr. *areté*, lat. *virtus*) generally means that, if a person possesses it, he 'is good – good at anything' (Kocijančič 2002: 570, Kocijančič 2004: 1100), or good at something (Flynn 2008). More precisely, virtue denotes 'excellence, the ability to act in the best possible ways in various fields' (Kocijančič 2002: 570), whereas even an animal or an object can be virtuous (Kocijančič 2002, 2004). However, human virtue primarily manifests itself in the use of reason, whereas it is not the same with animals (Aristotle 2002: 59). Spinoza similarly considered that people without moral virtues are to be seen as inhumane. Spinoza thus attributed virtues only to the human being and his nature, with the assumption that it is within his power (Spinoza 2004).

'*Areté* of a human lies in the fact that he can function well as a human being' (MacIntyre 1993: 26). Virtues were, just like ethics, a subject of discussion very early on in Greek philosophy[10] (Heraclitus), whereas the two most important virtues were represented by thoughtfulness and wisdom (Kocijančič 2004: 1101). Further, the Greek philosophers understood fairness, courage, temperance and prudence as the cardinal virtues.[11] For the ancient Greek philosophers, virtue, or excellence (*areté*), represented a characteristic that tended to influence life to become good or excellent (Mintz 1996). During the time of the Sophists, virtues especially came under the spotlight, specifically in relation to how man should live. The answer to that was that man was to be happy, however, this can only be achieved if he is good. Representatives of the school of Epicurus understood virtue as awareness of one's own maxim that leads to happiness, while the Stoics conceived of happiness as awareness of one's virtues (Kant 2003: 130). Given that *areté* means to be good at something, the word itself is often translated as *virtue*, whereas Aristotle understood that *areté* falls within the scope of moral character (for example, courage) or within the scope of the virtues of reasoning and thinking (for example, being good at planning) (Flynn 2008: 45).

The basic ethical and moral question already of integral importance for Ancient Greek philosophers such as Socrates and Plato deals with understanding which virtues constitute and contribute to a good character – it does not, however, deal with which *conduct* or *behaviour* is right and correct. According to Plato, virtue mainly denotes a 'natural virtue with a strong semantic emphasis on "goodness" in general' (Kocijančič 2004: 1100). Plato placed virtues in four main categories (reasonableness or wisdom, temperance or prudence, justice,[12] and courage); all of them reflect the 'idea of good' (Mintz 1996, Trompenaars and Voerman 2010). Because of this, virtues 'lose outlines in between them, thus suggesting the profoundest secret of Plato's ethics: a deep unity and oneness of all virtues' (Kocijančič 2002: 572). As such, if the core of a virtue is knowledge about good and bad, 'it is impossible to have one virtue without having the others' (Kocijančič 2004: 1103). Before Plato, Socrates had, in dialogue with Menon, concluded that all virtues are of one and the same form. As a result, it is impossible to list them and it is impossible for the virtues to be 'learnt' or trained as there are no sufficiently competent mentors. Man as such receives these virtues by divine destiny (Plato 2004: 887–914), whereas the human goodness is in his soul and not in his body or his riches (Kocijančič 2004: 1101). Socrates believed that a good life is the same as a virtuous and righteous life and that virtue and happiness are identical, with wisdom being the fundamental and necessary condition for happiness. With wisdom, as such, we are able to identify good acts, morals, conduct and so on (Mintz 1996). Socrates also believed that 'one, who knows[13] what is good and just, cannot act in opposition to that which is good and just, thus behaving ethically and morally' (Jerman 1992, 42). With this, just acting is possible only on the basis of knowledge (Jelovac 1997).[14] MacIntyre notes that it is not completely clear why Socrates equates virtue with knowledge because Socrates was very thorough regarding consequences: 'Nobody is willingly wrong, which means that the cause of the bad deed is in the intellectual error and not in moral weakness' (1993: 34). However, Price (2003) thinks that humans act unethically because of 'problems' with our own will and not because of 'problems' with our own beliefs and knowledge, as our sole interests are those that lead us into conduct that is contrary to what is expected.

According to Socrates and Plato, Aristotle defended the thesis that man must align his acting[15] with the ethical-moral virtues (justice,[16] courage, nobility, decency, moderation, calmness, friendship, generosity) and the rational-dianoetic virtues (wisdom, clarity, discernment).[17] There is a close connection between the two types of virtues (Jerman 1992: 41, Mintz 1996: 829, Barnes 1999: 92, Gantar 2002: 21). Their common objective is the management of human affects, which can represent happiness; in other words, with moral virtues man can subordinate his instincts, desires and emotions to reason (Jerman 1992: 41–2). The difference between them lies in the fact that intellectual virtues develop through learning, experience and time, while ethics derive from the nature of man (Aristotle 2002). Virtues are not innate and man thus becomes virtuous on the basis of virtuous conduct (Mintz 1996). Aristotle understood virtue as the *golden mean* between two extremes – exaggeration and deficiency (Mintz 1996, Gantar 2002). The measure or the ideal of this was accounted for by 'a wise man' (Gantar 2002: 20, 390). 'Exaggeration is misguided and deficiency is shunned upon, while the midfield between them reaps praise and success: both of these are, in fact, the characteristics of virtues' (Aristotle 2002: 85). Aristotle understood that it is the golden mean (moderation) that upholds a virtue, whereas a deficiency or exaggeration leads to its dissolution. In other words, a virtue exists inside a right relationship between good and bad. Aristotle saw the opposite of virtues as 'weaknesses', while at the same time he understood that because 'virtues are neither passions nor abilities', it is imperative that a virtue is 'withholding' from a 'certain action'. Thus, if we wish to explain the essence and its conceptual side, we can say that 'a virtue is the golden mean, however, if we wanted to explain its value and importance, we can say that a virtue is the end goal and peak of all things' (Aristotle 2002: 85–6). Consequently, a virtue, as balance and an end goal at the same time, can today be understood as *an ideal* (Gantar 2002), whilst Jelovac (1997) notes that an honest and intelligent man always looks for the ideal balance, thus avoiding unnecessary and prohibited conduct. Aristotle, in general, summed up that a virtue is a will to find the right balance, the golden mean, shaping human actions and at the same time being the result of them. As such, virtues are attainable and favourable, with common sense being the criteria for them (Aristotle 2002: 109–10). His answer to the question of whether it is the action or the action's purpose that is more important was that 'virtue consists of both; as such, it is clear that it is complete if it encompasses both' (2002: 319). Knowing this, the most important fact here is that 'it is not enough to "know" for a certain virtue, but that it is of the highest importance for us to attain it and to act in accordance with it' (2002: 322). Moreover, Aristotle recognised happiness within virtues and acting in accordance with them, whilst noting that 'the wise man is appreciated because of his characteristics and these characteristics are seen as virtues' (2002: 73). He understood wisdom as the most complete level of knowledge and as a link between knowledge and smartness. At the same time, he argued that as is with creation of an opinion – in a form of mental ability and as smart-ness, as is also with the construction of a character: one is a natural virtue or ability, while the second is a virtue in the true sense of the word. The virtue in the true sense cannot be developed without smartness'. Socrates was, as Aristotle put it, thus correct when he argued that 'there is no virtue without smartness.

(2002: 204)

Aristotle defended the thesis that the cause that enables a virtue to manifest itself also strengthens it; if the cause changes, so does the virtue decompose' (2002: 80). Virtue 'depends on our actions in the same way that wickedness depends on our actions' (2002: 106). This also applies to integrity and acting in accordance with it, whereby actions, 'which are in accordance with virtue, are noble and are com-mitted because of noble motives' (2002: 127).

Based on the foregoing, Aristotle's ethics is understood as virtue ethics where personal integrity is in the spotlight (Solomon 2004: 1025). At the same time, Solomon (1992: 331) believed that Aristotle can still be considered one of the greatest proponents of strengthening human excellence.

Spinoza (2004) considered the efforts of man to preserve his own being as the most perfect virtue, taking the view that the more someone seeks and is able to maintain his own being, the more he is endowed with virtue. In addition, he defended the thesis that man can act in accordance with virtue only when he pos-sesses adequate ideas and when he lives and works under the guidance of reason. Spinoza described man as one who always acts with honesty and is never insidi-ous, and always consistent in his words and deeds. The gap between true virtue and the helplessness of man, Spinoza understood as the gap between the man with true virtue, one that lives under the guidance of reason and the man who allows to be led by things beyond him, consequently being powerless. Accordingly, Kant (2003) also defined virtue as a moral condition, understood as a duty. He showed that 'seeing virtue in its true image does not mean anything other than to show the moral nature free from all admixtures of the sensuous, repayment and egocen-trism' (Kant 2005: 42).

Rousseau (1993: 48) ascribed man with only one natural virtue, namely, mercy from which all social virtues stem (1993: 49). Rousseau understood mercy as a natural emotion which, in the 'natural state', supersedes law, moral nature and virtues, while enabling man to calm the effects of egocentrism and encouraging the maxim of natural goodness: 'Do good to yourself with harming the other as little as possible' (1993: 50).

Moore understood virtue as a 'permanent disposition of the implementation of certain actions, which generally produce the best possible outcomes' (Moore 2000: 243). At the same time, he realised that both weakness and virtue are ethi-cal terms,

which means that we intend to, when seriously applied, to utter praise with one, and reprimand with the other. Praise means something to declare: either that something is a good thing in itself or that it is good as a means to something. Virtues are thus generally regarded as something inherently good.

(Moore 2000: 242–3)

According to MacIntyre (2006), a model of all virtues is a thorough-thinking man who must be both an independent and practical thinker, capable of reception and interpretation of his own independent decisions. As he says, for virtuous behaviour something more must be present than just simply following a rule. He states that 'without virtue, we cannot adequately protect ourselves and others from neglect, lack of compassion, stupidity, egoism and evil' (2006: 108). At the same time, the author believes that temperance is very important for virtues, 'because whoever becomes moderate, starts to enjoy moderation, while overdoing becomes uncomfortable and even painful' (2006: 98). MacIntyre sees honesty as one of the main virtues; in other words, recognising the truth about ourselves and others.

According to Kocijančič, 'virtues of man include every perfected skill in any profession' (2002: 570) or, in other words

virtue is any capacity of a man's right attitude and behaviour towards others and to oneself, especially to one's own passions and other absurd tendencies. This regularity is always determined by a code of ethics of the community, but can never be completely reduced to it.

(Kocijančič 2002: 571)

Man can be virtuous by nature, 'but needs to be philosophically informed and educated, if he is to reach true virtue. We need to achieve philosophical virtue', Kocijančič observes (2004: 1102).

Whetstone (2001) defines virtue as a qualitative characteristic that is normally associated with human character, that it is in man, meaning that it is not material and not biological. The author believes that virtue is an internalised value, as a kind of spiritual human essence, which is not static but directs, motivates and regulates man's moral thinking and behaviour. In this context, to determine whether a person has acted in accordance with conscious conduct, a real motive is required that is not linked to personal gains or quasi-intentions, and a dynamic equilibrium of human character regardless of the situation. In other words, virtuous behaviour can therefore be considered as rational acting based on a wise evaluation of the actual situation, the right motivation and a balanced character.

Audi and Murphy (2006) distinguish between two basic categories of virtues, namely *substantive virtues* and *adjunctive virtues*. Substantive virtues are morally good in themselves (for example, honesty and fairness), while complementary virtues in themselves are neither good nor bad, but are necessary for maintaining and strengthening the moral posture (for example, courage, conscientiousness). Integrity, in their view, falls into both categories, while in terms of integration into a whole, it falls into the second category – the complementary category. Their thesis is clarified by stating that 'integrity, in terms of integration into the whole, contrary to its aretaic sense, is not a self-sustaining ethical standard, nor does it contain one, which makes it a complementary virtue' (Audi and Murphy 2006: 12).

Koehn (2005b) believes that a virtuous man or someone who deals with business will never knowingly violate the rules in order to provide happiness to himself or others. In this regard, the author also notes that anthropological studies show that humans have changed over time. Consequently, he believes that it is questionable whether happiness or satisfaction still represents the human 'good'. Batson et al. (2006) consider virtues as moral excellence and as a distinction between pragmatic and prescriptive virtues, wherein the first virtues lead to a desired goal, while the others are desired as goals in themselves. Žalec sees virtues as 'human qualities which the latter must have, in order for his life to be good' (2006: 187), wherein everyone must ask himself what kind of person he should be. According to Whetstone (2001), virtues benefit a man and the people he is in contact with, while Grant (2011) sees virtue as a character quality that enables an individual to come closer to their own self-fulfilment (Figure 1.9).

Given that Aristotle understood justice as one of the highest and most perfect virtues and that it is a cornerstone of virtue ethics, which includes personal integrity, and given the fact that sometimes, when defining the desired characteristics of leaders, justice is more emphasised than integrity, we specifically define justice in the following chapter.

Justice in relation to integrity

As can be seen from Socrates' words, a just man (a man of integrity) does not allow his soul to perform inappropriate tasks because that would undermine his mental state (Plato 1995).

Plato answered the question of how justice itself can separate from any self-interest and be more beneficial from injustice in his works on the state and the human soul (MacIntyre 1993). Metaphorically, as was already mentioned, he used a tripartite division of the state or government (leaders, soldiers, workers) to mimic the constitution of the soul, whereby people are classified in classes depending on what part of the soul prevails. Justice is found in the fact that everyone knows their place which is given to them at birth. In doing so, Plato realised that man is

> wise because of his intellect, and brave because of the role that is played by his spiritual part. An individual is prudent if his lower bodily desires are governed by intellect. Justice, however, does not belong to this or that part of the soul or connections between them, but resides in its overall consistency.
> (MacIntyre 1993: 50)

At the same time, MacIntyre notes that Socrates and Plato differed in the fact that 'Socrates understood that for the use of ethical predicates, only a certain criteria is needed, while Plato believed that for such objective standards of use of such predicates, it is necessary that these predicates relate to objects, objects of external existence' (1993: 52).

Virtue generally means that if a person possesses it, he "is good - good at anything"

Heraclitus
- the two most important virtues are thoughtfulness and wisdom

Sophists
- virtues in relation to how Man should live
- man was to be happy, however this can only be achieved if he is good

Plato
- virtue mainly denotes a natural virtue with a strong semantic emphasis on goodness in general
- wrote what later would be known as cardinal virtues: fairness, courage, temperance and prudence

Socrates
- believed that a good life is the same as a virtuous and righteous life and that virtue and happiness are identical, with wisdom being the fundamental and necessary condition for happiness

Aristotle
- defended the thesis that Man must align his acting with the ethical - moral virtues (justice, courage, nobility, decency, moderation, calmness, riendship, generosity) and the rational - dianoetic virtues (wisdom, clarity, iscernment)

Spinoza
- understood the gap between true virtue and the helplessness of Man as the gap between the man with true virtue - one that lives under the uidance of reason - and the man who allows to be led by things beyond him, consequently being powerless

Rousseau
- ascribed Man with only one natural virtue, namely, mercy from which all social virtues stem

Moore
- understood virtue as a permanent disposition of the implementation of certain actions, which generally produce the best possible outcomes

Macintyre
- a model of all virtues is a thorough - thinking man, who must be both an independent and practical thinker, capable of reception and interpretation of his own independent decisions

Whetstone
- believes that virtue is an internalised value, as a kind of spiritual human essence, which is not static but directs, motivates and regulates Man's moral thinking and behaviour

Audi and Murphy
- distinguish between two basic categories of virtues (honesty), namely substantive virtues and adjunctive virtues. Substantive virtues are morally good in themselves, while complementary virtues in themselves are neither good nor bad, but are necessary for maintaining and strengthening the moral posture (courage)

Koehn
- believes that a virtuous man or someone who deals with business will never knowingly violate the rules in order to provide happiness to himself or others

Figure 1.9 Meaning of virtue through history.

Source: Authors.

Aristotle (2002) believed, as mentioned, that justice marked the highest and most perfect virtue, namely because it represents something good for others and that it also reflects in relations with others. Just conduct is understood as intentional conduct and as a path of moderation between profit and loss, in other words, between too much and too little, wherein at the definition of justice, he used Tognis's quote, that already in their time functioned as a common saying: 'in just behaviour all virtues are present' (2002: 156). According to Mintz (1996), Aristotle considered just conduct as the highest form of excellence. A just man was, for Aristotle, a man who acts justly out of free will, whereby when it came to a just distribution

> between himself and others, or between two other persons, the just man did not act in self-interest or in a harmful way towards others, but allocates everything to each person in accordance to the principle of fairness and proportion.
>
> (Aristotle 2002: 168–9)

Without justice, values would cease to be values and values would become worthless, whereby justice resides only in the man who realises it in practice (Comte-Sponville 2002). Therefore, this means that a just man only takes what belongs to him, including his share of that which is bad (Aristotle 2002). Here, he must take into account the equality in a relationship[18] with others. In this way, justice represents a balance between excessive humanitarianism and excessive selfishness or the path between 'too much' and 'too little' (Aristotle 2002: 160). Spinoza also saw justice in the fact that each person has what really belongs to them (Šajković 2004). Yet Comte-Sponville (2002: 102) believes that justice is inexistent in the natural state as such, it only exists if people are just and if justice is desired on the basis of a general consensus. For him, all justice is human justice and all justice is historical: there is no justice without laws (in the legal sense) and without culture (in the moral sense). The author notes that there is no doubt that justice is socially beneficial. He concludes that justice that would only serve the strong would not be just – consequently, this reveals the essence of justice as a virtue: the essence is the acknowledgment of the equality of legal subjects, and not the acknowledgment of power, individuals or authorities (2002: 113).[19]

John Rawls understood justice as fairness. In addition to the fact that all citizens receive reasonable shares of social goods, his doctrine of fairness constitutes restrictions in relation to what people can do to each other in obtaining these goods (Palmer 2007: 428). According to social contract theory as designed by Rousseau (2001: 26) in this context, everyone should renounce part of their own 'natural freedom' in favour of the 'citizens' freedom' and the community.

Integrity as a virtue

Integrity can therefore be classified as a moral virtue – in the set of virtue ethics. Plato and Aristotle believed that man's ultimate goal, which is also consistent with virtue ethics, is to be happy. The main prerequisite for this, however, is that man is virtuous. The fact is that the concept of integrity has hitherto failed to be defined clearly – it has not been defined in a way that renders it suitable for use in various everyday situations.[20] Yukl (2002) observes that the reason for this lies in the fact that today there is still no universal definition of integrity. In this connection, Palanski and Yammarino (2007) consider it necessary to define integrity in relation to other virtues that are closely related (such as courage, honesty, fairness and so on), *before* it is defined by itself.

As in the past, even today integrity is still occasionally used as a synonym for justice, as well as honesty, trustworthy, respect, openness and even empathy and compassion. Solomon (1992: 328) understands integrity as the key to Aristotle's ethics and as a common denominator and linchpin of all virtues, and which represents a necessary condition for their mutual coherence. At the same time, it represents a counterweight for personal disintegration. The author also considers that personal and individual wholeness depends on the community in which a person lives and where the person's integrity comes to the fore. However, it can also be understood in a social and organisational context and in conjunction with other organisational virtues such as trust, loyalty and cooperation. In addition, Paine (2005) considers that the trademarks of integrity, often understood as authenticity and sincerity, are also associated with a high degree of self-control and self-awareness; such is also in stark contrast with dogmatic devotion to incredulous belief, hypocrisy, dishonesty and so on.

Becker (1998) is, however, in conflict with the aforementioned; he is convinced that integrity[21] cannot simply be equated with honesty, diligence or a positive set of personality characteristics. As an example, he establishes a difference between integrity and honesty, which he considers to be essential, yet not a condition to suffice for integrity. Moreover, the abuse of fairness is reflected in relation to the outside world, whereas the abuse of integrity is reflected in relation to one's own values and virtues. Consequently, the author advocates an objectivist concept of integrity (loyalty to general truths, principles and values), which means 'to be principled, do what you say and mean, whatever your emotional or social pressure is, without tolerance for any irrational reason that might dictate one's own rational convictions' (Becker 1998: 157). The author is convinced that integrity is not just linked to words, but also to conduct which must be consistent with one's principles and values. As Becker notes, this does not mean that a man of integrity cannot ever change his own opinions and positions, but that this can be done if one has good intentions and that such a change is a result of new realisations and findings.[22] He believes that the use of the objectivist interpretation prevents errors that may occur in the case of 'subjectivist, morally relative perceptions related to understanding of integrity as such' (1998: 160) (Figure 1.10).

Audi and Murphy (2006) note that integrity is generally used in two different ways. The first concept is wider and has an integrational meaning, in the sense of the wholeness of the character, while the other concept is primarily focused on the aspect of virtue (an areatic sense – from the Greek word *areté* – virtue).[23] Integrity can be identical with an individual moral virtue or with moral virtues in general. As the authors note, 'integrity, in the integrational sense, is useful in a variety of cases that require strict adherence to high moral standards' (Audi and Murphy 2006: 13). The authors believe that if we do not think about integrity in relation to honesty, sincerity, taking responsibilities for one's own conduct, fulfilling promises and so on, but instead see integrity on its own, it can best be

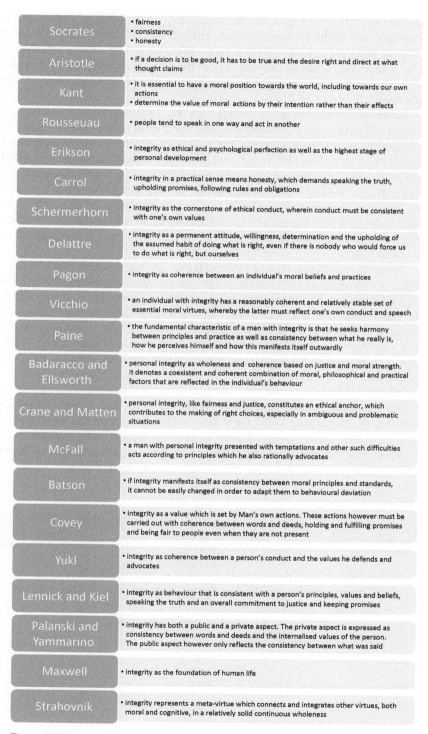

Socrates	• fairness • consistency • honesty
Aristotle	• if a decision is to be good, it has to be true and the desire right and direct at what thought claims
Kant	• it is essential to have a moral position towards the world, including towards our own actions • determine the value of moral actions by their intention rather than their effects
Rousseuau	• people tend to speak in one way and act in another
Erikson	• integrity as ethical and psychological perfection as well as the highest stage of personal development
Carrol	• integrity in a practical sense means honesty, which demands speaking the truth, upholding promises, following rules and obligations
Schermerhorn	• integrity as the cornerstone of ethical conduct, wherein conduct must be consistent with one's own values
Delattre	• integrity as a permanent attitude, willingness, determination and the upholding of the assumed habit of doing what is right, even if there is nobody who would force us to do what is right, but ourselves
Pagon	• integrity as coherence between an individual's moral beliefs and practices
Vicchio	• an individual with integrity has a reasonably coherent and relatively stable set of essential moral virtues, whereby the latter must reflect one's own conduct and speech
Paine	• the fundamental characteristic of a man with integrity is that he seeks harmony between principles and practice as well as consistency between what he really is, how he perceives himself and how this manifests itself outwardly
Badaracco and Ellsworth	• personal integrity as wholeness and coherence based on justice and moral strength. It denotes a coexistent and coherent combination of moral, philosophical and practical factors that are reflected in the individual's behaviour
Crane and Matten	• personal integrity, like fairness and justice, constitutes an ethical anchor, which contributes to the making of right choices, especially in ambiguous and problematic situations
McFall	• a man with personal integrity presented with temptations and other such difficulties acts according to principles which he also rationally advocates
Batson	• if integrity manifests itself as consistency between moral principles and standards, it cannot be easily changed in order to adapt them to behavioural deviation
Covey	• integrity as a value which is set by Man's own actions. These actions however must be carried out with coherence between words and deeds, holding and fulfilling promises and being fair to people even when they are not present
Yukl	• integrity as coherence between a person's conduct and the values he defends and advocates
Lennick and Kiel	• integrity as behaviour that is consistent with a person's principles, values and beliefs, speaking the truth and an overall commitment to justice and keeping promises
Palanski and Yammarino	• integrity has both a public and a private aspect. The private aspect is expressed as consistency between words and deeds and the internalised values of the person. The public aspect however only reflects the consistency between what was said
Maxwell	• integrity as the foundation of human life
Strahovnik	• integrity represents a meta-virtue which connects and integrates other virtues, both moral and cognitive, in a relatively solid continuous wholeness

Figure 1.10 Personal integrity.

Source: Authors.

defined in relation to ethics, but not necessarily on the basis of already existing concepts such as the Kantian approach, virtue ethics, utilitarianism and so on. All of these concepts already include honesty, fairness, loyalty, charity and free will. The authors consequently advocate use of the concept of integration (integration as a whole) in a broad sense and in the light of a better understanding of moral demands.

However, Comte-Sponville (2002) believes, because integrity as a virtue is taught effectively via a personal example role model rather than by books, that being virtuous is very demanding. The author understands virtue as an embodied moral value or a force that makes a man worthy, excellent, human and enables the realisation of 'good'. Living and acting with integrity means that a man lives authentically. To live authentically, according to Sartre's existentialism, means to 'live with the consciousness of full responsibility for everything that is happening in the world' (Jerman 1992: 126). In doing so, Cloud (2009: 41) believes that having integrity means to act with power, while simultaneously leaving positive results.

However, as already noted by Aristotle, we are not debating about virtue 'in order to determine what a virtue is, but in order to become good ourselves' (2002: 77), which means knowledge alone does not suffice – correlative acts should also be carried out. Aristotle also added that whatever is done in accordance with a virtue is not done fairly and in moderation merely because it was done, but that it is of paramount importance *how* such an act was done (Gantar 2002: 81). The fact *how* is, *per se*, the essence of ethical behaviour and integrity as a virtue (Figure 1.11).

Integrity therefore represents a complex concept that integrates conventional moral standards (telling the truth, being honest, frank and so on) and personal ideals at the same time, which are to be considered as one of the most important virtues of the 'higher order'. It represents the so-called integrated personality characteristic that also includes other personal characteristics such as honesty, reliability and trust. Given that we are interested in the integrity of leaders, we

FACTORS THAT DETERMINE PERSONAL INTEGRITY

- a man is honest, fair, independent and reasonable
- a man evaluates and assesses his own intentions and reasons
- his values, goals and behaviour are consistent
- he is willing to do everything necessary to live according to one's own, most respected values

Figure 1.11 Factors that determine personal integrity.

Source: Becker (1998).

will deal with personal integrity in the next chapter where we will discuss the connections between personal integrity and human character and the moral development of the individual, which affects both the integrity and character of man.

Personal integrity

Earlier on, Socrates was aware of the importance of personal integrity as he himself represented an example of moral life and behaviour. He alone reflected a high level of integrity, and, to this day, he is considered one of the most ethical people of all. Socrates had, at the cost of his life, represented someone who unbrokenly, void of calculation[24] and self-interest, defended his position before the Court that had sentenced him to death. This was all done precisely due to his firm conviction in his own right (Plato 2003: 83). As Bratož notes, Socrates 'paid for his principled fairness, consistency and honesty with his life' (Bratož 2003: 141). Moreover, shortly before his death, he affirmed to his cellmate that a fair, truthful, forthright and modest man need neither fear for his own destiny nor the fate of his soul (Plato 2003: 233).[25]

Aristotle also thought about a person's consistency without using the concept or the word 'integrity'. According to Barnes (1999: 102), Aristotle explicitly and implicitly – in his works – represented a model for the human ideal throughout his lifetime. Aristotle wrote in one of his works that

> what assertion and denial represent in thinking, desires and moderation reflect in one's willingness. Natural virtue is a retention from an act, while a decision is a deliberate volition. From this follows: if a decision is to be good, it has to be true and the desire right and directed at what thought claims.
>
> (Aristotle 2002: 187)

As already mentioned, Aristotle also realised that a virtue depends on the human will and that 'for the same reasons from which it arises, it also strengthens and (if these causes change) it decomposes' (2002: 80). This also applies to integrity and acting accordingly.

As is with moral (and amoral) conduct, it is likewise with acting in accordance with integrity (and without integrity); it is imperative to take the teachings of Kant's moral philosophy into account, namely that 'it is essential to have a moral position towards the world, including towards our own actions, as seen from the perspective of other people. We have to put ourselves in 'the shoes of others' (Palmer 2007: 326). This is, in fact, fully in line with the essence of integrity and the consistency of words and deeds. It is also contrary to saying something and then doing the opposite of what was said because as soon as someone puts himself into the position of another, they can see the correctness or incorrectness of their own actions. This means that it is not only our duty not to carry out specific acts, but it is also certainly our duty to choose those acts that can *be generalised*; what makes them moral is the fact that we chose them because we wanted to carry out our *duty*.

(2007: 329)

Here we can meet with authentic and pseudo-authentic actions. Because of this, Kant determined the value of moral actions by their *intention* rather than their *effects*. This is also consistent with the moral intuition that people themselves should not be exploited as a means for achieving certain goals and objectives.

Rousseau touched on the modern and contemporary conception of personal integrity in the eighteenth century when he described the situation in society at that time. He wrote that people 'tend to speak in one way and act in another' (Rousseau 1993: 19). This quote stems from an ancient moral principle – that we should practice what we preach. Greenleaf (2002a: 157) paraphrased it for today's use: 'do not do what you preach; just do'.[26]

The following contains an understanding of personal integrity from the perspective of our contemporary perspectives. Erikson defined integrity as ethical and psychological perfection as well as the highest stage of personal development (Paine 2005: 248).

Carroll (2009) believes that integrity in a practical sense means honesty, which demands speaking the truth, upholding promises and following rules and obligations. It denotes a life and conduct that complies with written and unwritten ethical principles. Schermerhorn et al. (2008) understand integrity as the cornerstone of ethical conduct, wherein conduct must be consistent with one's own values (for example, fairness, reliability) and statements. Delattre defines it as a 'permanent attitude, willingness, determination and the upholding of the assumed habit of doing what is right, even if there is nobody who would force him to do what is right, but himself' (Pagon 2003a: 23). He understands integrity as an irreplaceable basis for good friendship, marriage, parenting, sport and civic spirit as well as good public service. Pagon et al. (2000) see integrity as coherence between an individual's moral beliefs and practices. At the same time, the authors believe that an individual with a high degree of integrity acts in accordance with their own beliefs. Such a person does not act opportunely, which means that he acts according to his understanding of what is morally correct, regardless of both the opinions of others and the consequences.

Vicchio (1997) believes that an individual with integrity has a reasonably coherent, connected and relatively stable set of essential moral virtues, whereby the latter must reflect one's own conduct and speech. According to Pagon (2003a), this means that a person's words and actions must be one and the same. Personal integrity therefore requires consistency of words and actions, which reflect the fundamental values and virtues to which the individual is genuinely and voluntarily committed (Vicchio 1997). However, in that regard, Paine (2005) believes that moral coherence between belief and expression is impossible and probably even undesirable. According to Paine, the fundamental characteristic of a man with integrity is that he seeks harmony between principles and practice as well as consistency between what he really is, how he perceives himself and how this manifests itself outwardly.

Badaracco and Ellsworth (1992) see personal integrity as 'wholeness' and coherence based on justice and moral strength. It denotes a coexistent and coherent combination of moral, philosophical and practical factors that are reflected in the individual's behaviour. It is consistency between one's purpose, values and acts in an uncertain, changing and unpredictable environment. Crane and Matten (2004) understand personal integrity as dedication to moral values and principles as well as consistency between beliefs and behaviour regardless of the external circumstances. Personal integrity, like fairness and justice, constitutes an ethical anchor, which contributes to the making of right choices, especially in ambiguous and problematic situations. A man of integrity is completely fair; that goes for his private as well as his professional life, wherein he is characterised by his firm moral stance, notwithstanding the strong influences of different pressures (Fitsimmons 2008). McFall (1987) believes that a man with personal integrity presented with temptations and other such difficulties acts according to principles that he also rationally advocates. Batson et al. (1999) argue that if integrity manifests itself as consistency between moral principles and standards, then these principles and standards cannot be easily changed in order to adapt them to behavioural deviation. If human self-awareness encourages integrity, then this means that greater awareness contributes to the direct pressure on behaviour, according to moral principles and standards.

Covey (2004) sees integrity as a value which is set by man's own actions. These actions, however, must be carried out with coherence between words and deeds, holding and fulfilling promises and being fair to people even when they are not present. Covey (2006) adds that through integrity and personal principles wisdom of a person is reflected, while integrity is reflected in person's modesty and courage. Yukl (2002) understands integrity as coherence between a person's conduct and the *values* he defends and advocates. Such a person is also honest, ethical and trustworthy. Koehn, on the other hand, believes that integrity is intrinsically valuable, yet 'not an end in itself, but a prerequisite to man being truly human' (Koehn 2005a: 132). It means doing what is right, wherein the majority of people are merely intuitively aware of what integrity really means (Kampanakis 2000).

Huberts et al. (2007) consider integrity to be acting in accordance with socially accepted moral values, principles and rules. Lennick and Kiel (2009, 2011) see integrity as behaviour that is consistent with the principles, values and beliefs, speaking the truth and an overall commitment to justice and keeping promises. This leads to the belief that the person's words will match their deeds. The authors also consider integrity as an indication of an intelligent person, someone who acts in accordance with universal human principles, wherein moral intelligence[27] thus involves knowledge about what to do and moral competence by denoting a skill of doing what is right.

Palanski and Yammarino (2007, 2009, 2011) rank integrity amongst virtues and understand it to be consistency in acting entity's words and actions. At the same time, they recognise that integrity has both a public and a private aspect.

The private aspect is expressed as consistency between words and deeds and the internalised values of the person. The public aspect, however, only reflects the consistency between what was said (Palanski and Yammarino 2007). The same view on integrity, namely, as consistency between words and deeds, is held by Simons (1999, 2002), whereas Maxwell (2007) sees integrity as the foundation of human life. McFall (1987) considers integrity as coherence between the assumed principles and those principles in action. Lennick and Kiel (2012) see it as coherence between behaviour that is consistent with one's principles, values and beliefs, striving for righteousness, speaking the truth and holding promises. Woiceshyn (2011) considers integrity to be a virtue that manifests itself in the devotion to moral principles and as consistency between words and deeds. According to Strahovnik, integrity represents a meta virtue, 'which connects and integrates other virtues, both moral and cognitive, in a relatively solid and continuous wholeness' (Strahovnik 2012: 135). However, in the field of professional ethics, Strahovnik considers integrity as 'consistency between an individual's moral beliefs, his moral judgements and one's conduct' (Strahovnik 2010: 13).

Integrity does not denote something you either have or do not. Instead, it stands for a *path* of personal growth, which pays off in the long run. As such, people develop it throughout their lives (Cloud 2009). Family, education, friends, the environment and so on, all of these factors have a major influence on a person throughout their adolescence, and consequently, on their integrity. As such, it impacts on one's positive and negative experience as well as one's characteristics. Girodo (2003) understands integrity as a result of social interaction. Consequently, it is also an individual's personality trait. Kaiser and Hogan (2010) consider integrity to be more a component of a moral function of an individual's conduct rather than the standard of coherence between words and deeds. Laabs (2011) defines it as behaviour that is consistent with the individual's moral principles, enabling one to 'live with oneself' and to 'sleep peacefully' at night. It also reflects one's courage, tolerance and perseverance in difficult situations. Integrity thus does not mean that the individual merely resists or avoids unethical conduct but takes a pro-active stand on what he believes in, even if it is associated with problems (Gavin et al. 2003).

In addition to all these concepts, we believe that personal integrity can be understood as coherence between what the individual thinks, believes, speaks and what one actually does. We could, however, add here consistency between this and what one feels. This consequently manifests itself in the fact that man, as such, is emotionally at peace with himself.

Notwithstanding all that has been said, it is important to note that we can only speak of integrity in the case where the individual's acts are consistent with ethical principles. If someone believes that stealing from a corrupt organisation is acceptable, we cannot say that they have a high degree of integrity. Various studies show that it is precisely a lack of personal integrity that often leads to career stagnation. Becker (1998) sets out three general reasons that have negative impacts on

- In summing up, we can observe that personal integrity in today's world can be understood as a multi-dimensional phenomenon. We can define it as a set of virtues (to be fair, honest, modest, transparent, and so on), as consistency between words and deeds and as the absence of unethical behaviour.

Figure 1.12 Definition of integrity.

Source: Authors.

personal integrity. The first reason is the fact that people do not always act rationally. The second is the fact that people tend to have desires and preferences that are inconsistent with the principles of morality, wherein the third reason is associated with a variety of influences from the environment (for example, co-workers) (Figure 1.12).

Personal integrity and character

Human nature, or character, has occupied the centre of the philosophical study of ethics since ancient times. Socrates then realised that human character traits, like one's beliefs, desires, fears and so on, have a changing nature (Plato 2005). Aristotle, however, as Grant (2011) notes, saw great importance in one's character. He also thought that a good character enables a good judgement about what is best in each situation. This consequently means understanding what to do in every concrete situation and in accordance with 'integrity'.

According to Solomon (1992), the concept of virtues can be used as shorthand for defining the qualities that make up a good character. Yet Mintz (1996) notes that virtues are 'assumed human qualities or character traits that enable humans to achieve a good life. In business, they promote successful cooperation and facilitate the achievement of common goals'.

Palanski and Yammarino (2007) believe that integrity as a virtue can be understood as an integral part of a good character, which consists of other virtues (for example, honesty, justice, compassion, trustworthiness and credibility besides integrity). However, if it is used to explain wholeness and completeness, it can also be understood as a multi-faceted concept that joins several aspects. In this case, we can consider integrity as a synonym for character. Worden (2003) believes that integrity is dependent on the character of a person, while Becker (1998) notes that a good character, at least in part, means that a man has integrity.

Audi and Murphy (2006) believe that integrity is an essential but not a sufficient element of good character. It is, however, the first among the virtues that form a good character. According to the authors, we can search for integration between character and conduct on the personal level or on the group level, that is, between the individual and an organisation, between an organisation and society, between society and a region and so on. The authors see the said integration in a positive sense, wherein this is particularly true for the moral aspect of the consistency of thoughts, behaviour and so on. At the same time, they consider that when integrity is understood as being of good moral character it has at least as many aspects as there are moral virtues (honesty, fairness, loyalty, sincerity).

Howard (2010) believes that good leadership depends on being of good character, which manifests itself in positive qualities such as integrity, honesty, authenticity, courage and so on. Conversely, Kaiser and Hogan (2010), in their search for the answer to how to measure the integrity of leaders, use the concepts of integrity and character interchangeably.

Cloud (2009) believes integrity to be the coordinated acting of all aspects of the character that are independent; however, one cannot function without problems without the other. The author considers that people with good character can be trusted. This is a result of assumed ethical principles and personal integrity. Consequently, we can be sure they will not act unethically or harmfully in any way. At the same time, Cloud notes that integrity, as well as character, are subject to change – both can be strengthened or modified. In other words, this means that a person can always improve for the better.

The ability to make genuine connections contributes to building mutual confidence and trust. The tendency to focus on the truth leads to being aware of the reality of a situation. Actively dealing with problems leads to solutions, while focusing on development leads to progress. Abstract thinking helps to overcome adverse selfishness (Cloud 2009).[28]

Carroll (2009) believes that it is easier to talk about character than it is to act in accordance with it. The author notes that character is defined by reliability, sensitivity, responsibility, fairness and diligence. The ethical aspect, which deals with the importance of character, falls within the framework of virtue ethics. Girodo notes that the concept of integrity is bound with the power of character that is derived from the coherence of five elements: beliefs, emotions, perceptions, intentions and actions (Girodo 2003: 215).

Whetstone (2001) considers that a person's good character enables virtues to manifest themselves, while playing a central role in the absence of defects and weaknesses. Sarros and Cooper (2006) define character as visible expressions of an individual's values and integrity. These expressions tend to strive to achieve morally acceptable goals, while human activities 'without character' are thus only routine and often irrelevant.

Jelovac noted that 'character is a category, which includes the whole of all moral characteristics of a person. It is a person's symbol of individuality which is a result of his inheritance, upbringing and education' (Jelovac 1997: 33). In his opinion, this means that a person with character is someone with a constructed personality, which is resistant to common influences and changes in life's circumstances and the social environment. Harman (1999) considers that the findings do not confirm that individuals would vary according to personality traits, but that the situations themselves differ along with our perceptions of these situations, our objectives, strategies and so on.

We believe that human character shows who we really are and what we are like 'on the inside'. Character can thus be equated with personal integrity, which is regarded as an intact and solid state of completeness, wherein the individual has a consistent relationship between his beliefs and practices. We believe that good character and personal integrity are a basic premise for good leadership and denote an upgrade of the individual's physical, intellectual or psychological level. Therefore, being concerned only with a leader's physical and mental state does not suffice. The leader's character, his personal integrity and spirituality are just as important. Personal integrity provides the inner strength of character that allows a person to make difficult decisions and commits them to a common good for everyone around them.

A good character and a high level of integrity are directly linked to moral maturity. Given that moral maturity depends on the individual's moral development and is, at the same time, connected to leadership, the next section will feature an analysis of it.

Moral development

Jean Piaget, Lawrence Kohlberg and Carol Gilligan are generally considered to be strongly related to the theory of moral development.[29] In 1932, contrary to the views of psychoanalysis and behaviour, Piaget argued that the development of one's morality is a result of the internal, rational process of the individual. After Piaget, Kohlberg[30] offered a more detailed scale of moral thinking, as Piaget had initially only discovered two levels of moral thinking. Piaget's second phase denotes early adolescence, while Kohlberg discovered more phases that are typical of both adolescence and adulthood. Kohlberg (1975) continued to develop Piaget's findings in 1955, while also taking John Dewey's cognitive ever-developing approach into account.[31] On the basis of his 20-year empirical study of 50 boys and his other subsequent studies, he found that there are three stages of moral development, each of which has two sub-phases.[32] All of them, however, contain the concern for justice. The latter seems very important for Kohlberg (1975: 673) because decisions made on the basis of universal principles of justice are going to be accepted by all moral people.

Kohlberg found that moral development, except in the case of strong trauma, always develops itself from the lower to the higher level of moral development, whereby man can never skip individual levels. Moral stages were understood in the form of a hierarchical structure of moral reasoning and judgement. Such moral reasoning included judging right and wrong, where every higher level included the lower one. He believed that an individual who does not understand moral principles or does not believe in them simply cannot follow them. On the other hand, the individual can think about moral principles and at the same time, not live in accordance with them. Consequently, for Kohlberg, the Socratic method of debating dilemmas about moral principles and values seems important. The Socratic method is believed to contribute to moral development aimed at a higher level of moral thinking.

The lowest level of moral development, according to Kohlberg, is associated with satisfying one's own needs, selfishness and external rewards and punishment. The second level is associated with compliance with social norms that are expected by others, organisations and society. The third level presupposes that the main motivation for behaviour is being consistent with internalised values and moral principles, while not being too dependent on external factors. As mentioned, Kohlberg divided each level into two sub-phases (Kohlberg 1975: 671) (Figure 1.13).

The pre-conventional level is divided into two orientations: the first is oriented by punishment and obedience, which leans toward obedience, avoiding punishment and fear of punishment. The second level is the instrumentalist relativist orientation combined with instrumental purpose and exchange, which is characterised by the utilitarian principle of reciprocity.

The conventional level, which is divided into the inter-personal concordance or 'good boy, nice girl' orientation, is when an individual obeys in order to gain approval from others. The second orientation, or sub-level, is the law and order orientation social accord and system maintenance, which is characterised by

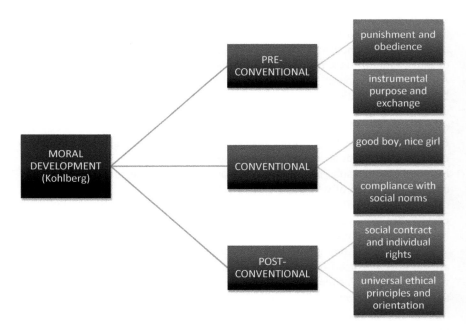

Figure 1.13 Moral development.

Source: Kohlberg (1975).

compliance with social norms. Such behaviour plays the main role in maintaining order in society, namely, for the sake of man himself. Hence, the ability of abstract thinking is required for this sub-level.

The post-conventional, autonomous or principled level is reached only by a few adults and, as such, is oriented more to the benefit of society than to the benefit of oneself. The first sub-level is the social contract and individual rights (legalistic orientation), which are directed to the general social good and acting in accordance with social norms. It does, however, have a slight utilitarian touch – the greatest good for the greatest number of people. Social norms are understood as relative and are, as such, subject to change by agreement. The second sub-level is the universal ethical principles orientation that strives for justice, equality and reciprocity. These principles do not reflect concrete moral rules like the Ten Commandments. This sub-level manifests itself where decisions are made according to one's own moral conscience and where universal ethical principles, human rights, fairness, justice, equality, dignity and so on, are at the forefront. This sub-level is represented by Kant's categorical imperative and the golden rule.

Each stage has its own characteristic values and provides an appropriate basis for the following stage. Moral development as a rational process of learning and acquiring moral values can only be assumed if understood conceptually and emotionally. These factors are instrumental in the resolution of interpersonal problems. Crane and Matten (2004) argue that Kohlberg developed his theory with the aim of clarifying the different thought processes people engage in when making ethical decisions in the decision-making process; as such, it is not of great importance *what* the subject of decision may be, but *how* the decision was made. Peterson (2004) notes that man progresses through these various stages, but also in terms of moral thinking. The higher it is, in this respect, the more ethical decisions are made. In light of this, being able to differentiate cognitive processes contributes to the understanding of how people make their choices about what is morally right or wrong. Similarly, Crain (1985) notes that Kohlberg's scale focuses on moral thinking and not on moral behaviour, whereby it is not necessary that an individual who thinks and talks in a morally high manner also behaves like that in practice. According to the author, it would be best for society if every person understood the need for social order, which falls into the fourth sub-level on Kohlberg's scale. As such, the individual could think and reflect upon universal principles such as justice, which falls into the sixth sub-level on Kohlberg's scale. Messick (2005) believes that assuming higher levels on Kohlberg's scale denotes a more mature attitude to morality. People, however, differ in how fast they progress. In view of this, we think that Kohlberg's exploration of the stages of moral development in the process of socialisation is particularly relevant to the field of moral judgement and the related strengthening of personal integrity.

Ethics is certainly associated with the moral development of the individual from childhood onwards. In view of Kohlberg's theory of moral development, an individual in the first stage of development (the pre-conventional stage) does not understand why one's conduct is moral or immoral. Most adult behaviour is located in the second stage (the conventional stage), while the last stage (the post-conventional stage) is characterised by the fact that one understands the moral principles that are adopted and internalised voluntarily. All three phases are inter-twined, resulting in the fact that the cognitive moral development of an individual seems continuous and connected. Kohlberg's theory clearly shows that an individual can change their own moral beliefs and behaviour through education and on the basis of experience gained from resolving conflict situations.

Musek notes that

> the motivational hierarchy and the hierarchy of values quite clearly show that conflicts between values and needs are more difficult and disadvantageous if the individual's fundamental needs remain unmet. The urgent tendency to satisfy disadvantaged motives does not strive so much at whether it will be realised in a truly morally correct manner.

(Musek 1993: 132)

At the same time, the author adds that the moral attitude may be easier if the individual is not exposed to unpleasant hardship and conflict and that

> a crisis of values is generally a moral crisis of the personality, its integration and its self-development. Personal fulfilment adds order into an individual's system of values, which, as such, bridges the moral hesitation and diver-gences between morality and deeds.

(1993: 133)

Based on the conclusion that moral principles and the hierarchy of values in humans are differently shaped, Musek (1993) formulated a four-level develop-mental hierarchy of values; he ranked Dionysian values on the first two levels, while the second two were ranked with Apollonian values. The first level is ranked with hedonistic values that are associated with pleasure, while the second level is ranked as values of potency, focused on achievements and accomplish-ments. The third level is the stage of moral values that are associated with duties and responsibilities, while the fourth and final level is ranked with values of sense and fulfilment that focus on self-actualisation and spiritual growth. Musek found that the higher an individual advances on the scale of values, the more ethical they become. As such, and with maturity, the role of moral values increases.

We agree with Burns (2010) that people on the highest level of moral develop-ment generally act under the influence of universal ethical principles (for example, justice, equality, respect, dignity) and on this level represent an opportunity for good leadership. However, an individual on the highest level of moral develop-ment (the principle level) is less susceptible to the influence of others, which also applies to one's leaders, while the individual who achieves the highest level of moral development is guided by those values and principles of morality that they assume on their own, thus thinking beyond rules, rules of law and authorities. An individual on the second level of moral development adjusts his behaviour to the expectations of others (family, colleagues, society). Peterson (2004) notes that people who believe less in universal moral values are more susceptible to the influence of others; for example, their leaders.

Organisational integrity

In addition to personal integrity, organisational integrity seems to be vitally important.

Most research on the topic of integrity focuses primarily on the individual's behaviour. Integrity can be analysed on three different levels, namely the levels of the individual, the group and the organisation. Palanski and Yammarino (2009) found that integrity can also be a subject of research in the organisational context. Simons (2002) made similar findings, namely that the concept of behavioural integrity can be applied to the individual and the group level.

On the organisational level, two different types of integrity can be found, wherein the conceptualisation is different than that for the individual level. On one hand, Petrick and Quinn (2000) understand organisational integrity as the behaviour of an organisation, which reflects a held concern about moral development on all organisational levels, organisational processes, the existence of ethical codes and other formal documents about organisational values. On the other hand, some authors see integrity as one of the organisational values, but do not elaborate as to where and how integrity reflects in the organisation (Palanski and Yammarino 2009).

They first establish entities, namely, the individual, the group and the organisation. These entities can be addressed mutually or separately. This means that the integrity of a group can be studied and defined separately from both the individual (lower level) and the organisation (higher level). The authors then conceptualised these three entities and separated them from each other with respect to the internal variability of each entity. The said variability leads to four categories:

1 Within the entity there is homogeneity and there is no significant variability that characterises the difference between the entities
2 Within the entity there is significant variability, although variability between entities is not valid
3 Significant variability exists within an entity as well as between entities
4 There is no significant variability within and between entities

On the basis of these conceptualisations of all three levels (individual, group, organisational), they present various examples of practices that are in accordance with integrity and contrary to it. Here, the authors used Simson's (2002) concept of behavioural integrity (consistency of words and deeds and promises given and lived up to). Because the authors are convinced that group and organisational integrity can best be defined as consistency of words and deeds or, put differently, as consistency between the declarative and the real. This includes emphasising and respecting values and keeping promises (Palanski and Yammarino 2009).

In support of what is stated above, Brown (2006) believes that the public is very interested in organisational integrity which manifests itself when individuals in the organisation are sincere, care for organisational security, advocate what is right, cooperate with others and care for the environment. Huberts et al. (2007) also understand organisational as well as personal integrity as an essential factor of functioning in public and private organisations.

Brown (2006) believes that leaders can assume integrity in an organisation without organisational integrity, but only up to the point or degree to which they themselves are active, thus reinforcing the integrity of the organisation as a whole. At the same time, Brown identifies five interrelated factors of organisational integrity: cultural factor (openness to different cultures, their inclusion and integration); interpersonal factor (different relationships that individuals develop or bring into the organisation); organisational factor (the organisation's purpose and objectives that are to be followed); social factor (interaction between private and public institutions); and natural factor (social responsibility to those involved, including environment and nature). These factors can either enable or inhibit its effects. The author also adds verbal communication (statements about objectives, everyday conversations and so on), non-verbal communication (work processes, organisational structure and so on) and considers that the personal integrity of leaders is a necessary condition.

Becker (1998) notes that the integrity of the employees has a positive impact on the organisation. Common sense, fairness and justice, which are assumed by employees with a high degree of integrity, benefit both the employees and the organisation. Consequently, in such an organisation there is a smaller number of deviant and unethical practices. At the same time, employees with a high degree of integrity can be good candidates for managerial positions (Figure 1.14).

Simons (1999) believes that when official policies and strategies of the management of an organisation are not in accordance with everyday practices, employees rapidly adapt their behaviour, thereby potentially undermining the organisational integrity. Simultaneously, Johnson (2007) found that organisational integrity promotes and enhances the personal integrity of employees. The author continues that employees who assume ethical codes also consider themselves as more ethical than those employees who work in organisations where ethical codes do not exist.

Paine (2005) notes that much research shows that organisational integrity is significantly affected by the organisation's structure, the system of work and the organisational strategy. As such, an organisation that reflects a high level of integrity seems to increase the confidence of the internal and external public.

In addition to the above, organisational integrity is a key factor in the sustainable development of an organisation, wherein the conditions for its implementation and dissemination are supposed to be ensured by the organisation's management (Lennic and Kiel 2009). In order to achieve this, the management needs a communication strategy through which the internal and external public can present their organisational values. The latter must first and foremost manifest itself in the

ORGANISATIONAL INTEGRITY

Brown believes that leaders can assume integrity in an organisation without organisational integrity, but only up to the point or degree to which they themselves are active, thus reinforcing the integrity of the organisation as a whole. At the same time Brown identifies five inter-related factors of organisational integrity:

CULTURAL FACTOR
openness to different cultures, their inclusion and integration

NATURAL FACTOR
social responsibility to those involved, including environment and nature

ORGANISATIONAL INTEGRITY

INTERPERSONAL FACTOR
different relationships that induvidual's develop or bring into the organisaton

SOCIAL FACTOR
interaction between private and public institutions

ORGANISATIONAL FACTOR
the organisation's purpose and objectives which are to be followed

Figure 1.14 Organisational integrity.

Source: Brown (2006).

practice of managers where control and feedback on their values from employees must be ensured.

Research on integrity

Carroll (2009) and Palanski and Yammarino (2007) concluded that empirical studies confirm integrity plays a significant role in successful leadership and that research in this area is therefore necessary. Vicchio (1997) also advocates this – he believes that the mere absence of unethical behaviour does not mean that someone has integrity. Craig and Gustafson (1998), on the other hand, noted at the end of last century there was a lack of empirical research on the role of integrity with regard to leadership. They concluded that this is a result of the difficulties of measuring the personal integrity of leaders and their moral behaviour in organisational situations. Northouse (2010) agreed with this and noted that researchers in this particular field face a specific problem, namely that research into leaders is not very popular because it is very personal in nature. People do not like it when they are evaluated and judged by others. The author's opinion is that the probable reason for this is the fact that there are very few measurement instruments/questionnaires on this topic. In addition, Dineen et al. (2006) concluded that integrity was equated with fairness, honesty and trust up until the 1990s. After that, the concept was expanded to, for example, cover consistency between behaviour and assumed values (Becker 1998), between words and deeds (Simons 2002) and so on. Thus, in the last decade, the importance of integrity has been increasingly studied through research into the importance of values and virtues in relation to leadership (Fitsimmons 2008).

Most of the current instruments for measuring integrity emerged in the field of psychology as an attempt to evaluate the fairness of employees and their tendency to steal. Ones et al. (2003) noted that evaluating integrity in the phase of recruitment can be a good predictor of unwanted behaviour and absenteeism. The measured unreliability, irresponsibility and dishonesty indicated a greater likelihood of unwanted behaviour and reduced employee productivity. Such tests included elements of the awareness of the work ethic, following the rules, reliability, control of reactions, confidence, friendliness, emotional stability, resistance to stress and so on.

In the field of leadership, two measurement instruments provide a basis for the research. They are designed to assess personal integrity, although each instrument measures a different aspect of integrity. The first instrument is PLIS (the Perceived Leader Integrity Scale), which was developed by Craig and Gustafson (1998). The second instrument is BI (Behavioural Integrity), which was developed by Simons (2002). They are both based on the same methodology, namely identifying the employees' subjective perception of the behaviour of their leaders. Simons (1999) believes that leaders and managers are an unreliable source of information regarding their own behavioural integrity. Such an approach, which rejects the exploration of the ethical conduct of leaders through the use of self-evaluation tests,[33] is also advocated by Craig and Gustafson (1998), Becker (1998), Simons (1999), Berlogar (2000), Parry and Proctor-Thomson (2002), Brown et al. (2005), Brown and Trevino (2006), Sarros and Cooper (2006) and Kaiser and Hogan (2010). The latter believe in this regard that individuals employed are in a weaker position relative to their leaders because the employees are in hierarchically subordinated roles. Consequently, the employees are more vulnerable to the leader's influence, thus making them all the more motivated to monitor the leader's behaviour. As Simons (2002) notes, employees are more sensitive to detecting the integrity of their leaders. They are also more sensitive than the leader's colleagues (other leaders), and their superiors. According to Kaiser and Hogan (2010), the hierarchically subordinated employees are in the best position because they can directly detect and experience the darker side of their leaders (exploitation, unethical behaviour and so on). On this basis, the authors conclude that such employees are the best source of information regarding the integrity of their leaders. They also believe that the past behaviour of leaders is the best predictor of their future behaviour.

Below we present a detailed presentation of the two measurement instruments (PLIS and BI). The first one was used for our research and study.

PLIS measurement instrument

The PLIS questionnaire is focused on the perception of the personal integrity of leaders through the prism of the leader's conduct. The questionnaire is designed in such a way that it enables the assessment of the presence or absence of unethical behaviour of leaders (Craig and Gustafson 1998). However, it is not necessarily designed to assess the presence of exemplary ethical behaviour. The PLIS is underpinned by the utilitarian theory of ethics and thus based on assessing the impact and consequences of individual behaviour and conduct (Craig and Gustafson 1998). In practice, the questionnaire is carried out by giving the employees the opportunity to assess their immediate superiors and leaders. The evaluation is based on their leader's compliance with the rules, which provide the greatest good for the greatest number of people.

Most variables in the PLIS questionnaire are designed so that respondents evaluate their leader's unethical behaviour as a result of experiencing and observing the leader's conduct (Craig and Gustafson 1998). As Brown and Trevino (2006) note, the PLIS instrument measures the negative aspects linked to the performance of managerial functions. The design of the questionnaire is also consistent with Schermerhorn's understanding of unethical behaviour and defining factors that are contrary to personal integrity.

The main questionnaire of Craig and Gustafson (Cronbach's alpha > 0.97), which meets the criteria of validity and reliability (Parry and Proctor-Thomson 2002, Peterson 2004) is one-dimensional. It has a one-factor structure and consists of 31 claims (Craig and Gustafson 1998). The one-factor structure of the questionnaire was also confirmed by Parry and Proctor-Thomson (2002) and Datta (2005). Craig and Gustafson (1998: 130) developed the final version of the questionnaire from a set of 100 variables that were previously classified in seven different categories, namely, training and development, allocation of resources, speaking the truth, illegal discrimination, compliance with regulations and strategies, treachery and protecting oneself. About half of the variables are focused on the perceptions of employees regarding the attitude of leaders in relation to their colleagues. They also added six variables that measure the overall perception of the integrity of leaders (for example, my leader has high ethical standards). With the help of a study, Kaiser and Hogan (2010) found that the PLIS instrument has different dimensions, such as character weaknesses (for example, revengefulness), unwanted conduct, violation of the rules and alarming prospects (namely, the leader would let me be blamed for his mistakes). As such, it is suitable for evaluating the integrity of leaders.

The statements of the respondents are assessed using a four-point Likert scale (Datta 2005, Baker and Craig 2006) which, according to Craig and Gustafson

(1998) disables the use of the mean value (3). If the option of selecting the mean value (3) was available, the respondents would be able to avoid replying to sensitive content. Peterson (2004) adjusted the PLIS instrument for the purposes of his own research, namely, he used a seven-point Likert scale instead of a four-point one.

Kaiser and Hogan (2010) noted that there are several necessary conditions for use of the PLIS instrument. The said conditions are ensuring the anonymity of the respondents and the complete confidentiality of the employees' responses. This encourages a respondent's sincerity in their answers and safeguards them from possible retaliation from their leaders. Other necessary conditions are a clearly expressed purpose of such data collection and processing and open support from the organisation for the purpose of strengthening integrity in the organisation in which the survey is being administered.

The PLIS questionnaire has so far been used to determine the relationship between the perception of the integrity of leaders and employee satisfaction, transformational and transactional behaviour, satisfaction with leadership, the perception of the efficiency of leaders, motivation and investing in additional efforts of employees in their work (Datta 2005). The questionnaire of Craig and Gustafson (1998) was adapted by Northouse (2010) for the purposes of leader's training.

BI measurement instrument

The measuring of BI is designed to determine the employees' perception of the behaviour of their leaders. In the foreground of this instrument, however, is not the morality of principles but the consistency of words and deeds (Simons 1999, 2002). As Palanski and Yammarino (2007) note, BI would be specifically suitable for measuring the consistency of values a leader advocates and practices as well as the leader's tendency to keep promises. At the same time, the authors note two potential limitations of this instrument, namely, that the findings are based on a perception that is not reliable and the focus is solely on individual behaviour.

After the introductory part, the following section first presents the empirical findings of researchers that used both measurement instruments. After that, we will present the remaining findings of the empirical research on the topic of integrity.

The empirical findings on the role and importance of integrity

Leader integrity is gaining in importance. This is confirmed in the scientific research of leadership conducted over the last 30 years, as was mentioned in the introduction to this chapter.

Carroll (2009) notes that studies show that the behaviour of leaders is the most important factor of influence in relation to the ethical behaviour of employees in an organisation. The author found a positive correlation between employees who believe in the ethical behaviour of their leaders and their sense that there is less deviant behaviour in their environment. At the same time, the author notes that leaders who talk to or converse with their employees about the importance of ethical conduct is a positive activity. Informing employees, holding promises and leading by example are also positive activities. In addition, Carroll notes that leaders themselves consider personal integrity as one of the most important factors in successful leadership. This discovery is also backed by the fact that personal integrity is characterised by honesty, righteousness, speaking the truth, coherence between words and deeds, wisdom and prudence and accountability, as well as strong family values.

Craig and Gustafson (1998) used the PLIS instrument and found a strong positive correlation between the integrity of leaders and employee satisfaction. The authors also found a negative correlation between leader integrity and those employees who wish to leave their job.

The PLIS questionnaire was also used by Parry and Proctor-Thomson (2002). They found a positive correlation between the perception of the integrity of leaders and the absence of unethical behaviour and conduct. Simultaneously, a positive correlation was established between transformational leadership and the organisational efficiency and the effectiveness of leaders. The authors also found a negative correlation between the perception of leader integrity and passive management by exception and laissez-faire leadership. On the basis of their survey, Parry and Proctor-Thomson (2002) thus conclude that the perception of a high level of leader integrity is associated with a high level of cooperation with employees (developmental exchange behaviour), a low level of leader absenteeism and the transmission and correction of employees' decisions (corrective and avoidant behaviour). For the purposes of their own research in the for-profit and non-profit sectors, the authors adapted the PLIS instrument to their own needs. The adapted instrument was thus named PLIS-R because the authors used 28 variables instead of all 31. The key adjustment lay in the fact that it was prepared for the evaluation of leader integrity on all organisational levels and in different ways (not merely bottom-up, but also top to bottom and between colleagues). They found that measuring leader integrity top-down (from leaders who are hierarchically superior) is significantly better than measuring leader integrity on the same organisational integrity (peer rating, assessing leaders through colleague leaders). In their view, this indicates the important unreliability of such evaluations of leader integrity.

Peterson (2004) also used the PLIS questionnaire to assess the connection between the ethical behaviour of leaders and their employees (subordinates). The author concludes that both the perceived high level of integrity of employees as well as their firm belief in universal moral principles positively correlates with ethical behaviour and conduct. The author also notes that employees who firmly believe in universal moral principles are less vulnerable to the influence of unethical behaviour, not according to their perception of leader integrity. By contrast, employees who are not devoted to the belief in universal moral principles are more susceptible to unethical behaviour, which increases and decreases in proportion to their perception of the level of leader integrity. Based on these findings, the author concludes that leader integrity only affects those employees who are not devoted to the belief in universal moral principles. Conversely, employees who respect such principles base their moral decision on their own and personal criteria.

Palanski and Yammarino (2011) note that different theories of leadership emphasise the importance of leader integrity. However, the said theories fall short in clarifying the impact of leader integrity on individual and significant leadership results, for example, the confidence in leaders, satisfaction with leaders, employee performance and so on. Therefore, the authors carried out a survey in which they assessed how leader integrity influences employees and impacts on their job performance. To measure integrity, they used Simson's measurement instrument for detecting the behavioural integrity of leaders (BI) with eight variables, which focus on the consistency of the words and actions of leaders. They found that leader integrity is not directly related to the work performance of employees. However, it is related indirectly through employee confidence in leaders, employee satisfaction and through employee integrity. The authors found the importance of employee integrity and its impact on their work performance. They established a direct as well as an indirect impact, which is reflected in their confidence in their leaders and employee satisfaction.

Palanski and Vogelgesang (2011) purposely tried to find out how the ethical conduct of leaders impacts the creativity of employees. They also used Simson's BI measurement instrument. They found that the perception of the consistency between the words and deeds of leaders has a positive impact on the psychological safety of employees, employee creativity and their willingness to accept responsibility (risk-taking behaviour).

Reave (2005) reviewed over 150 studies and found consistency between spiritual values (including integrity as such) and efficient and effective leadership. As the author notes, successful leadership starts with integrity, which is then reflected in ethical behaviour. Leader integrity does not only affect motivation and employee integrity but also their ethical conduct. The author concluded that leader integrity affects the 'ethical' climate of the organisation as well as ethical decisions made by employees (even outside of the organisation).

In a survey regarding students, Mumford et al. (2003) placed themselves in the roles of leaders and found that people who are more focused on getting and achieving their personal benefits are more prone to unethical behaviour. The same was found in the context of values; such values that are associated with satisfying personal interests (financial security, status, pleasure) have a negative correlation with both personal and organisational integrity, which is reflected in the decision-making related to sustainable development and not meeting short-term benefits. A positive correlation was found between organisational ethical values and the relationship between employees and the organisation. Andrews et al. (2011) also established a positive correlation between organisational ethical values and relations among employees, commitment and employee satisfaction.

In a survey assessing leaders of for-profit and non-profit organisations, Ahn et al. (2012) found that leader integrity is considered the most important value. Badaracco and Ellsworth (1992), on the other hand, established that leaders consider personal integrity as a prerequisite for successful leadership. Datta (2005) noted that integrity is as important for leaders as intelligence and competence, while Mayer et al. (1995) found a positive correlation between a high degree of leader integrity and employee trust in leaders. Integrity was also understood as a core competency in a study of competencies by Lennick and Kiel (2009).

Peterson (2004) found that the personal integrity of leaders has a positive effect on the moral behaviour of employees. Dineen et al. (2006) established that a high level of leader integrity is positively correlated with the desired social behaviour of employees (organisational citizenship behaviour) and, vice versa, a low level of leader integrity is associated with deviant behaviour of employees (Figure 1.15).

On a sample of university students, Posner (2001) found that integrity is regarded as the most important virtue of leaders. At the same time, the majority

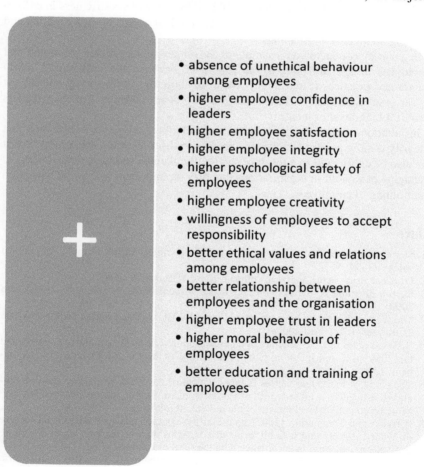

- absence of unethical behaviour among employees
- higher employee confidence in leaders
- higher employee satisfaction
- higher employee integrity
- higher psychological safety of employees
- higher employee creativity
- willingness of employees to accept responsibility
- better ethical values and relations among employees
- better relationship between employees and the organisation
- higher employee trust in leaders
- higher moral behaviour of employees
- better education and training of employees

Figure 1.15 Positive impacts of leaders' integrity on organisations.
Source: Authors.

of respondents considered that the biggest benefit from acting in accordance with integrity is the good feeling about oneself or satisfaction with oneself.

Schafer (2010) determined that American police officers consider honesty and integrity as the most important characteristics of a successful leader. The first five important features included a concern for the needs of other employees, good communication skills, ethical conduct and listening skills. On the other hand, the author found that the first three features that lead to unsuccessful leadership are ineffective communication, the neglect of the needs of other employees and questionable ethics and leader integrity.

Huberts et al. (2007) found that employees imitate the behaviour of their leaders in a sample of Dutch police officers. They imitate their moral standards through which leader integrity is related. In addition to leading by example, the authors established that employee conduct is affected by the leader's strictness in enforcing the rules, sanctioning deviant behaviour and their accessibility for talking and debating about ethical dilemmas.

In a survey conducted on a sample of Slovenian police officers, we found that employees understand integrity as coherence between the individual's moral beliefs and practices (Šumi 2006). We also, similarly to the survey carried out a year later (Šumi 2007), found that the employees consider that their leaders assume a high level of integrity.

In addition, with colleagues (Šumi and Lobnikar 2012), we established that integrity is an important factor in the professionalisation of the said profession. It can also be considered as a result of a carefully planned and long-term process of managing behaviour in organisations that play an important role in the education and training of employees.

Notes

1 Šter thus believes that it is 'absurd to say moral-ethical values or moral and ethical values' (1994: 5).
2 Practical issues being abortion, euthanasia, etc. (Blackburn 2008).
3 Such a dilemma is, for example, the social responsibility of companies (Blackburn 2008).
4 The idea is thought to have originated from Buddhist ethics, dating back more than 2,500 years (Greenleaf 2002a).
5 Berlogar notes that the structure of an organisation reflects the structure of society and that 'there is as much culture (ethics) in society, as there is culture (ethics) in a company' (2000: 46).
6 The study of individual factors is more typical of the USA, while the study of situational influences is more typical of European researchers (Crane and Matten 2004).
7 More on cognitive development of the individual follows.
8 Palanski and Yammarino (2007) note that the concept changed through the course of history, namely that it firstly denoted a virtuous man, while later on, it was more focused on behaviour in accordance with the rules of conduct.
9 About the differences between virtues and values, Strahovnik notes that 'values form and guide Man at his practices. The core values of ethics are elements that are important for human life and survival and denote a necessary condition. Virtues, on the other

hand ... are morally significant human qualities or dispositions for existence and can be understood as personality traits. They are closely related to the human character. The opposite of virtues are defects and/or shortcomings. Moral virtues of Man are thus honesty, benevolence, compassion, courtesy, generosity, while defects are cruelty, selfishness, etc.' (Strahovnik 2010: 10–12).

10 Ciulla (2004) noted that ancient Greeks did not distinguish between individual personal ethics and professional competencies, which people need in order to perform different types of work.

11 Peterson and Seligman identified six universal virtues that are respected in all cultures around the world, namely: wisdom, courage, humanity, justice, temperance and transcendence (2004, Lennick and Kiel 2009: 34).

12 In ancient Greek philosophy, justice was a social virtue, according to which people 'regulated mutual relationships, namely that everyone got what they deserved or that everyone got the same' (Kocijančič 2004: 1143). According to Mintz (1996), a just individual is the one who controls his desires and does not wish to commit an act that is unfair.

13 According to Socrates, virtue is knowledge, which is based on the right understanding and the practical management of things (Jerman 1992: 30).

14 The author concludes in a thesis, that if virtue would not be knowledge, it therefore would not be possible to teach morals to others (Jelovac 1997).

15 According to Aristotle, virtues and weaknesses reflect in Man's voluntary deeds (MacIntyre 1993).

16 Given that Aristotle considered justice to be one of the most important virtues (Aristotle 2002, Gantar 2002) and that it is inextricably connected to personal integrity, we will discuss it in greater detail in this chapter.

17 MacIntyre noted that Aristotle's list of virtues was made according to what was in ancient Greece understood as 'the gentleman codex of the then Greek society', which he personally approved (MacIntyre 1993: 75).

18 Berlogar (2000) notes that in assessing relationships and actions, fairness is just as frequently discussed as ethics and honesty.

19 Comte-Sponville's answer to the question 'how to describe a righteous man' would be analogous as the answer to the question 'how to describe a man with a high degree of integrity', leading us to conclude that a man with a high degree of integrity would be:

> Someone who uses his power to serve law and justice and who determines others as equals, despite the de facto inequalities or the inequalities in talents, establishes order, which does not exist, even though without him, no order would be able to suffice. The world resists, as does Man. Both must be challenged, but first, challenge the injustice which everyone carries within themselves. Therefore, the struggle for justice will never be completed. This Kingdom is prohibited, or rather, we are in this Kingdom as much as we strive to be in it and reach it: blessed are those who hunger for justice, as their hunger will never be quenched.
>
> (Comte-Sponville 2002: 115)

20 For this reason, in the following chapter that discusses personal integrity in relation to leadership, we define various categories of conceptions of integrity.

21 The author considers that integrity and fairness are interrelated but conceptually different (Becker 1998).

22 The author believes that morality is at the heart of integrity (Becker 1998).

23 In this respect, virtue is identical with either a particular virtue, for example, fairness, or with virtue in general (Audi and Murphy 2006).

24 Opportunism as opposed to personal integrity.

25 Because of his ideals and integrity, which led to his demise, the Christian Church believed Socrates to be 'almost as a pre-Christian Christian' (Raeper and Smith 1995: 9) which, for example Rousseau, who is also considered to be a man with an upright ethical stance, is not the same (Bahovec 1993).

26 In this connection, it is worth taking into account the thinking of Hesse, namely, that words distort human thoughts and that their meaning is relative (Hesse 2007).

27 In their work, the authors use the phrase 'moral intelligence' for which they believe represents an ability of mental knowledge to understand how the universal principles (e.g. the golden rule to treat others in the way you want to be treated yourself) can be used or expressed through personal values, goals and actions (Lennick and Kiel 2009: 7).

28 At the same time, according to Cloud (2009), in addition to character, genes, temperament and past experiences also influence integrity.

29 Zupančič (1993) and Whetstone (2001) conclude that the psychological school of moral growth and the stages of moral development both evolved from Aristotle's philosophy.

30 Crane and Matten (2004) argue that Kohlberg's theory of cognitive moral development is the most widespread and accepted theory in this field.

31 In terms of moral development, the cognitive approach is linked to active contemplation, while the developmental approach is linked to passing through different moral development stages.

32 An explanation follows.

33 Mumford et al. (2003) noted that values and beliefs before this were always evaluated by means of direct self-evaluation instruments.

2 Leadership

Definition of leadership

Dictionaries define leadership as guiding and leading, showing the path to others and taking the helm (Oxford 1989b, 2004, 2009, Cambridge 2003). A leader is defined as a person who leads others to action and is responsible for the situation. Brewer's dictionary (1995) compares a leader with the first violin of an orchestra. Conversely, management is defined as managing, supervision, guidance and succeeding in doing something.[1] A manager is someone who controls and supervises an organisation or a part of it (Oxford 2009).

In the next few chapters, we will distinguish between leadership and management, which is important for our topic because we are studying the field of personnel management. After that, a definition of leadership will be provided from the perspectives of different authors. The next chapter will deal with the relationship between personal integrity and leadership with the aim to demonstrate and emphasise their interconnected tendency. We will then elaborate the theories of leadership and define ethical leadership. Different management styles will be presented, including the servant leadership style, which represents the heart of our study.

Distinguishing between leadership and management

Leadership falls within the framework of management (Schermerhorn 2008). On one hand, it is a process that is in many ways similar to management because they both involve deciding on what to do, influencing people,[2] working with people and a concern for the effective achievement of objectives (Kotter 1990, Northouse 2010). On the other hand, there are also differences between them (Kotter 1990, Fairholm 1991, Bennis and Nanus 2003, Northouse 2010) or, as noted by Greenleaf (1998), Griffin (2002), Carroll (2009) and Keohane (2010), while management and leadership are connected and intertwined, they are not identical. Thus, some authors regard leadership as one of the functions of management. This means that, as concepts, leadership and leading are narrower than the concept of management. Other authors treat leadership and management as equivalents, which differ in several aspects.

The first difference between them lies in the fact that leadership has been an object of study since Ancient Greece,[3] while the scientific study of management only began at the turn of the twentieth century. Such scientific research arose with the rise of mass production (Schermerhorn 2008).[4] Another difference stems from the meaning 'to manage'. 'To manage' means to exercise and carry out duties, while leading or 'to lead' means to influence co-workers and staff. Leading also means to shape a goal and the vision of it, contributing to change (Northouse 2010: 11).

The third difference exists in the functions of management and leadership. The basic functions of management were defined by Fayol in 1916. In the opinion of Northouse (2010), Fayol's work is still valid today in relation to planning, organising, staffing, directing and controlling. Schermerhorn (2008) believes the functions of management can be summarised in four basic categories: planning (setting the direction and goals), organising (creating a structure), managing (inspiring, motivating and supporting colleagues) and monitoring results. Možina et al. (2002) also agree with that division. In addition, the authors include creative problem-solving. On the other hand, Adair (1997) combines the functions of management in three categories: planning, management and monitoring. According to the author, leadership includes the same factors, with one difference: leaders upgrade the said factors with will and employee enthusiasm for achieving the desired objectives (Adair 1997).

According to Greenleaf (1998), management is related to monitoring and controlling a situation. Leadership, however, is leading by example, 'at the helm' or at the forefront, showing the right way and direction. In this way, leaders assume responsibilities for the decisions. As the author notes, the only reliable test of effective leadership is whether the employees follow voluntarily or not (Greenleaf 1998). In contrast, Carroll (2009) notes that management is more focused on the processes that lead to achievement of the organisation's objectives (for example, planning, organising). It is therefore more focused on tasks than people. According to the author, a manager can create an excellent organisational strategy or a plan of work but they are often not skilled enough to put them into practice and motivate employees to participate. Unlike a manager, a leader dedicates himself to the employees as people through the creation of a vision, creativity, making changes, etc.

The above already points to the fourth difference, which is reflected in the functions of the manager and the leader. In this connection, Bennis and Nanus (2003) note that 'managers do things right, while leaders do the right things'. Schermerhorn (2008) defines a manager as a person who supports and encourages activities, supervises and is responsible for the work of employees, while a leader encourages enthusiasm and inspiration in order to achieve objectives. According to Fairholm (1991), leaders have a more personal approach to their employees and are more focused on values and content, while managers are more focused on results and controlling processes. At the same time, the author believes that both functions are needed for an organisation to operate effectively; the function of the manager and the function of the leader as they both share a common point in integrity, responsibility and vision. The author sees the difference between them in the metaphor that managers reflect on yesterday's and today's results of work and the problems of today, while leaders reflect on tomorrow and the day after tomorrow (Fairholm 1991).

Alban-Metcalfe and Mead (2010) note that the distinction between management and leadership was established in the early 1980s, with John Kotter being the main contributor (1990). His and Northouse's (2010) division is shown in Table 2.1.

Table 2.1 shows that the role of management is to ensure a well-functioning organisation or, as Kotter (1990) notes, management must ensure that even the most complex organisations are in touch with the times and that it possesses the necessary financial resources. At the same time, the main purpose of management is to provide order and consistency within the organisation (Northouse 2010). Thereby, it differs from leadership, which initiates change and ensures constant development (Kotter 1990, Northouse 2010). In other words, managing denotes the concern for order and stability, while the function of leadership is to ensure flexibility and introduce constructive changes (Crane and Matten 2004, Northouse 2010). Despite their substantive differences, a successful operation needs both management and leadership (Kotter 1990, Griffin 2002). As Northouse (2010) notes, both competent management and skilled leadership are needed. The author illustrates the urgency of the latter by showing that an organisation with good management and bad leadership is rigid and bureaucratic, while an organisation with good leadership and bad management can go wrong when introducing organisational changes (Northouse 2010). As Kotter (1990) notes, leadership without proper management can introduce changes just for the sake of change and without a real basis for them.

Table 2.1 The role of management and leadership

Management: concern for order and consistency	*Leadership: introducing changes and the concern for development*
Planning and budget	Establishing guidelines
• Setting goals and programmes	• Creating a vision
• Scheduling work	• Providing a comprehensive picture of the situation
• Providing funds	• Developing strategies
Organisational structure and staffing	Connecting people
• Defining the organisational structure	• Informing people about the established vision
• Recruitment of qualified people	
• Determination of rules and procedures	• Creating alliances and being supported by staff
Monitoring and problem-solving	Motivation and inspiration
• Monitoring the achievement of objectives	• Motivating employees
• Identifying problems	• Empowering employees
• Problem-solving	• Meeting the ends

Source: Compiled according to Kotter (1990: 3–8) and Northouse (2010: 10).

Given the similarities and differences, it is therefore apparent that management and leadership overlap. When a manager influences employees in order to achieve organisational goals, he is in a way leading and exercising his leadership (Northouse 2010). When a leader is planning work, organising it and the employees, he is performing management duties. Both management and leadership therefore entail influencing employees in order to achieve organisational goals (Northouse 2010). Griffin (2002) sees the functional difference in the fact that when implementing their plans, managers monitor the results, compare them with the set goals and take action in the case of deviation. Conversely, leaders are focused on encouraging and motivating employees to overcome bureaucratic obstacles on their way to achieving these goals. Griffin, as well as Northouse (2010), shows that when a person monitors the results of the employees that person is playing the role of a manager. When that same person is encouraging and motivating employees to perform work, that person is playing the role of a leader. Griffin (2002: 521) also substantiates the theory that every successful organisation needs both managers and leaders (Griffin 2002: 521). Management connected to leadership can implement the right changes, while leadership in conjunction with management maintains an appropriate relationship between the organisation and its environment.

Berlogar (2006) believes that management, irrespective of the prevailing style of leadership, is responsible for achieving the set objectives. However, the choice of the style of leadership is affected by four different factors. The said factors are employees (professionals, experience, status in the organisation and environment), organisational characteristics (nature of work, location, organisational regulations, etc.), environment limitations (legislation, financing etc.) and the professional-personal characteristics of the leaders and managers (knowledge, experience, character, motivation, etc.) (Berlogar 2006: 105).

Based on the foregoing, we side with those authors who believe that management and leadership are one and the same process, they both overlap and involve differences. In doing so, however, we mostly agree with the opinion of Greenleaf (1998); he believes that leadership denotes working 'at the helm', in the forefront, showing the right path and at the same time taking responsibility for their own decisions. In addition, we agree with Adair (1997, 2004), Griffin (2002), Audi (2008) and Burns (2010) regarding their definitions of management, which are presented in the next section.

Defining leadership

There are many definitions of leadership and over the last 60 years more than 60 different classifications of dimensions of leadership have emerged (Northouse 2010).[5] Bass and Riggio (2006) believe that leadership is likely to be one of the most complex and evolving activities. Burns (2010), Fry and Kriger (2009) and Riggio and Pirozzolo (2002) agree with Northouse, while DePree (2002) also contends that this is why leadership cannot be defined by some formula. Consequently, Smith et al. (2004) note that there is still no universally accepted definition of leadership as well as the fact that there is still no right notion of what constitutes good and successful leadership. Riggio and Conger (2007) agree that leadership is a complex and evolving activity, yet they also consider that successful leadership is a very complex process, which was confirmed after decades of research; they provided important data on good and bad practices. Successful management requires a lot of time, effort, personal motivation and dedication. The authors believe leaders include their employees in the process of leadership and set a good example when they are pro-active and are committed to monitoring, measuring and adjusting activities. At the same time, a leader is aware of the fact that successful management is a long-term process. Riggio and Conger also assert that leadership is both a science and a practice. Science requires constant monitoring and checking of whether something is successful or not, while practice requires the leader to continually learn how things can be done even better (Riggio and Conger 2007).

Avolio (2005) believes that the development of leadership skills requires learning and practice. The said process is affected by the talents, strengths and experiences of the leader, which gives the author a reason to suspect there is no best possible route or way to reach the said goal. The author adds that, if a best way did exist, it would still be subject to change due to the dynamics of the development of leadership (Avolio 2005). Adair (1997, 2004) contends that, in addition to the necessary personal qualities (integrity, inspiration, strength, honesty, modesty, human warmth and confidence) and general knowledge, leadership requires functional knowledge, which focuses on how one is required to lead, wherein the best and an irreplaceable mode of learning is leadership in practice. In light of the above, Avolio (2010) states that a good leader is trained and made rather than born, while for Drucker (2005), a good leader is neither born nor trained but self-made on the basis of experience.[6]

Burns defines leadership as a structured collective process which includes individuals from various organisational levels. The said process runs between them as well as in relation to their external environment (Burns 2010). Leadership involves leaders and employees mutually influencing each other, thus forming and developing relationships over time (2010: 425). The author emphasises the difference between the two functions and ascribes substantially greater responsibility to the leader, who must cater to the needs and wishes of employees, objectively resolve conflict situations, and be on the level of employees as well as above them. At the same time, a leader must respect the fundamental values and principles (2010: 78). All this, according to Burns, helps ensure that employees follow the leaders and are inspired.

For Greenleaf, leadership means to 'go out ahead and show the way' (2002a: 109). For a leader, any person who has relevant skills, values and character is suitable. This means that the leader has a good sense about when some activity should be done. As such, the leader is ready to assume responsibility in the 'let's do this now' way (2002a: 256). Senge (2002) believes that if leadership means anything, it means the courage to stand 'at the helm' upfront. At the same time, Greenleaf (1998) sees leadership as a field where much is discussed, but where there are still several unknowns.

Audi (2008) notes that real leadership means a reciprocity of influence and leading by example. In practice, this means that when an employee begins to be inspired by the leader, the leader consequently stands to influence him in one way or another. As the author notes, 'where leadership is being practiced, behaviour is under its influence. Where behaviour is under its influence, ethics depend on the influence' (Audi 2008: 198).

According to Adair (1997), leadership is not simply 'to be at the helm', in the forefront of a group, organisation, etc., but also denotes directing staff, giving instructions, a concern for social interaction and attention to the individual needs of employees. As a condition for labelling someone as a leader, Adair (2002) identified three criteria a leader must meet: achieving the set goals, working in harmony with colleagues and meeting the individual needs of employees. Further, the author believes that leadership is a 'gift' from employees because a person, despite their formal appointment to the position, truly becomes a leader when he is understood as one on the rational and emotional level by his staff (Adair 2004). Griffin (2002) similarly believes this to be the case when he notes that he considers a leader to be someone who can influence the behaviour of others without coercion, while the same person must also be accepted as a leader by others.

DePree (2002) states that leadership seriously affects the lives of all people involved and thus each leader must realise the importance of confidentiality, a wide range of leadership competencies, the importance of ethical conduct and respect of values. The author also notes that leadership skills demand that leaders think like custodians of the assets and resources of the organisation, the quality of products and services, sustainable development, the legacy for future generations, the development of employees, new managers, organisational values, etc.

Keohane (2010) believes that leadership involves finding appropriate solutions to collective problems and searching for ideas on how to realise the objectives of the group. The leader thus connects the activities of members of the collective or group with a view to achieving the objectives that could not otherwise be achieved by the said individuals alone.

Barker (2006) defines leadership as a process of transformation and structural change in which the ethics of employees is integrated into social ethics and social habits with the goal of social development. At the same time, the author notes that where there is no need for change there is no need for leadership since maintaining stability management alone is sufficient.

Kaiser and Hogan (2010) define leadership as a mechanism that affects the employees in such a way that they replace their short-term selfish interests with long-term care for the welfare of all employees in the organisation. In their view, leadership can be understood through the cost-benefit analysis intended for managers and employees because following the leader's example brings benefits, while poor leadership comes at a cost. Griffin (2002) sees leadership as influence without coercion with which the leaders motivate employees to achieve the organisational goals. We believe that the legitimacy of leadership is a prerequisite for attributing success to a leader. With leadership that is not legitimate, where employees do not accept the implementation of the leader's influence, there is no essential dimension that would provide the leader-employee relationship with reciprocity and mutual acceptance.

Personal integrity in relation to leadership

Given that the aim of the research goal of this book is to determine whether the personal integrity of leaders impacts the mode of leadership, the findings and observations of some authors that follow below focus on their interconnected nature. We believe that a positive effect of leadership with integrity is the trust that employees have in their leaders. At the end of this chapter, in conjunction with the various elements of personal integrity we discuss the five basic categories of definitions related to leadership.

When we talk about the ideals of leadership, personal integrity is essential as society demands it from politicians and stakeholders from companies, and employees expect it from their leaders, etc. (Palanski and Yammarino 2007, Northouse 2010). This is confirmed by the fact that integrity is increasingly becoming an important content of organisational studies, particularly in the study of leadership.

The concept of integrity is mostly used in relation to leadership and in the literature dealing with business ethics, where it is very often used as a moral value. It is also used as such in statements about the mission of organisations. Regarding this, Goethals et al. (2004) note that literature on the personal integrity of leaders categorises integrity among the characteristics of good leadership and governance. Moreover, Palanski and Yammarino (2009: 405) consider that the importance of integrity plays a particularly important role in transformational, ethical, spiritual, authentic and servant leadership (Liden et al. 2008). On the other hand, the integrity research in relation to leadership is often inhibited by three factors, namely the patchy and inconsistent definition of integrity, the lack of available theories on the topic of integrity in leadership and management in the literature (which is largely focused on the personal integrity of leaders and a serious lack of empirical findings in this area) (Palanski and Yammarino 2007, 2009).

Some believe that integrity in relation to leadership is not only a moral imperative, but also a business necessity. Parry and Proctor-Thomson (2002) are also convinced that the introduction of ethical standards in business is no longer simply desired but essential for the long-run reputation and survival of the organisation. Petrick and Quinn (2000) believe that integrity is, apart from being an important factor in the moral development of the individual, a factor in organisational success and for a sustainable competitive advantage. At the same time, they advocate the view that leaders in organisations of high integrity, which otherwise constitutes an intangible strategic asset, are increasingly aware of the moral concerns of stakeholders and at the same time are quicker in responding to them. On the contrary, leaders of organisations with low levels of integrity undermine their reputation. The authors note that a very important factor in integrity in relation to leadership is good judgement and prudence, which includes responsibility for achieving good results (teleological ethics with set goals), taking rules into account (deontological ethics), strengthening the motivation for virtuous conduct (virtue ethics) and strengthening the environment, which supports the ethical aspect of conduct inside and outside of the organisation (systemic aspect of ethics).

Bass (1990) understands integrity as a central feature of successful leaders, while Fitsimmons (2008) considers that integrity is the first and most important standard of effective and efficient management. As Heineman (2008) suggests, it is therefore important that organisations aspire to a mix of business performance and a high level of integrity, wherein the obligation of all employees is to understand their own formal and ethical duties. They must also act in accordance with these duties, whereby they consequently implement organisational values. Russell and Stone (2002) and Northouse (2010) also see integrity and honesty as essential components of good leadership, which are also closely connected. Russell and Stone (2002) note that honesty is mostly reflected as truthfulness while integrity, on the other hand, is reflected more in adherence to the fundamental principles of morality. In the context of integrity, Cohen (2010) understands leadership a little more broadly than honesty as it means doing the right thing regardless of the circumstances and the problems which follow for the leader and the organisation.

Bracher (2008) is convinced that integrity is a keystone of leadership and the most important factor in the area where customers come into contact with ideas, products, individual organisations or companies. Koehn (2005a) considers the same, namely that integrity properly understood is not only one of the appendices to business, but also the core of good business. It is a synonym for excellence and efforts which pay off, wherein integrity is worthwhile in itself. It is a lever for identifying risks and recognising responsibility, where it enables the organisation and the leaders to achieve their missions (Bracher 2008). They occur in relation to one other (Koehn 2005a). Vicchio (1997) understands integrity from the perspective of achieving the goal of an activity (through the prism of professionalism) as a coherent set of values and virtues that are necessary for achieving objectives. At the same time, Schuyler (2010) believes that a key element of the personal integrity of leaders is their awareness of themselves and their awareness of the need for coherent practices that are pertinent to the situation. With this, they reflect their internalised values.

Miller (2003) notes that the most important factor of leadership is the employees' trust in the character and integrity of their leaders. This is crucial because we understand that leaders can successfully lead only those employees who are willing to follow them. Kirkpatrick and Locke (1991) understand the integrity of leaders and their fair conduct as the basis for gaining the trust of employees. Schermerhorn (2008) believes that trust is a key factor that ensures employees follow the leader in achieving objectives. Luthans et al. (2007) conclude that the integrity, trust and transparency of leaders encourage the reciprocity of employees and strengthen the organisational culture. Trevino et al. (2000) see integrity, honesty and trustworthiness as characteristics of a moral leader. However, Yukl (2002) considers that, without trust, it is difficult to maintain the loyalty of employees, or the cooperation and support of the staff. As the author notes, integrity is associated with different forms of behaviour. Fairness and truthfulness, living up to promises, acceptance, compliance and loyalty to colleagues are amongst the said forms of behaviour. Yukl (2002), as well as Northouse (2010), believe that the key factor regarding trust is the employees' perception of the leaders' coherence of actions and the values they permanently defend and advocate. As Bowie (1991) asserts, it is important to understand that if employees think or start to believe that the leader is not acting in accordance with what the leader advocates, it is difficult to convince the employees to act ethically.

In conjunction with this, Huberts et al. (2007) contend that leadership is the one key factor that influences the level of integrity and ethics of employees. Leaders can achieve such an influence if they lead by example and openly discuss ethical dilemmas. This is, of course, accompanied by their consistency in sanctioning the unethical behaviour of employees. Fitsimmons identified 10 universal characteristics of leadership with integrity, namely the recognition of small things, recognising the positive side of every situation, correcting errors, creating an atmosphere of trust, abiding by their word, a concern for the common good, being honest and modest, working as the leader would be watched, recruiting people with integrity and enduring a situation through to the end (Fitsimmons 2008: 25).

Schermerhorn, on the other hand, defined different factors on whose basis a leader is said to be lacking in integrity (Schermerhorn 2008: 342). Such factors are paying special attention only to certain people, a willingness to lie, blaming others for their own mistakes, enjoying the mistakes of others, falsification of documents, promoting conflicts and disagreements, ascribing the success of others to oneself and theft from the organisation (Figure 2.1).

LEADERS

WITH INTEGRITY	LACKING INTEGRITY
• recognise the positive side of every situation • correct errors • create an atmosphere of trust • are concerned for the common good • are honest and modest • recognise the small things • act as if they were constantly being watched • recruit people with integrity • endure a situation through to the end	• pay special attention only to certain people • are willing to lie • blame others for their own mistakes • enjoy the mistakes of others • falsificate documents • promote conflicts and disagreements • ascribe the success of others to themselves • steal from the organisation

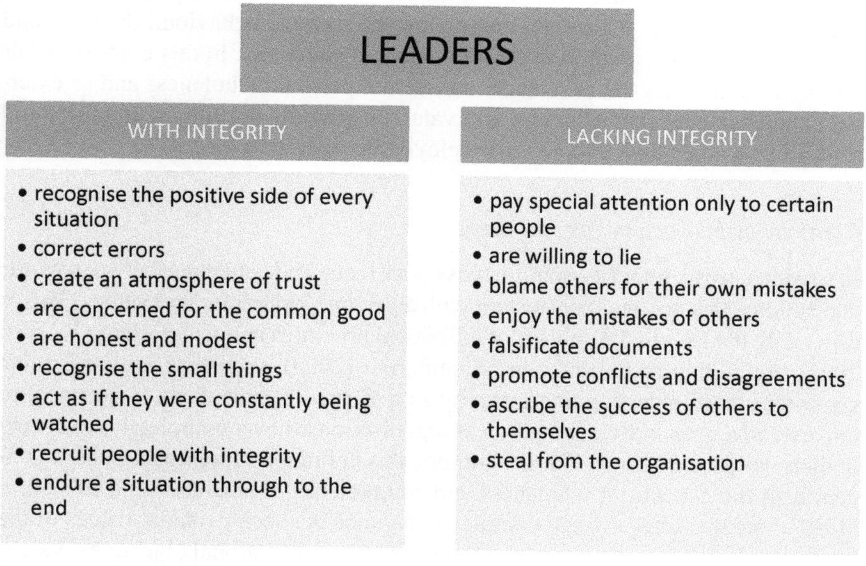

Figure 2.1 Leaders with and without integrity.
Source: Authors.

Five categories of personal integrity in relation to leadership

Given that personal integrity is differently defined or interpreted in the available literature (Yukl 2002, Audi and Murphy 2006, Palanski and Yammarino 2007, 2009, Laabs 2011), we will present five categories of integrity that are associated with leadership. Palanski and Yammarino (2007, 2009) defined them based on an extensive study of the different understandings of integrity in the literature on leadership. The five categories are:

1 Wholeness or completeness.
2 Consistency between words and deeds.
3 Consistency in the case of inconvenience and uneasiness.
4 Honesty to oneself.
5 Moral behaviour.

Although the concepts are mutually intertwined, we have also broadened the discussion with approaches that are also in some way connected to personal integrity and leadership. This was done for the sake of greater transparency and to facilitate a sharper distinction.

Wholeness or completeness

The first definition sees integrity as wholeness in a broader sense (Worden 2003, Palanski and Yammarino 2007) and through a prism of wholeness compares it to human character (Palanski and Yammarino 2007). In a broad sense, integrity is also understood as a general consistency between the behaviour, thoughts and emotions of an individual in different times and situations. In this context, Adair (2004) sees the integrity of a leader as internal personal wholeness and as external coherence between behaviour and values, especially dutifulness to others and truthfulness. They both encourage employees to trust their leader.

Consistency between words and deeds

In a stricter sense, integrity manifests as consistency and coherence between words and actions, that are again consistent with a person's principles and values. This is especially the case in the context of individual pressures and temptations (Worden 2003). According to Palanski and Yammarino (2009), such a definition is most consistent with understanding integrity as a virtue. In their view, it is crucial to understand that an individual, group or organisation is never completely consistent in their words and actions. For the authors, this definition represents a subtler concept than the concept of wholeness and completeness. Badaracco and Ellsworth (1992) note that integrity is a complex coherence between personal values of the leader, his/her daily actions and the fundamental organisational objectives. Values of fairness and honesty are at its heart. Paine sees integrity as coherence in different ways, namely between obligations, moral judgements, between beliefs and expressed beliefs and between words and actions (Paine 2005: 248).

Simons (1999, 2002) understands integrity as consistency between words and actions as well as coherence between the values a person advocates and lives by. The author names this *behavioural integrity*. He also adds that there is a difference between behavioural integrity and credibility, namely that behavioural integrity is based on previous coherence between words and actions, while credibility is focused on future actions.

Behavioural integrity reflects the degree to which employees believe in the consistency of their leader's words and actions. In addition, it reflects the degree to which leaders and the organisation uphold the advocated values in the context of communicating. In other words, 'behavioural integrity indicates the extent to which leaders are acting as they speak and speak as they act' (Simons 1999: 90). It follows from this that behavioural integrity is not so much focused on the morality of principles, but on the compatibility between these principles and actions. At the same time, the author notes that research shows a gap between the words and actions of leaders. The author also identified the general causes for this:

- the diversity of requirements, that are often in conflict, which leaders often face both inside and outside of the organisation;
- wishful thinking; and
- unwillingness to learn, change and adapt.

According to Simons (1999, 2002), this discrepancy creates considerable damage. It is caused by a lack of confidence and trust in leaders and their credibility. As such, it has a negative impact on employees who would be subject to changing habits and values for the benefit of the organisation if the leader were trusted. The author also believes that the longer the words and actions of an individual leader are incoherent, the less such a leader will be aware of the said incoherence, leading to the strengthening and increasing the frequency of such behaviour (Simons 1999, 2002). As a result, some employees become disillusioned with the behaviour of such a leader, some become cynical and contemptuous towards their leader, while the rest learn to distinguish between what has been said and what will be done.

Kirkpatrick and Locke (1991) and Brown (2006) also see integrity as consistency between words and actions, whereas Brown believes that such consistency is not sufficient, although it is a necessary condition for integrity and doing the right thing. Worden (2003) also believes that integrity denotes more than mere consistency between words and actions because morality involves the denial of satisfaction of current and momentary benefits for the benefit of the organisation. This strengthens both the credibility of the leader and the employees' confidence in such a leader. This is of course a very important disposition for successful leadership. In relation to this, Dineen et al. (2006) noted that behavioural integrity also reflects the level, that is, the field of exemplary behaviour that is provided by the behaviour of their leader.

Here, we agree that integrity can be defined as consistency between words and actions as this is the foundation of leading by example. Moreover, it represents a foundation for the integrity of the organisation, which affects employees in whether they will recognise aspects of new and different practices of their organisation as legitimate. It also represents the basis for higher levels of loyalty, employee satisfaction and their success.

Consistency in the case of inconvenience and temptation

Paine believes that a person with a high degree of integrity advocates and defends their position even in a situation where they are faced with inconvenience or temptation (Paine 2005: 248). According to McFall (1987), temptations and difficulties in taking unpleasant decisions represent an essential condition for integrity. The author believes that someone who cares only for their pleasure cannot enter into a conflict between principles and care for oneself. We are unable to assume a loss of integrity in such a person. The author continues and draws an assertion that 'where there is no possibility for loss, there is no possibility of talking about integrity' (McFall 1987: 9).

Worden (2003) notes that the trademark of integrity lies in the fact that we act transparently in accordance with principles, despite temptations, resulting inconveniences and problems that damage us. We believe that in this context we can only talk about integrity when it manifests in the stages of temptation, trouble, bad and negative consequences, risks and possibly negative outcomes for the individual.

Being true and honest to oneself

With the fourth definition of integrity, we can talk about integrity in the event that an individual is consistent with their conscience as such. This means that the leader acts in accordance with their own values. Howell and Avolio (1995) note that a leader with a high level of integrity is internally consistent and acts in accordance with their own values and beliefs. Koehn (2005a) notes that integrity is often understood as personal coherence and as compliance with moral norms and expectations. Batson et al. (1999) assume the same.

Morrison (2001) believes that a commitment to high moral principles prevents the risk of unwanted behaviour, and at the same time, brings many benefits, including the goodwill and trust of employees, which are key to successful leadership.

Most authors understand integrity as loyalty to one's own rational beliefs about what is right when carrying out certain activities. Posner (2001) noted that the good feeling that arises when an individual acts with integrity is achieved with internal fulfilment.

Moral behaviour and a lack of immoral behaviour

Craig and Gustafson (1998) define integrity as the absence of immoral behaviour, which may on one hand mean that it is enough if one does what is acceptable and not necessarily more than the minimum. Mumford et al. (2003) and Posner (2001) assume the same. In relation to this, Parry and Proctor-Thomson (2002) believe that integrity is not merely the absence of unethical behaviour or a lack of doing the wrong things, but it also means doing the right things and what employees expect and recognise as positive. Palanski and Yammarino (2007) note that integrity is more often associated with going beyond just the immediate and expected behaviour. They also add that the latter category includes the definitions of fairness, justice, compassion and trustworthiness. We agree with this because integrity does not only include a moral minimum but also a moral ideal, which is precisely what ranks integrity amongst virtues.

The moral minimum, in our view, is just a necessary precondition for achieving integrity; however, integrity manifests itself when an individual proves that as a moral individual one can act in accordance with moral ideals in concrete situations with the given effort in achieving them.

Studies of leadership

As mentioned above, leadership has been a subject of research and discussions since at least the days of Ancient Greece or the golden age of Greece (Kellerman 1984), wherein it has always been in the limelight of Western philosophers (Grob 1984). Socrates, as the pioneer of intellectual discussions on leadership as well as the first philosopher-leader, represented the exact opposite of an autocrat. He argued that leadership is always in relation to its situation and most dependent on the knowledge of the leader (Adair 1997). He believed that a person is suited to being a leader when they know what to do in a particular situation and that professional and technical competencies are a prerequisite of good leadership. People mostly follow a leader who knows what needs to be done. At the same time, Socrates was the first person to define the functions of leadership (Adair 1997: 30):

- The selection of suitable people for particular jobs.
- Sanctioning bad practices and rewarding good ones.
- Highlighting the positive qualities of subordinates and motivation (gaining the goodwill of those under them).
- Acquiring allies and assistants.
- Feeding on what was obtained and made.
- Being persistent and diligent.

From Socrates onwards, the study of various leadership functions continued through philosophical, often utopian and idealistic aspects. Plato, for instance, discussed the king-philosopher, Machiavelli, the prince-philosopher, Hobbes, the ruler-sovereign, and Nietzsche, the 'leader-overman' (*ubermensch*) (Grob 1984, Fairholm 1991).[7]

The development of scientific theories of leadership dates back to the early twentieth century when more and more theories gradually developed. Initially, they were spaced apart and today they have merged to form a complex whole. Ciulla (2004) noted that it was characteristic of leaders in the 1920s that they led by exercising their own will upon their employees. In the 1940s, they started with the persuasion of employees, in the 1960s by influencing them, and in the 1990s, they started with predominant interaction. Alban-Metcalfe and Mead (2010) noted that the leadership models of the late 1970s and early 1980s shifted from focusing on caring for employees and the tasks they carried out (the situational and contingent models) to understanding the characteristics of leadership. The said characteristics are crucial in the increasingly complex and changing environment. Thereafter, some three decades ago, Burns (1984: vii) concluded that the development of leadership models was no longer sufficient for the study of leader characteristics. These models, or the 'man-on-horseback theories of leadership', are no longer appropriate because leadership is based on the dynamics of the relationship between the leader and employees, which includes needs, requirements and motivation. At the same time, he realised that leadership is a learning process that begins in childhood, wherein crises, conflicts and dialogues are closely linked with creativity in relation to leading. He also considered that leadership is one of the most studied phenomena, but also one of the least understood phenomena in the world (Burns 2010: 2). Kellerman (1984) saw this as a result of the fact that there was more literature available that described how leadership should be carried out, and less literature explaining what leadership really is. In this connection, in 1978, Burns (2010) realised that the crisis of leadership in those days was a result of the irresponsible behaviour of leaders, where the cause of this situation was a lack of knowledge about leadership. He also drew attention to the deficit of a leadership model that would connect all previous observations. He was convinced that this would certainly be done on the basis of research in the 1980s (Figure 2.2).

INDIVIDUALISATION OF MANAGEMENT

- On the other hand, the practice of management over the last few decades testifies to an increased tendency towards individualisation (Hendry 2013), which started in 1980 with the onset of the neoliberal tendencies in economic policies, the functioning of organisations and globalization. Its basic characteristic is the existence, striving and domination of private interests of managers, which are given an advantage over common interests and working together for a common good. By creating individualized policies of evaluation of their performance and reducing the opportunities for career advancement, a specific role of the manager evolves, namely that the manager strives to achieve individual goals at the expense of many other objectives, participants and those affected. Such individualization of management is in clear conflict with the requirements for the integrity of leaders and leadership, which should be more focused on the interests of employees and organisations in which the organization operates.
- We could say that there is a basic contradiction between the fields of managerial and organizational practices and the requirements of the integrity of leadership. While managers pursue their own particular interests as well as those of shareholders, the employees expect them to work more ethically with taking the interests of employees, the community and the common good into account.

Figure 2.2 Individualisation of management.

Source: Authors.

In the last 10 years, Avolio et al. (2009) have acknowledged that in the field of leadership, the complexity and dynamism of leadership has been identified. A more holistic, comprehensive and positive approach has been developed in the said field, with an emphasis on the role of employees in the process of leadership. One reason for this, according to Alban-Metcalfe and Meade (2010), is that today's organisational environment is quite different from the one existing 10 to 15 years ago. They considered that more and more is expected for less and less from employees in both the public and private sector. Because of this, organisations have to stimulate their employees for work beyond expectations in order to ensure sustainable development. The latter is ever more difficult if one is merely using the traditional methods to motivate and reward employees, which makes the use of new methods of leadership increasingly urgent.

In relation to this, Yukl notes that in the 1980s, researchers started to analyse the emotional and symbolic factors of how leaders influence employees. Before that, the emphasis was on the rationally speculative aspects of the interaction between the leader and the employees. The difference between the newer and older approach lies in the fact that the newer theories involve several variables (or characteristics: behaviour, influence, situation). This consequently enables a more integrated approach. At the same time, Yukl notes that many of the 'new' findings only reflect the conclusions of the 1960s (teamwork, mutual trust, power-sharing, cooperation, etc.) and the 1970s (behaviour and conduct of leaders) (Yukl 2002: 262). In connection with this, Smith et al. (2004) noted that in recent years, transactional, transformational and servant leadership styles have been in the forefront of study.

Development of the models and styles of leadership

A short overview of the first models of leadership

In the early twentieth century, researchers first began with the study of leadership traits and characteristics of the leaders, wherein they originally derived from the belief that the best leaders are born as such. This belief changed in the 1940s as a result of findings that supported the fact that there are no universal characteristics that would make leaders differ from those who are not leaders, and the fact that personal characteristics are by themselves not sufficient (Stogdill 1948, in Northouse 2010: 16). As Yukl states, hundreds of studies on the characteristics of leaders were carried out, yet a reliable and significant correlation between them and the efficiency or effectiveness of leadership has not been established. Kirkpatrick and Locke (1991) concluded, even before these findings, that the positive properties of leaders were a prerequisite of successful leadership. They also noted that the possession of such properties increases the possibility of such leadership. In doing so, the authors identified six different types of positive leadership characteristics, namely:

1 the characteristics of drivers, which include the desire to achieve results (perseverance, initiative, ambition, etc.);

2   motivation for leading (the use of power in favour of the organisation and not as a means for manipulation or exercising personal interests);
3   integrity and honesty (integrity and consistency of words and actions);
4   confidence (including emotional stability);
5   cognitive ability (good analysis of situations and making the right decisions); and
6   competence to perform the work (knowledge, making plans and strategies).

In addition, they identified other, in their view, less important features such as charisma, flexibility and creativity.

Taking into account that the personality characteristics of leaders are an important factor of leadership, the research on leadership then shifted to the study of leadership skills, behaviours of leaders and the influences of situations on leadership.

The skills and competencies (skills model) of leaders, which unlike personal characteristics can be developed and/or trained, were classified in three categories (technical, human and conceptual) by Katz (1955, in Northouse 2010: 40). Yukl (2002) later differentiated between the three main categories of leadership skills, namely interpersonal, cognitive and technical. Their priority depends on the type of organisation, level of leadership and the situation. The study of the behaviour of leaders (style – behaviours approach) was focused on how leaders do what they do, with an emphasis on whether they are more focused on employees or their tasks, and how they combined this with the objective of influencing employees. In this respect, it is very different from studying the characteristics and skills of leaders as the core of this approach is what leaders do, not who the leaders are (Northouse 2010). The study of the influence of the situation on leadership or situational leadership has been focused on which style of leadership is the best in a particular situation, depending on the needs of employees. As Northouse (2010) notes, situational leadership consists of both directing and supporting employees, which stipulates that leaders must adapt their style of leadership according to their competencies and needs (from directing to delegation).

Later, the contingency theory of leadership arose, examining what style of leadership is most appropriate in a particular case, taking into account the influence of interactions of various elements on leadership (the type of organisation, organisational level, number of employees, type of work, etc.). According to Northouse (2010), the contingency theory of leadership points out that leaders are not effective in all situations. The path-goal theory dealt with how leaders motivate employees to achieve the set goals. The author adds that the goal of this theory was to increase employee satisfaction and productivity through proper motivation. This also applies to the contingency theory approach as it is important that the leader decides on the appropriate style of leadership that corresponds to both the employees and the situation.

This was followed by the theory of exchange (leader-member exchange theory – LMX), a theory about the exchange between the leader and members of the group or team. This theory examined the inter-relationship and process interaction. With this, it distinguishes itself from other approaches that were more focused on either the leader (the theory of personality characteristics of leaders, skill theory and the path-goal theory) or employees and the situation (situational leadership, contingency theory and the path-goal theory). The current findings of the LMX theory, which appeared in the 1980s, show that high-quality relationships between the leader and the members based on trust, respect and responsibility bring positive results for both the people and the organisation (Northouse 2010).

The above-mentioned theories of leadership were followed by the theories of transactional leadership, transformational leadership and laissez-faire leadership, which together form the integrative theory of leadership (or the full range leadership model).

At the same time as the theory of servant leadership was developed, so have transformational, authentic and spiritual leadership fallen within the scope of ethical leadership. Because of this logical sequence, we will firstly present the transactional, transformational and laissez-faire theories of leadership, which lie within the scope of the integrative theory of leadership. After that, in the context of ethical leadership, we will identify the authentic and spiritual leadership theories and, finally, the servant leadership theory.

Introduction to transactional and transformational leadership

In 1978, Burns (2010) identified two styles of leadership, namely transactional and transformational leadership. The first is based on a mutual exchange between the leader and their co-workers (employees), while the transformational[8] style is based on the active role played by the leader in influencing the motivation and goals of employees. In the first style, moral values/extrinsic or instrumental values are dominant, such as honesty, integrity, accountability and respecting requirements that represent a prerequisite for achieving an objective. In the second style, according to Burns, end values/intrinsic values are dominant, such as freedom, justice and equality. These are essential and are an objective in their own right.

After Burns, Bass[9] (1997) noted that this leadership paradigm is universal and applicable to various organisations and cultural environments. As such, the best leadership is a combination of both styles. He noted that transformational and transactional leadership, despite their differences, are not exclusive of one another. Bass and Steidlmeier (1999) found that transformational leadership does not replace transactional leadership but strengthens it. Bass and Rigio (2006) concluded that transformational leadership is an enriched form of transactional leadership. At the same time, Bass found that transformational leadership can be ethical or unethical (Palanski and Yammarino 2009, Northouse 2010), depending on the leader and the purpose of their activities (Liden et al. 2008). Bass and Steidlmeier (1999) further elaborated on this, namely, they defined ethical transformational leadership as genuine and authentic leadership, while unethical transformational leadership was defined as fake and pseudo leadership. Genuine transformational leadership is based on moral foundations, values and the integrity of leaders, which are reflected in the leader's vision and the morality of the methods used. Such a leader's actions go beyond their subjective interests of either utilitarian or moral reasons (Avolio and Bass 2002, Bass and Riggio 2006). In the case of genuine transformational leadership, the leader follows the interests of employees, organisations and the local environment and tends to want to realise the organisation's mission. In the second case, namely pseudo transformational leadership (or inauthentic leadership), the leader lacks integrity and may become immoral because of their megalomania and vanity. For the latter, it is typical that they are primarily focused on satisfying their own interests and their own satisfaction, even though in public they can appear the opposite (Bass and Steidlmeier 1999, Avolio and Bass 2002, Parry and Proctor-Thomson 2002, Bass and Riggio 2006). Notwithstanding this, Bass and Steidlmeier (1999) noted that a genuine transformational leader can be occasionally manipulative, but only when one is acting for the sake of the common good. The overall conclusion is that genuine transformational leadership is based on the principle of altruism and selflessness.

Price (2003) believes that ethics and genuine transformational leadership may be questionable in cases where a leader's own interests come into conflict with the required moral behaviour. By this, pseudo-transformational leadership means the absence of a will to the contrary. Conversely, the author believes that when a genuine transformational leader acts unethically, this is because the leader mistakenly believes that his/her actions are correct and helpful. Thus 'the ethical failures in leadership arise when leaders overestimate the importance of their own values' (Price 2003: 75). The author contends that in such cases, when this is consistent with social values and principles, the leader should 'sacrifice' their own values (their 'other-regarding' values). At the same time, Burns considers that 'the test of respecting values is the readiness for using them in relation to themselves and others' (Burns 2010: 75).

Bass and Riggio (2006) point out that transformational leadership is not the key to solving all problems because in stable work environments in which routine tasks are carried out such leadership is often inadequate. As such, transactional leadership meets the needs of the leader. At the same time, in their opinion, there is a possibility that transformational leadership, due to the greater dedication to work, has negative consequences (leader burnout, problems with family life etc.).

Transactional leadership

As mentioned, transactional leadership is based on a mutual exchange between the leader and the employees with the aim of achieving the expected results (Bass and Riggio 2006). A leader who employs this style uses the method of rewards and punishment. The personal growth of employees and their personal needs are not a concern of his, although he is focused on the tasks that are supposed to be carried out (Northouse 2010). As Bass and Riggio (2006) conclude, transactional culture is based on clear and unconditional contractual relations with employees, wherein the employees do not identify with the mission and vision of the organisation, innovation is not encouraged and the employees' most important goal is meeting their own interests.

The first factor of transactional leadership is positive and called contingent reward. A contingent reward occurs when the agreed work is done. A contingent reward is transactional when it is material and it is transformational when it is immaterial (e.g. a commendation). The second factor of transactional leadership is negative; it is divided into two parts, namely active management by exception and passive management by exception. In the first part, the leader monitors the employees and takes immediate action if there are irregularities in order to remedy the failure. In the second part (passive management), the leader acts subsequently when complaints emerge and problems have already arisen (Bass and Steidlmeier 1999, Bass and Riggio 2006).

Transformational leadership[10]

Transformational leadership is considered to be one of the most popular styles of leadership and it has received considerable attention from researchers. This approach to leadership emphases the inner motivation and development of employees (Bass and Riggio 2006), wherein the name alone indicates that the transformational leadership process is process that transforms people (Northouse 2010). The description originates from 1973 when it was first used by James Downton, whereas the transformational leadership style was first developed in 1978 by Burns and in 1985 by Bass[11] (Northouse 2010).

According to Burns (2010), transformational leaders can positively influence the moral development of employees, taking the leader's integrity as a prerequisite for moral conduct. Here, respect for end values and the focus on the wellbeing of all people is dominant. Transformational leadership is literally understood as a process that affects both, the leaders as well as employees who consequently encourage each other to achieve higher levels of morality, motivation and inspiration According to Burns, 'transforming leadership ultimately becomes moral in that it raises the level of human conduct and ethical aspiration of both leader and led, and thus it has a transforming effect on both' (2010: 20). The author also considered that moral behaviour and transformational leadership are inseparable as 'the moral legitimacy of transformational leadership comes from the conscious choice making between real alternatives'. In this context, Burns defended the interdependence between the leader role and the employee role as they both have a transformative effect on each other.

Burns' theory of transformational leadership puts a strong emphasis on values, morals and needs as well as the development of employees, wherein transformational leaders encourage employees to achieve higher standards in terms of moral responsibility (Yukl 2002, Parry and Proctor-Thomson 2002, Brown and Trevino 2006, Avolio 2010, Northouse 2010, Kaiser and Hogan 2010).[12] According to Yukl (2002), Burns saw the essential function of leadership in raising employees' awareness of the importance of both moral conduct and employee assistance in resolving ethical dilemmas. Parry and Proctor-Thomson (2002) consider that Burns' ethical model consequently strengthens organisational integrity. When ethics are understood as the fundamental characteristic in the process of transformational leadership, Burns' contribution is unique, according to Northouse (2010).[13]

Transformational leadership focused on encouraging and inspiring employees to move beyond the expected results of their work, the development of leadership skills among employees and their empowerment, as well as integrating the employees' personal objectives with the collective and organisational goals (Bass and Riggio 2006). At the same time, the authors contend that transformational leadership has much in common with charismatic leadership, wherein charisma is only an important part of transformational leadership (Simons 1999, Bass and Riggio 2006).

Yukl (2002) believes that the essence of transformational leadership also includes the inspiration, development and empowerment of employees. At the same time, Burns and Bass conclude it is appropriate in different situations at all organisational levels of any organisation. In relation to this, Price believes that the essence of transformational leadership lies in influencing changes in employees' personalities 'from the person they are into the person they are expected to be' (2003: 68).

Bass and Steidlmeier (1999) note that the critics of transformational leadership believe this style of leadership is unethical. Such criticism points out that the rhetoric of this style of leadership is based on emotions rather than on reason, it lacks checks and balances, and it manipulates employees with the goal of ignoring their interests, etc. The authors reply that such critics neglect the positive aspects of transformational leadership and do not distinguish between genuine and pseudo transformational leadership.

Transformational leadership consists of four factors, namely idealised influence, inspirational motivation, intellectual stimulation and individual care and concern for the individual (individualised consideration). These four factors are briefly summarised in below.

The first factor – idealised influence – defines a leader who provides a model for employees. He is respected and the employees trust him, they often identify with and imitate him. Such a leader generally reflects high ethical standards (Bass and Riggio 2006, Northouse 2010). Bass and Steidlmeier (1999) note that genuine and pseudo transformational leaders differ in defending different values, which they idealise. A genuine transformational leader defends common social values and the common good, while a pseudo transformational leader merely defends their own values and those with which he cannot identify, describing them as bad (our values and the values of others). Two different aspects of idealised influence exist, that is, the behaviour of the leader and the factors the employees ascribe to the leader (Bass and Riggio 2006).[14] Another term for describing this aspect of transformational leadership is charisma, which in this context is ascribed to people who are able to motivate employees to follow their own vision (Northouse 2010). Hunt (1984) believes that one of the characteristics of charismatic leadership is that the leader is able to give the organisation something special that is directly connected to him. House (1976) defined a charismatic leader as an individual whose influence is able to encourage others to achieve significant and exceptional action. The author also defined a charismatic leader as an individual who represents someone the employees identify with, by which the said employees assume their values and objectives and mimic their behaviour. House also emphasised the four personality traits of leaders, which are understood as charismatic properties, namely an extremely high degree of assertiveness, dominance, the need to influence others and greatly excessive enthusiasm in the moral correctness of their own beliefs. As the author states, these personality traits are reflected in practice, such as setting goals, creating a personal image, expressing high expectations, confidence in employees, etc.

Based on the belief that charisma is not in itself a dividing line between good and evil or moral and immoral, Howell and Avolio (1995) identified six fundamental differences between an ethical and an unethical charismatic leader. They found that ethical leaders chiefly use power for the purpose of caring for employees and their wellbeing, include the needs of others in their own vision, inspire employees, have good two-way communication, are open to the criticism and ideas of employees, encourage the latter in independent and critical thinking, promote and take care of their development, publicly recognise the achievements of employees and behave morally in accordance with their own values for the benefit of the organisation by which they show a good example for the employees. The authors also found that ethical charismatic leaders possess three fundamental virtues, namely courage, integrity and a sense of fairness and justice. As such, we can only speak about ethical charismatic leadership when positive changes are achieved in the organisation.

Yukl (2002) noted that some researchers equate the transformational and charismatic styles of leadership while others differentiate them, but they are not all convinced that both styles can be used simultaneously. The author believes that in addition to the similarities between the styles, there are serious differences and that charisma is a result of an interactive process between the leader, employees and situation. At the same time, the author notes that a charismatic leader can have a considerable impact on the organisation, although the impact is not always necessarily positive since it can degenerate into egotism, tyranny, manipulation, domination or remorselessness. The negativity manifests in the leader's personal will to power, while the positivity manifests in the opposite, that is, in social power and positive effects on the organisation.[15]

The second factor – inspirational motivation – defines a leader who motivates employees, expresses optimism, presents work as important and meaningful, encourages teamwork and involves employees in making the vision and planning the work (Bass and Riggio 2006). Such a leader uses symbols and the emotional approach to encourage employees to work and do more than they would do by themselves (Northouse 2010). Bass and Steidlmeier (1999) noted that a genuine transformational leader provides a challenge for employees with his inspirational motivation and raises awareness of the importance of cooperation and achieving common goals. The leader's inspiration is focused on the desired social behaviour (e.g. charity). Pseudo transformational leaders, in contrast, are characterised by the fact they do not take such inspiration seriously. The same applies to the empowerment of employees, about which pseudo-transformational leaders only talk about.

The third factor – intellectual stimulation – means that a leader encourages employee independence, creativity and innovation by supporting the introduction of new ideas and solutions. Employees are involved in diagnosing and solving problems and the leader avoids public criticism of their mistakes (Bass and Riggio 2006). Bass and Steidlmeier (1999) consider that intellectual stimulation includes an open and dynamic process of assessing situations, the creation of the organisational vision and a behavioural model. On the other hand, a pseudo transformational leader uses his/her power to undermine and underestimate employees' arguments, claims other people's ideas as his/her own and blames others for his/her mistakes.

The fourth factor – concern for the individual – defines a leader who is responsible and cares for the development of employees, knows their needs, the individual differences between them, knows how to actively listen and allows 'private', two-way communication between him and others. Such a leader is able to delegate tasks and acts as a mentor or coach when he helps the employees do their best in their work (Bass and Riggio 2006). Bass and Steidlmeier (1999) see the difference between authentic and pseudo transformational leaders in the fact that genuine transformational leaders truly care for employees, even by becoming leaders themselves. In contrast, pseudo transformational leaders enjoy it when others are dependent on and blindly follow them.

With regard to all four factors of transformational leadership, including transactional leadership, Bass and Riggio (2006) note that in practice, the factors are reflected in a genuine or pseudo manner. Thus, for example, the idealised influence and inspirational motivation are used in a genuine manner when aimed at strengthening employee loyalty and enhancing motivation in order to achieve the benefit of all concerned. The same applies to the factor of concern for the individual when a genuine leader truly cares for the wishes and needs of his/her employees and their personal development. Such a leader sees the employees as their ultimate goals and not as a means to achieving goals. In this connection, Bass and Steidlemeier (1999) note that both a genuine as well as a pseudo transformational leader can fail any of the four factors of transformational leadership, wherein pseudo transformational leaders typically neglect the factor of concern for the individual.

The integrative theory of leadership

The integrative theory of leadership is made up of seven different factors, the first four of which were already mentioned (transformational) along with the second three (transactional). We also have the laissez-faire factor, which represents the absence of leadership (Bass and Riggio 2006). Given that we have already defined the transformational and transactional leadership factors, we will now provide a brief explanation of the laissez-faire factor.

Such leadership is inactive and its designation actually denotes the absence or avoidance of leadership (the French translation would say 'putting your hands away'). Leaders who lead in such a way refuse to accept responsibility, decision-making, giving feedback and make very little effort to meet the needs of their employees. Compared with the transactional leadership style, here we cannot talk about a transaction (Bass and Riggio 2006). As Northouse (2010) adds, there is no exchange and cooperation between the leader and the employee. Schermerhorn describes this leadership style as 'do the best you can without encumbering me' (Schermerhorn 2008: 326).

The positive effects of transformational leadership

The findings of the last 30 years show that use of the transformational leadership style is more effective, that it has a better impact on productivity and innovation and that it is more demanding than use of the transactional leadership style (Bass and Steidlmeier 1999, Avolio and Bass 2002, Bass and Riggio 2006). Bass and Steidlmeier (1999) also note that employees led by transformational leadership are more satisfied than employees led by transactional leadership. It leads to moving beyond the expected results, it contributes to the investment of additional effort and reinforces employee commitment. We also consider greater motivation and greater satisfaction to be positive effects of such leadership, to which the leader's commitment in eliminating stress and conflict contributes considerably.

Tracey and Hinkin (1994) and Parry and Proctor-Thomson (2002) empirically confirmed a positive correlation between transformational leadership and the perception of the leader's integrity. Tracey and Hinkin (1994) found that successful transformational leaders increasingly strive for consistency in their words and actions, which are coherent with the values they advocate.

In addition, Yukl (2002) noted that the theory of transformational conduct demonstrates the influence of leaders on their employees (individual level), while their influence on the group and the organisation is not yet sufficiently understood.

Ethical leadership

Individuals strengthen and develop integrity throughout their whole lives, leaders develop in the same way, and in the recent period, the leader's role has been increasingly shifting in favour of the employees (Bass and Riggio 2006). Accordingly, theories of leadership are being developed and employees are beginning to change with their increased education.

In conjunction with this and the fact that personal integrity occupies the centre of our interest, ethical leadership is especially relevant for us. Ethical leadership includes a different leadership style (Reed et al. 2011) or, in other words, ethical leadership manifests in different previously mentioned leadership styles (Dion 2012).[16] Thus, we can understand authentic leadership, spiritual leadership and servant leadership as ethical leadership. All of the mentioned leadership styles have a common focus on the personal integrity of the leader and values such as honesty and fairness. Reed et al. (2011) note that all of the aforementioned styles also include a concern for others (altruism), leading by example and a concern for ethical behaviour (2011: 420).

Given the above, we will first present ethical leadership as a theoretical frame-work of all four leadership styles. After that, we will present authentic, spiritual and servant leadership separately, while transformational leadership was already presented and discussed in the previous chapter.

The basics of ethical leadership

Goethals et al. (2004) believe that leadership is ethical by definition; therefore, unethical leadership is not leadership. At the same time, they show how this dilemma's origin is in the works of Plato who argued that every rule seeks to ensure what is right in both a private and public sense.

In the field of contemporary understanding of ethical leadership, Heifetz, Burns and Greenleaf (Yukl 2002, Northouse 2010) made a considerable impact; they all studied the ethics of caring. They focused on the needs of employees and the relationship between the leader and the employees (Northouse 2010). Yukl (2002) notes that ethical behaviour has been gaining in importance in recent years. The author sets out the criteria on which a study can analyse the individual's behaviour. These are personal values and virtue, the level of moral development, purpose, freedom of choice, ethical and unethical behaviour, external influences, etc. At the same time, the author adds that in assessing whether certain behaviour was ethical or not a study must take its purpose into account, as well as its compliance with ethical standards and consequences. With this, similarly to Brown et al. (2005), the author adds that personal integrity is an important factor in ethical leadership.

As mentioned in the introduction, Northouse (2010) notes that the study of ethical leadership is concentrated on what the leaders do and who the leaders are. In other words, it is focused on the leader's behaviour and character. The study of the moral behaviour of leaders and its consequences is made possible through the prism of ethical egoism, utilitarianism and altruism. At the same time, the author identifies five principles of ethical behaviour that derive from Aristotle's philosophy, namely, respect for others, serving others, fairness, honesty and concern for the community. Based on the grounds that behaving merely in accordance with the law does not mean that certain behaviour is ethical, Schermerhorn et al. (2008) noted that ethical leadership is defined by care, integrity, principles, acting according to ethical standards, discussing ethical behaviour, rewarding ethical behaviour and sanctioning unethical behaviour. Regarding the latter, Carroll (2009) believes that effective ethical leadership requires a balance between rewarding ethical behaviour and penalising immoral behaviour.

Burns (2010) also defined ethical behaviour as a relationship between leaders and employees. This relationship is based on common needs, aspirations and values (Figure 2.3). At the same time, the author adds that 'ethical leadership is not merely preaching ... but always derives and returns to the basic needs and desires, aspirations and values of the employees' (Burns 2010: 4). Burns believes that the only ethical behaviour that exists is that which works for the benefit of the people.

CRITERIA THAT DEFINE ETHICAL BEHAVIOUR

- caring for employees and the organisation
- balancing and integrating various interests of those involved (stakeholders)
- inclusion of the needs, ideas and values of employees in the vision of the organisation
- behaviour that is consistent with the declared values, such as integrity
- being personally responsible for achieving the objectives and implementing the vision
- timely and effective informing of employees with the necessary information about events, issues and solutions
- encouraging critical thinking of employees with the aim of looking for the best possible solution
- providing instructions, mentoring and training for the employees which contribute to their development of skills and their self-confidence

Figure 2.3 Criteria that define ethical behaviour.

Source: Authors.

Despite the growing interest in ethical behaviour, Yukl (2002) noted that this field still contains considerable disparities concerning the preferred definitions and empirical methods. Schermerhorn et al. (2008) concluded that there is no simple definition of ethical behaviour because, as Yukl (2002) adds, empirical research of the ethical aspects of leadership is relatively new. This is why this field is still quite open to further research. In addition, Bass and Steidlmeier (1999: 182) note that ethical behaviour is based on the following three pillars:

- The moral character of the leader
- The ethical aspect of values that are woven into the leader's vision and expressions and an organisational programme that employees accept or reject
- The morality of the decisions and actions of the leader and the leader's employees

Johnson (2007) further divides ethical leadership into two components, namely leading by example/moral conduct of the leader, and the formation of an ethical culture in the organisation. Both of these roles are intertwined because the leader also shapes the ethical culture by his/her exemplary behaviour.

In conjunction with the above, Carroll (1991) and Carroll and Buchholtz (2000) distinguish between immoral, amoral and moral leadership. An immoral leader deliberately acts immorally for the purpose of personal benefits. An amoral leader acts in two distinct ways: intentionally and unintentionally. An intentionally amoral leader does not think about the ethical significance and implications of their decisions and behaviour. The authors believe that such a leader is someone who is neither moral nor immoral. Such a leader also believes that the business world has different rules than the outside world. Accidentally amoral leadership also does not include a reflection on the ethical implications of decisions and behaviour, however, such a leader is not morally conscious, while the leader's moral judgement ability is weak. In spite of their good intentions, this prevents the leader from behaving in an acceptable manner. Kreitner (2004) defines such a leader as a lazy leader. Tavčar (2008), on the other hand, believes that the common cause of the amorality of a leader is the leader's internal ethical vacuum.[17] Unlike the first two types, the third type of leader – moral leadership – understands moral behaviour as a personal goal in the spirit of fairness and altruism (Carroll 1991, Carroll and Buchholtz 2000).

Robbins and Langton (2003) see the difference between ethical and unethical leadership in the fact that ethical leaders use their influence in a socially accept-able way (for the benefit of the employees). Unethical leaders, on the other hand, exploit their influence to gain power over the employees, with the aim of satisfy-ing their own interest. Schermerhorn believes moral leaders are ethically mindful; this means that an ethical leader has a positive impact on the employees and the organisation through his/her constant promoting of ethical values and leading by personal example (Schermerhorn 2008: 44). The author also understands ethical leadership as leading with ethical standards, which meet the criteria of 'being good and righteous'. Schermerhorn is convinced that ethical leadership begins with the personal integrity of the leader (2008), which up until quite recently was a rela-tively neglected topic of leadership (Carroll 2009). The author adds that an ethical leader is an ethical person at first and that ethical leaders follow high standards of moral behaviour. With this, the leader influences the employees in a fair and honest way. Employees are thus inspired to achieve success, while legal provisions only represent a minimal level of moral behaviour. The author also believes that ethical leadership requires a balance between power and responsibility (Carroll 2009).

According to Fry and Kriger (2009), ethical leadership is based on three fac-tors, the moral character of the leader, the ethical legitimacy of the leader's vision and the values of the decision and actions in which the leader is involved. In con-trast, Trevino et al. (2000) noted that ethical leadership depends on two factors: how others perceive the leader as a moral person and as a moral leader. Being a moral person is connected to what the personal characteristics of the individual are, what the individual does and how they decide and behave. Being a moral leader, in contrast, means leading by example in the context of moral conduct, communicating about ethics and values as well as rewarding ethical behaviour. The authors believe that ethical behaviour pays off and manifests in commitment and employee satisfaction because, as Den Hartog and De Hoogh (2009) state, it is objective, respectful to employees and worthy of trust. For an ethical leader the characteristics are integrity and principled, ethical, fair and just decisions. Bennis and Goldsmith (2010) note that if an organisation is successful in the implementa-tion of ethical leadership, based on values such as integrity, it can function as a unified system, which is both consistent internally as well as with the environment in which it operates. Caldwell et al. (2008) are convinced that ethical leadership strengthens the confidence and commitment of employees in their organisation, and consequently, leads to a substantial competitive advantage of the organisation in the market.

Brown et al. (2005) understand ethical leadership as moral behaviour of leaders in the context of their work and performance and their personal relationships as well as the encouraging of employees to engage in such practice with the help of the leader's two-way communication and empowerment. In other words, 'ethical leadership is a combination of the personal characteristics of the leader and their behaviour, which reflects their integrity and high ethical standards, considerate and honest attitude towards employees and demands accountability for ethical behaviour' (Brown et al. 2005: 130). The authors conceptualised ethical leadership as social learning because they are convinced that imitating the behaviour of a leader who leads by example (modelling) is the best way of learning and internalising ethical behaviour and leadership. On this basis, Brown et al. (2005) and Brown and Trevino (2006) found that leaders are those who offer employees a model for ethical behaviour in the workplace. The authors found that leadership by example covers a wide range of psychological processes, such as identification, imitation, learning by observation, etc.

The thesis that the majority of employees imitate and identify with the ethical conduct of their superiors and other relevant persons (significant others) was already advocated by Kohlberg. Yukl (2002) believes that the differences between leaders' ethical behaviour can be explained with the help of Kohlberg's theory of moral development. According to this theory,[18] every higher level reached by an individual enables them to develop a broader understanding of the principles of fairness, social responsibility and human rights. Dienhart (2005) believes that the internalisation of values takes place on the rational level and leaders' progress in this way when they are better at solving problems.

Crane and Matten exemplify Kohlberg's six stages of moral development through the prism of work and engagement in activities (2004: 120). Thus, they note that in the first phase, employees behave unethically as they believe, for example, that they are going to be rewarded or at least not punished. In the second stage, employees protect the unethical behaviour of co-workers because they expect the same in return. In the third phase, for example, employees use the organisation's resources (e.g. a phone) as this is widely acceptable and 'everyone does it'. In the fourth phase, for example, the leader adjusts the pay of employees who go beyond their minimum work standards due to the pressure of other interest-based groups, customers and the wider community. In the fifth stage, for example, the leaders and employees carry out socially beneficial activities that reach beyond legal norms and social expectations. The sixth stage represents a stage where, for example, leaders and employees act and make decisions only according to their own values and principles, which they believe are beneficial to everyone else.

Basing on Kohlberg's division, Carroll and Buchholtz (2000) note that the majority of leaders still act ethically in order to avoid penalties or receive a prize, while many leaders act ethically because they want to be responsible towards their family, friends, superiors or they are simply good people. A small portion of leaders act ethically as they believe this is the right thing to do, striving to achieve values and ideals. Yukl (2002) adds that it is not necessary that all people mature morally, which consequently means that some leaders remain at lower levels of moral development. Waddock (2007) came to similar findings, namely that surveys show that the majority of leaders do not reach the post-conventional level of moral thinking and reasoning. For the latter, the author believes that, contrary to conventional moral thinking, it is one of the key factors in successful leadership and management in today's challenging business environment (Figure 2.4).

Crane and Matten (2004) note that Kohlberg's theory has been subjected to numerous criticisms and that it was originally developed in the non-profit environment, in interviews with young American men, which was the reason for doubting the validity of generalising the results. At the same time, they believe that people can also backtrack in their moral development and that they use different strategies of moral reasoning in a variety of situations and circumstances. Nevertheless, the authors assert that Kohlberg's theory of cognitive moral development is widely accepted as an important factor in explaining individual effects of the taking of ethical decisions.

It is necessary to take account of the impact and influence the situation has on the ethical behaviour of leaders. This was studied by Brenner and Molander (1977), who demonstrated the concept of situational ethics with empirical methodology. The conflict between the creation of profit and ethical behaviour represented an ethical dilemma, which lead to the dissatisfaction of leaders, the fall of ethical standards and confirms that the situation affects the ethical behaviour of leaders,

Figure 2.4 Ethical leadership.

Source: Caldwell et al. (2008).

while economic pressures make business ethics relative and situational (Brenner and Molander 1977, Berlogar 2000: 196).[19]

Brown and Trevino (2006) identified three situational factors (in addition to the individual characteristics of leaders, namely, character, motivation, level of moral development, self-control, internal or external locus of control, etc.) that influence the perception of employees about the morality of their leaders (Figure 2.5). The first factor is connected to whom the leaders looked up to in their own careers, and who was their mentor, because a good leader, in addition to setting a good example, also means a greater likelihood of future leaders behaving ethically. The second factor is related to the organisational climate and the level of ethical culture in the organisation. If the organisation supports and advocates an ethical culture and supports ethical behaviour, it has a positive effect on the presence of ethical behaviour. The third factor is the intensity of moral judgements, which is associated with leaders' level of ethical awareness and their ability to recognise moral challenges. Berlogar (2000) found that exercising organisational ethics largely depends on the organisational environment and those involved.

Authentic leadership

Given that we have already discussed transformational leadership, we are going to briefly introduce the philosophy of authentic leadership.

The concept of authenticity stems from Greek philosophy (Avolio and Gardner 2005). The authors present the difference between authentic leadership and other styles of leadership with the fact that authentic leadership is more generic

Figure 2.5 Situational factors affecting the perception of employees about the morality of leaders.

Source: Brown and Trevino (2006).

(common) and represents a so-called root construct of other 'positive' leadership styles such as transformational, servant, spiritual, etc. Dimovski et al. (2009) made similar findings, namely that authentic leadership differs from other styles in that it does not define any style of leadership a leader should assume, but instead it highlights the personality of a leader, which should be pursued.

Authentic leadership is one of the new areas of research. Northouse (2010) adds that its very name denotes that it deals with the authenticity and credibility of leaders and their leadership. In contrast to the previously mentioned theories of leadership, it is still in the phase of research and development (Bass and Riggio 2006, Northouse 2010). Interest in it emerged at an early stage of exploration of the transformational leadership style (Bass in Steidlmeier 1999, Burns 2010).[20],[21]

A uniform definition of authentic leadership has not yet been accepted among researchers (Northouse 2010). It can be defined from the intrapersonal aspect, the development process and the interpersonal aspect. The first aspect is focused on the leader and the processes happening in the leader's interior (for example self-control). The second aspect is based on the assumption that authentic leadership is a process a leader develops throughout his life. The third aspect emphasises the fact that authentic leadership arises in the interaction between the leader and the employees (Northouse 2010). In defining authentic leadership, the researchers used both the practical and theoretical approach where they defined four basic factors of the authentic leadership style in the development process. These four factors are self-awareness, inner moral perspective, balanced and objective acting and transparency in relations (Northouse 2010: 217). In addition, the researchers discovered that the positive psychological characteristics of the leader (trust, hope, optimism, adaptability), the ability of moral judgement and critical life events all influence the authentic leadership style.

Palanski and Yammarino (2007) noted that authentic leadership includes transparency and integrity, wherein authenticity is based on consistency of words, actions and internalised values. Howard (2010) believed the same, while Noble (2008) noted that authentic leadership stems from the genuine motivation of the leader to, for example, help employees in their department. Schermerhorn et al. (2008) believed that authentic leadership is based on the leader's knowledge of himself and on authentic behaviour, which is consistent with personal values.

Avolio and Gardner define an authentic leader as someone

> who is profoundly aware of how they think and act. The leader's employees also perceive him as an individual who is aware of his own values and the values, moral principles, knowledge and virtues of others, is aware of the real situations, is trustworthy, hopeful, optimistic, flexible and highly moral.
>
> (2005: 321)

At the same time, the authors believe that authentic leaders encourage employees to develop their own authenticity. The leader achieves this with his high level of self-awareness, self-restraint and leading by example. George and Sims (2007) noted that authentic leaders are primarily loyal to themselves and their principles and beliefs, which is the main reason for the employees' trust in them.

Similarly, Brown and Trevino (2006) acknowledge that authentic leaders are deeply aware of how they think and act, wherein in addition to self-awareness, they are distinguished by openness, transparency and authenticity. Goethals et al. (2004) considered that leaders achieve authenticity with a successful balance between ambition, competence and personal integrity. Bennis (2002) added that the more the leader is authentic and adapted to the times, the better the leader can manage changes in the organisation.

Similar to the transformational and servant leadership styles, the authentic leadership style also has a clearly expressed moral dimension and emphasises the duty of the leaders to do what is right and beneficial for the employees and the organisation (Northouse 2010). Moreover, according to Northouse, an authentic leader will first take care of the needs of employees and only secondly of his own personal needs, which is also a central feature of the servant style of leadership that will be presented below.[22]

Given the above, we believe that authentic leadership represents the foundation of ethical leadership and that it is a necessary component of other ethical forms of leadership, whereby we concur with the beliefs of Avolio and Gardner (2005) and Dimovski et al. (2009).

Spiritual leadership

Fry (2003) defines spiritual leadership as a method of leadership based on internal motivation and through which values are reflected, together with beliefs and behaviour, which motivates and inspires employees. Here, integrity is one of the key foundations. Brown and Trevino (2006) agree with this and add that employees trust and appreciate their leader because of this.

According to Fry (2003),[23] the theory of the spiritual leadership style can be seen as an attempt to design an integrated approach to leadership, bringing together the four fundamental factors of the human being in the workplace, namely the body (physical factor), thinking (logic), heart (emotions, feelings) and the soul. Conversely, Smith and Malcom (2010) see the concern for spirituality (values, vision, mission, ethics, etc.) as part of an integrated approach to leadership in addition to the physical condition of employees (welfare and good working conditions) and their mental state (knowledge, understanding, etc.). The authors believe that spirituality is the most difficult factor, which leaders prefer to avoid. With the aim of ensuring an integrated approach, the authors advocate a balance of all three factors.

Gavin et al. (2003) argue that human spirituality brings awareness of the importance and meaning of life and is separated from religion which, according to the authors, does not fall into the framework of the workplace. The fact that spiritual leadership is not related to religion is also agreed upon by Schermerhorn et al. (2008). It denotes a deep sense of the fact that everything is interconnected and can be an inexhaustible source of hope and will, which benefits humans in all areas of life. In the field of leadership, it provides a view through everyday tasks, understanding the mission and long-term objectives, not only in the interest of leaders, but also in the interest of the entire organisation and all concerned. Moreover, according to the authors, spirituality also affects relationships between people, wherein it helps people from different religions to jointly advocate the implementation of the organisational mission. This gives purpose to work and a more important role than understanding it merely as the fulfilment of obligations and financial compensation (Gavin et al. 2003).

Tourish and Tourish (2010), however, hold a more critical view on the topic of spirituality because, as they believe, spirituality is only a means to achieving organisational benefits and the benefits of the leaders. At the same time, they are convinced that the workplace, especially in the for-profit sector, is not an appropriate place where people realise their deepest mission and purpose of being. To this end, neither leaders nor organisations are qualified for this. The authors advocate that work is naturally important, but it should not be a substitute for social networking, life interests, obligations, etc.

In conjunction with other leadership styles, Crossman (2010) noted that spiritual and transformational leadership are both related to the element of inspiration. According to the author, this is the main difference from the transactional leadership style, which is based on everyday exchanges between the leader and the employees. Transformational leadership was defined as inspirational by Burns (2010). It was understood as an ability to inspire employees to adopt moral behaviour and higher motivation, consequently delivering results above expectations.

Crossman (2010) noted that the connection between spiritual and servant leadership, as was also demonstrated by Fry (2003), is that the servant leader is in tune with spiritual values. The relationship between spiritual and servant leadership styles, without any element of religiosity, was also researched by Nandram and Vos (2010).

Ethical leadership as an independent model of leadership

Given that some authors understand ethical leadership as a stand-alone leadership style, which is also contained in other leadership styles, we would like to present their observations on the similarities and differences between the ethical leadership style and other styles below.

Brown et al. (2005) and Brown and Trevino (2006) found that both ethical and transformational leadership contain common characteristics in their focus on the care for employees, on behaviour in accordance with integrity and moral principles, on the care for the consequences of the decisions taken and on leading by example. We believe that this is also true for the servant leadership style.

Brown et al. (2005) also assert that ethical leadership is closely linked to the ethical aspect of the transformational leadership style, which includes honesty and integrity. It is also included in the transformational leadership model in the factor of idealised influence, which emphasises leadership by example. The key mutual difference is that ethical leadership also contains the elements of transactional leadership, which does not apply to transformational leadership (Brown and Trevino 2006). The basic characteristic of the ethical leadership style lies in the fact that the leader advocates and acts in accordance with high ethical standards and demands the same from his/her employees. To this end, the leader uses both positive measures (reward) and negative measures (penalty), with which the leader encourages employees to behave ethically. The authors note that in this regard such a transactional relationship, in the context of social exchange, has a significant impact on the behaviour of employees who are consequently enabled to efficiently recognise desired behaviour, which is beneficial and vice versa. In addition, the ethical and transformational leadership styles differ in that the ethical leadership model does not emphasise the formation of a vision and the intellectual stimulation of employees, which is a basic characteristic of transformational leadership (Brown and Trevino 2006).

Similarly, the ethical leadership style is intertwined with the authentic and spiritual leadership styles. This manifests in the personal characteristics of leaders, namely in their high degrees of integrity, concern for employees, concern for the morality of the decisions taken and leading by example. The difference between them lies in the fact that self-awareness and being true to oneself, which both determine authentic leadership, and a concern for the vision and emphasising the organisation's mission, which are part of the spiritual model of leadership, are not present in the ethical leadership model (Brown and Trevino 2006). According to the authors, ethical leadership is somewhat more pragmatic, and with the help of transactional leadership, it is aimed more at influencing the employees, which is not as typical for the authentic and spiritual leadership styles.

Research of ethical leadership

Before we move on to the study of servant leadership, a brief overview of the findings of empirical research of ethical leadership follows below.

Northouse (2010) noted that, to date, relatively little research has been published on the theoretical foundations of ethical leadership, while Brown et al. (2005)[24] and Brown and Trevino (2006) concluded that studies so far on ethical leadership have mainly focused on the philosophical aspect and the question of how leaders ought to behave. To this end, there has not been enough research on which factors form ethical leadership.

Den Hartog and De Hoogh (2009) noted that many researchers and experts consider ethical leadership to be important. Similar to De Hoogh and Den Hartog (2008) and Northouse (2010), they noted that only a few empirical data on ethical leadership and the impact of personal characteristics on ethical leadership are available. Den Hartog and De Hoogh (2009) concluded that these studies are generally solely focused on one element of ethical leadership, for example, integrity (Craig and Gustafson 1998) or the general perception of ethical leadership (Brown et al. 2005).

Thus, De Hoogh and Den Hartog (2008) found that ethical leadership has a significant impact on employees' perception of their leader's performance, on optimism and the positive attitude of employees relative to the future of the organisation as well as their role within it. In another study, the authors found a positive correlation between the perception of employees about the ethics of their leaders and the employees' confidence in their leaders, other employees, employee commitment and the wellbeing of the organisation. In this connection, they also found a positive correlation between employees' perception of the integrity and fairness of their leaders and the emotional commitment of the employees to the organisation or the group in which they work (Den Hartog and De Hoogh 2009). Similarly, Caldwell et al. (2010) found that when employees see the behaviour of their leader as trustworthy, their confidence in the organisation grows and the leaders are perceived as more ethical.

Russell (2001) reported that values influence the behaviour of leaders and that they have become an important part of research in the field of leadership. The author considers honesty and integrity to be the two most important values; he believes that both values have an important impact on the establishment of interpersonal trust between a leader and the employees, the confidence of employees in the organisation and the organisational performance (Figure 2.6).

Bass and Steidlmeier (1999) are convinced that the character of the leader is an important factor in ethical leadership, while Trevino et al. (2000) add that,

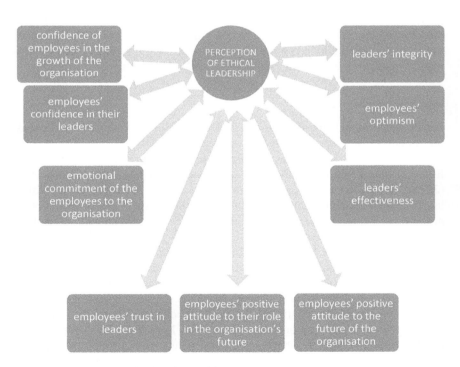

Figure 2.6 Perception of ethical leadership.

Source: Authors.

in the eyes of leaders, integrity is the most important factor. Sarros and Cooper (2006) noted that in addition to the integrity of leaders as the key factor, honesty, self-discipline and cooperativeness should be considered. In relation to fairness, Cotterell et al. (2006) stated that employees see it as inextricably linked to integrity and the character of the leader and that ethical leadership is understood as the leader's consistency between values and standards. Similarly, Rickards and Clark (2006) noted that the ethical standards of an individual leader are reflected in his leading by example and the level of his integrity.

At this point, it is worth mentioning the findings of Berlogar (2000: 195). On the basis of a survey on the ethical leadership of managers, the author found that, with respect to certain principled positions, they can be placed very high on Kohlberg's scale. Taking all of the results into account, they can be ranked between the third and fourth levels on Kohlberg's scale.

Servant leadership

Introduction to servant leadership

As already mentioned, a good leader is determined by his personal values and virtues, with integrity being one of the virtues (Figure 2.7). If a leader lacks integrity, the employees will not trust the leader as they have no reason to do the opposite (George and Sims 2007: xxxii). It is the same with the inspiration of employees because an immoral leader who is not respected can hardly influence his employees in such a way (Lennick and Kiel 2009). The authors believe that the best leader is neither charismatic nor heroic. The best leader is one who is able to inspire others to achieve high efficiency and takes the employees into account and is sensitive to their needs. At the same time, Bass and Riggio (2006) add that it is important for leaders to take care of the development of leadership skills amongst all employees who are being led (Figure 2.8).

In spite of the above, Adair (1997, 2002) noted that people are still not accustomed to thinking about leaders as service-minded colleagues and still prefer to emphasise the position of the leader rather than his/her responsibility. At the same time, the author (2002) noted that Socrates identified a common element of servility in all forms of leadership. Socrates believed that it is the fundamental responsibility of leaders to meet the needs of the people. In the author's opinion, it is paradoxical that the leader who does not put himself in front of the employees is always ahead of the leaders who do the opposite (Adair 1997).

All of the mentioned and more characterise the servant leadership style. This style will be the subject of our study that now follows.

Definition

In dictionaries, servility, in relation to leadership, is defined as 'being useful' (Oxford 1989b), 'helping to achieve something useful' or 'to assure and accomplish something urgent' (Cambridge 2003). In relation to the leader, he is defined

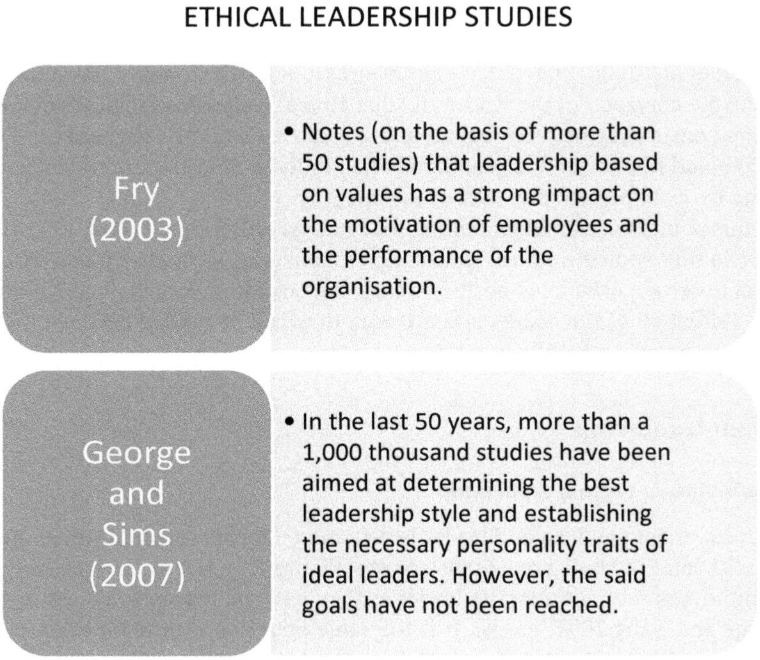

ETHICAL LEADERSHIP STUDIES

Fry (2003)

- Notes (on the basis of more than 50 studies) that leadership based on values has a strong impact on the motivation of employees and the performance of the organisation.

George and Sims (2007)

- In the last 50 years, more than a 1,000 thousand studies have been aimed at determining the best leadership style and establishing the necessary personality traits of ideal leaders. However, the said goals have not been reached.

Figure 2.7 Ethical leadership studies.

Source: Authors.

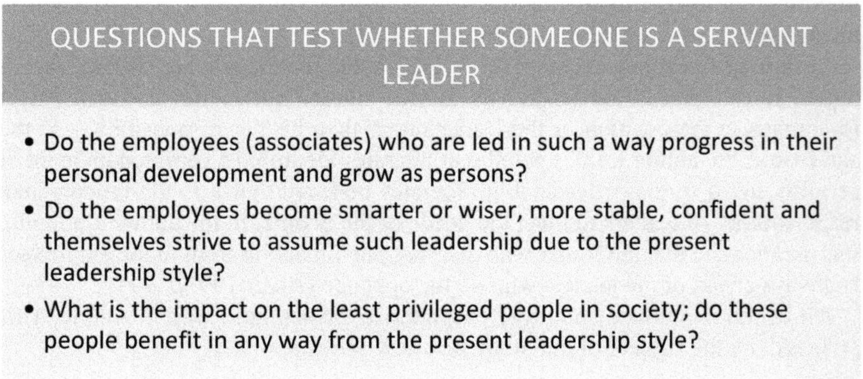

QUESTIONS THAT TEST WHETHER SOMEONE IS A SERVANT LEADER

- Do the employees (associates) who are led in such a way progress in their personal development and grow as persons?
- Do the employees become smarter or wiser, more stable, confident and themselves strive to assume such leadership due to the present leadership style?
- What is the impact on the least privileged people in society; do these people benefit in any way from the present leadership style?

Figure 2.8 Questions that test whether someone is a servant leader.

Source: Greenleaf (2002a, 2002b).

as a person who performs tasks for others and who is loyal and hospitable to associates (Oxford 2004).

Sendjaya et al. (2008: 406) note that the relationship between the terms 'servility' and 'leader' is already shown in the ancient Greek words *diakonos, doulos, therapon, huperetes, sundoulos, oiketes* and *pais*. None of these terms denotes a lack of self-esteem or low self-esteem. However, they denote voluntary subordination for the benefit of others. Sendjaya and Sarros (2002) point out that servant leadership is not a sign of weakness of the leader, while Lewis (2008) believes that servant leadership cannot be understood as a soft approach to leadership. Page and Wong (2000) are convinced that it does not reflect weak and indecisive leadership because a servant leader acts in the same way as other leaders: realistically and flexibly.

The source and etymology of the word 'servant', in our context, is focused on leadership and the organisational functionality. It is rich with concepts that underpin the moral behaviour of participants (Boyum 2006).

The development of servant leadership

The roots of the philosophical study of servant leadership stem from ancient Greece (Nandram and Vos 2010, Trompenaars and Voerman 2010, Searle and Barbuto 2011), where Aristotle, similarly to Socrates before him, stated that servant leadership means serving others and doing what is right (Nandram and Vos 2010: 236). As Trompenaars and Voerman (2010) note, Aristotle regarded serving others and doing what is right as representing the essence of life. Aristotle discussed the noble sacrifice for others and the fact that a good and noble man distributes his wealth among his friends in such a way that they have more than him (Gantar 2002).[25] It is interesting that Aristotle believed that a tyrant's interest is only that of his own, while a king's interest is aimed at all of his serfs, which is also the difference between a kingdom and monarchy (Aristotle 2002). As previously mentioned, Aristotle also noted that actions 'that are in accordance with virtues, are noble and done because of noble motives' (2002: 127), which also applies genuinely to servant leadership. Using the analogy from Aristotle's characterisation of a generous man, who 'gives almost too much and retains the smaller part of distributed wealth; as a generous man does not look only after himself' (2002: 127) and Aristotle's definition of a righteous man who 'does not allocate more assets to oneself than one is proportionally supposed to, and puts effort into serving and aiding others', we can see the point of contact of the philosophy of servant leadership in the fact that a leader first and foremost takes care of his employees and then himself. This is also in line with the thinking of Rousseau who believed that 'the one who believes to be the master and leader of others is himself a greater slave than the ones he believes are lead' (Rousseau 2001: 13) because a leader who adheres to the servant leadership style does not behave in front of his subordinates as their master. In the context of our research into the authenticity and inauthenticity of servant leadership, we can understand Biant's saying that Aristotle used to interpret justice, namely: 'When a man has authority and power, his true nature is revealed' (Aristotle 2002: 156). It should be added that servant leadership, according to Trompenaars and Voerman (2010), is based on Plato's four main virtues, namely wisdom, justice, courage and temperance.

The concept of servant leadership can also be identified in the early Christian teachings on the role of leaders and their qualities (Boyum 2006, Greenleaf 1998), while the model of servant leadership as we know it today was designed by Robert Greenleaf in 1969 in his essay 'The Servant as Leader'[26] (Spears 1998, 2002, Greenleaf 2002a, Yukl 2002, Smith et al. 2004, Boyum 2006, Washington et al. 2006, Barbuto 2007, Carroll 2009, Northouse 2010, Trompenaars and Voerman 2010, Nandram and Vos 2010). In the mid-1930s, Greenleaf was employed by the US company American Telephone and Telegraph Company (AT&T) where he worked in senior posts for almost 40 years. When he retired, he founded the Centre for Applied Ethics. When the Centre was founded, the American society was faced with a crisis in leadership and management (Bartholomew 2006), which was why he decided to present the servant leadership model to the public.

The idea and theorem, which was not initially popular, was first justified with the belief that until the right people hold decision-making positions even the best systems are unable to contribute to a better society (Figure 2.9). In relation to this, he saw a danger in the situation where people who have an innate sense of 'being servant' and the potential for leadership and do not lead, and where people have decided to follow unethical leaders.

It seems that for Greenleaf, it was very important to be aware of the fact that the opportunity of influencing change and creativity is only in the hands of those within the organisation, as those outside it can only criticise its policies. According to Greenleaf (2002a), for the leader who is servant and capable of creativity, the greatest joy is precisely creativity.

Greenleaf (2002a)

- Greenleaf got his idea during the time during his student days (in the early 1930s), namely the subject 'The Sociology of Labour Problems', which was taught by Professor Oscar Helming. The latter considered that in American society large organisations had started dominating (business, government, religions, university etc.) which had failed to serve their people and society well enough. Thus, the professor suggested to his students, that as part of their career they should also be active in this area, whereby he believed that the most effective way of influencing the organisational culture is from within. For a definitive understanding of the professor's advice, Greenleaf noted that he himself needed almost 50 years.
- According to Boyum (2006), Greenleaf saw the reason for the crisis of leadership and management in the ever-stronger tendency towards individualism and self-efficacy against social efficiency.

Figure 2.9 The first concept of servant leadership.

Source: Greenleaf (2002a).

Given the definition of leadership, Greenleaf was aware of the negative over-tone of the word 'servant', but decided to keep the term because he believed that no other word can cover the width of its notion (Greenleaf 2002a). Greenleaf imported the idea and inspiration for designating a leader as a servant from the novel 'The Journey to the East' by the author Hermann Hesse. As he wrote, the idea did not come to his mind on the basis of logic but in an intuitive manner, where a model of a true servant was his father (Greenleaf 1998, 2002a). Whetstone (2002) believed that Greenleaf interpreted Hesse's story as a doctrine in which the real leader is servile and helpful, which is also the key to his greatness. Through use of the terms 'servility', 'leadership' and 'persuasiveness', he tried to restore dignity to leadership, which had been substantially weakened by the impersonal functioning of industrialisation (Greenleaf 1998). He was convinced that it was dignity that gave power to employees as well as organisations in the terms of servant leadership. Spears (1998) believed that Greenleaf shaped the term 'serv-ant leadership' for the purpose of defining leadership that was then lacking in organisations. With the combination of contradictory concepts, the servant and the leader were brought together in a positive and efficient framework, allowing Greenleaf to construct a new insight into the function of leadership (Spears 1998, 2002, 2009). Trompenaars and Voerman (2010) believed that leadership and ser-vility are two sides of the same coin, while Greenleaf (2002a, 2002b) added that both roles (servant and leader) can be combined within a single person on any organisational level.

Increased interest in the study and exploration of servant leadership is a characteristic of recent years and the new millennium (Burkhardt and Spears 2002, Russell and Stone 2002, Sendjaya and Sarros 2002, Ramsey 2003, Liden et al. 2008, Sendjaya et al. 2008, Northouse 2010). Spears (2002, 2009) and Dierendonck and Patterson (2010) believe the reason for this is that the start of the twenty-first century brought with it the realisation that, instead of the tradi-tional, hierarchical and overtly aristocratic leadership styles, primarily focused on the benefit of the owners and shareholders, a number of more suitable models had arisen based on ethical behaviour, caring for employees, their development, care for the community, employee involvement in decision-making, a long-term vision of development, etc. In their view, servant leadership is specifically sufficient for these criteria, which have been gaining ever more followers since its creation. As Peete (2005) adds, more and more organisations are adopting the servant leader-ship style as part of their organisational philosophy. Burkhardt and Spears (2002) and Ramsey (2003) also see the reason for the rise of servant leadership style in the development of society and its constant changing, which consequently applies equally to leadership models and the understanding of the role of leaders in for-profit and non-profit organisations.

Spears (2010) noted, in relation to this, that in the fourth decade after Robert Greenleaf had designed the idea of servant leadership, it started to spread in the education process and in leadership practice because many organisations had woven the mentioned principle of leadership into their own development phi-losophy. Interest in the study of this model also spread in the field of scientific research,[27] as reflected in the growing number of research studies, papers and books. This confirms the thesis of Bass (Sendjaya and Sarros 2002: 57), who, at the turn of the millennium, expressed the belief that servant leadership would grow in importance in the future. Similarly, such expectations were expressed by Senge (2002) and Blanchard (2002).

Role and importance of servant leadership

The servant leadership style stems from the view that the primary purpose of organisations is to serve human needs (Covey 2006). As Schermerhorn et al. (2008) note, the basic purpose of every business and transaction lies in the positive effect it has on the employees, the organisation and society. Servant leadership emphasises the moral responsibility of leaders (Sendjaya and Pekerti 2010) or, as Schermerhorn (2008) believes, its berth, in addition to caring for employees, is in the ethical behaviour of leaders. In this relation, by analogy with Kohlberg, it falls within the highest level of moral development of the leader, 'post-conventional' leadership (Graham 1995). On the other hand, Whetstone (2001) notes that the servant leadership model is based on a complementary three-tier ethical approach, namely the teleological that is focused on the consequences of acts, the deontological which is focused of duty and commitments and on virtue ethics which is focused on ethical principles and virtues. The author also notes that a servant leader is 'servile' towards his employees because of his character, wherein he functions on the basis of both the conceptual and intuitive ethical level.

Servant leadership denotes practical application of the philosophy of altruism and includes individuals who have chosen to serve and only secondly to lead. It is applicable to both formal and informal leadership roles and encourages cooperation, trust, care, listening and the ethical use of power and empowerment (12Manage 2009). It is based on values, ethical principles and the empowering of employees (Boyum 2006) and emphasises integrity, attributing it with importance (Page and Wong 2000, Greenleaf 2002a, Smith et al. 2004,[28] Boyum 2006, Liden et al. 2008, McNenery 2008, Sendjaya et al. 2008, Lennick and Kiel 2009) because it represents the foundation of social relations (Greenleaf 2002a).[29] Locander and Luechauer (2006) add that servant leadership is based on a paradox, as supposedly the best way to 'use' power is to not use it. Senge (2002) sees the paradox in the fact that servant leadership is very personal and at the same time intrinsically collective, while Henry (2008) considers that the key factor in servant leadership is precisely the availability of the leader to anyone in need of help. This is also understood as the 'open door policy'.

A servant leader is primarily servile and only secondly a leader (Greenleaf 2002a, 2002b, Northouse 2010), which means that for him, the concern for employees, customers and the community takes first place (Spears 1998, Page and Wong 2000, Yukl 2002, Fry 2003, Schermerhorn 2008, Carroll 2009, Lyons et al. 2009, Searle and Barbuto 2011).[30],[31] Another very important factor in servant leadership is the moral development of employees (Rickards and Clark 2006, Sendjaya and Pekerti 2010), which is the essence of ethical leadership (Yukl 2002).

Covey (2002b) adds that the essence of servant leadership has the same meaning as ethical leadership. In this connection, Covey (2002a) notes that the core of servant leadership consists of four factors of moral authority and conscience, by sacrificing one's own ego for more noble purposes, inspiring the realisation of the organisation's mission, understanding the indivisibility and equal importance of goals and the means with which to achieve objectives, and the understanding of the wholeness and connectedness of everything to everything. The author also believes that when people strive to live according to their own conscience, this strengthens their integrity and simultaneously weakens the influence of the ego on their behaviour.

The inner feeling of the desire to serve is most significant in the servant leadership style. The said feeling then grows into a conscious decision and the will to lead (Spears 1998, Greenleaf 2002a, 2002b, Sendjaya and Sarros 2002, Sendjaya et al. 2008, Carroll 2009, Trompenaars and Voerman 2010, Prosser 2010). With this, Greenleaf emphasised the distinction between the individual who is initially servile and only secondly a leader, and the individual who is initially a leader and only secondly servile (Greenleaf 2002b, 12Manage 2009). He believed that the key difference between servant leadership and the other leadership models is in the motivation of the leader to firstly take care of others (Peete 2005), wherein this concern includes the education, protection and empowerment of employees (Yukl 2002). Mumford et al. (2003) consider that people who strive for the welfare of others and believe they can manage their behaviour despite external influences have a higher degree of integrity. Greenleaf always defended the thesis that the most important step towards becoming a great leader is to first become a great 'servant' (Spencer 2007). He believed in the fact that almost every man at a young age has the potential to develop in this area, wherein the most important element is education (Greenleaf 2002a). The author contended that preparation for servant leadership must start in high school at the latest, where a man learns how to resist the dominant culture of power and mutual competition (Greenleaf 1998). Rickards and Clark (2006) believe that the idea of servant leadership is very suitable for leaders who have a highlighted system of humanistic values.

A servant leader is therefore an individual who wishes to lead in accordance with his own beliefs by serving, thus achieving the maximum benefit for others (Greenleaf 2002a, Boyum 2006). The fact that a genuine servant leader is firstly servile and only secondly a leader gives him grandeur (Greenleaf 2002a), to which his integrity and modesty also contribute (Page and Wong 2000). In this connection, Greenleaf (2002b) believed that there is a big difference[32] between genuine and non-genuine servant leadership because a leader who is firstly servile has no interest in power, influence and acquiring material interests.[33],[34] For genuine leaders, the desire to serve people is the primary one. Sendjaya and Sarros (2002), Sendjaya et al. (2008), Sendjaya and Pekerti (2010) and Trompenaars and Voerman (2010) consider servant leadership to even be a way of life, a mission focused on care for others. Prosser (2010) even believes it to be a life process.

Despite the fact that Greenleaf idealised the servant leadership model, he always justified its practical value and maintained realistic expectations. Years of practical experience helped him not to live in illusion (Vaill 1998), wherein he was aware that servant leadership does not happen overnight (Spears 1998). He was aware of the gradual and long-term impact, drawing on the view that initially one individual is sufficient with whom the philosophy expands further. He also considered that if the top management of each organisation functions according to the principle of equality, wherein the leader is the first among equals (*primus inter pares*), we can reasonably expect the faster development of leaders and other people on other levels of the organisation. As Vaill (1998) noted, the servant leader, as was defined by Greenleaf, finds his purpose in the organisational development processes, while Greenleaf (1998) personally believed that the organisation can become more servile to shareholders only when the employees work together, are servile and create synergy. According to Greenleaf, it is necessary that the leader uses persuasion in order to achieve decision-making and not coercion or manipulation. According to Dierendonck and Nuijten (2011), this is in accordance with leading via the *primus inter pares* principle. The authors noted that another of the servant leadership characteristics is the courage to adopt unconventional decisions that are consistent with the leader's values and beliefs ('walking one's talk'), regardless of the consequences (Dierendonck and Nuijten 2011: 264). According to Sendjaya and Sarros, the primary desire to serve others stems from one's own notion of the moral and altruistic leader (2002: 60). The fact that the concept of servant leadership strongly expresses altruism is agreed with by Northouse (2010), Sendjaya and Pekerti (2010) and Searle and Barbuto (2011), wherein Northouse (2010) notes that, in addition to caring for employees, there is an emphasis on empathy with, and the education of employees. Painter-Morland (2008) adds that the servant leadership model also allows for the creation of conditions for employees' personal growth because this process is not disturbed by the egoism of their leaders.

With the selfless concern for others and only a secondary concern for oneself, the servant leader creates trust among employees, according to Greenleaf (2002a). Walsh (2008) believed that this is the most important aspect of leadership. In this context, Manz and Sims (1987) argued that such an approach would contribute to developing and maintaining strong interpersonal ties between the leader and the employees and that this helps employees achieve their greatest potential and at the same time become increasingly motivated.

From the above mentioned, we can conclude that servant leadership is in line with the concept of an ethical leader who is sensitive to the needs of the employees, treats them fairly and takes care of them (Northouse 2010). As Spencer (2007) adds, servant leaders are aware that the organisation is represented by the employees, thus including them in the creation of the organisational vision, while the goals and needs of the employees are expressed in the goals and needs of the leader. The leader and the organisation are successful because the employees are successful. Consequently, one of the key tasks of servant leadership is to foster the achievement of consensuses, namely voluntary and permanent ones (Greenleaf 1998). Yukl (2002) adds here that Greenleaf understood social responsibility as one of the fundamental objectives of the organisation, where the importance of

providing quality products and services to customers was equated with the creation of the importance of the business in the eyes of the employees.

Greenleaf later added an extra condition, namely that no one should be directly
or indirectly harmed by the leader's behaviour (1998: 43). At the same time, the
author stated that he judges the quality of a society according to what the least
privileged members achieve in it. Moreover, Greenleaf was also convinced that
if someone is truly a servant leader then they continuously explore and seek to
progress and believe in it (2002b).

Similar to Greenleaf, Burns (2010) believed that a 'great' leader helps his
employees develop themselves into leaders, and that the function of leadership
is to include the needs, aspirations and goals of employees in the organisational
strategy.

In addition to what is mentioned above, below we list some conceptions of
servant leadership from the perspective of other authors. Thus, Passmore (2010)
sees the servant leader as someone who understands the importance of employee
development not only for the benefit of the organisation but also for their own
benefit and the wider social benefit. Such a leader is also someone who knows
how to listen, be emphatic and is able to introduce beneficial changes as part of
realising the organisational mission. Dierendonck and Patterson (2010) believe
that servant leadership is a model of leadership in which the main concern is
the professional and personal development of employees. At the same time, the
authors expose two fundamental elements of the servant leadership style, namely
the emphasised concern for the employees, and the leader as one who is first
among equals (*primus inter pares*) without using the position's power. Fry noted
that the servant leader combines two in one, that is, the activity and service on
one hand, and his mission on the other (Fry 2003: 708). The leader is in tune with
the basic values and serves all participants through these values, wherein servant
leadership includes assisting in identifying and promoting the internal inspirations
of employees, the acquisition and retention of trust, services that go beyond one's
own interests, and active listening. Chen et al. (2011) found that servant leadership has a positive impact on the awareness of employees, trust in the leaders and
the organisation, a willingness to learn and the inspiration for work. The authors
also believe that servility is the foundation of the servant leadership style and that
putting the needs and interests of employees in first place is the most important
function of servant leaders.

Reed et al. (2011) are convinced that one of the fundamental tasks of the servant leader is to develop future servant leaders and that Greenleaf's argument that
servant leadership should reflect on the individual, organisational and societal
level is very important if we want to have the maximum effects of such leadership. Even Jones-Burbridge (2012) believes that servant leaders have a priority of
caring for the needs of their employees and all others for whom they care. With
such care, the leader achieves positive results for the organisation. At the same
time, Graham (1995) concludes that the organisation is most successful when the
leaders succeed in encouraging the employees to constructively participate in the
organisation's management.

Trompenaars (2009) noted that, in addition, servant leadership is useful in times of crisis (for example, economic downturn). In the context of crisis management, caring for the employees does not preclude the adoption of difficult decisions. On the other side, Searle and Barbuto (2011) note that servant leadership can be very effective in work environments where unethical behaviour has taken place in the past, as this style of leadership encourages moral behaviour among employees. Carver (2002) adds that servant leadership can be helpful in managing administrations and decision-making bodies. The leader is in the function of the servant leader of the decision-making body, while the decision-making body is in the function of the servant leader of the owners, who can be public or private. This in turn means that the leader is in the function of a servant leader of servant leaders and the guardian of the integrity of the decision-making body.

Characteristics and dimensions of servant leadership

The following section presents the different characteristics and dimensions of servant leadership identified by different authors. Greenleaf was the first to discuss the characteristics of servant leadership, although he never published them in the form of a list (Spencer 2007). Given that we have already discussed all his points of view, they will not be repeated below. Finally, we present the findings of Liden et al. (2008), which were studied in the empirical part of the book.

Spears understands servant leadership as a long-term, transformative way of life and work, which holds the potential for positive changes in society (Spears 1998: 5). As he says, this leadership model offers hope and implies a new era of human development and the path to a better and more caring organisation.

After several years of studying Greenleaf's work (Avolio et al. 2009), Spears identified 10 basic characteristics of servant leadership: listening, empathy, healing (conversion, the ability of transformation and regeneration of an organisation), awareness, persuasiveness, conceptuality – abstractness, predicting outcomes of decisions in the future by understanding the experience from the past with a correct assessment of the present, stewardship[35] (managing with entrusted sources and things that benefit the organisation and community), a commitment to the personal and professional development of employees and care for development of the community (Spears 1998, 2002, 2010). Spears (2002) believes that the list of characteristics is certainly not finished, but nevertheless considers that this leadership style offers a different way of working with employees and more caring organisations.

Page and Wong (2000) note that servant leadership, besides integrity and modesty, combines empowerment,[36] teamwork, quality and participation in leadership and ethics, which are also the reasons that being service oriented is not a sufficient condition for someone to be characterised as a servant leader.

However, Lewis and Noble (2008) do not see servant leadership as a set of techniques and tips on how to improve productivity or improve the welfare of the employees. They see it as a way of leading, which the leader adopts, because he believes that this is the right way. Noble (2008) notes that the fundamental characteristic of servant leadership is defined by caring for employees, an integrated approach to work, promoting care for the community and empowering employees for their own important decision-making. The author believes that servant leadership is not merely a theoretical concept as it is important for it to be reflected in daily practice.

Trompenaars and Voerman (2010) defined seven basic characteristics of servant leadership that can be efficient on all organisational levels (not only for middle and upper management), namely leading through serving, linking theory and practice, integration of creative individuals into a team, emotional intelligence, strategic thinking by combining various activities within a whole, designing a short-term and long-term vision and integrating the internal organisational culture with the external environment. Regarding the integration of opposites in terms of creating an integrated whole, according to Trompenaars and Voerman (2010), servant leadership is unique. As an example, they posit that leaders become more powerful by serving others because the more they serve their employees, the more they are successful. At the same time, they are convinced that the personal growth of the leader is connected to care for the personal growth of employees (Trompenaars and Voerman 2009), where their concern for the employees is returned by way of the employees' good care of the customers.

Trompenaars and Voerman (2010) also illustrate their view on servant leadership in the form of a pyramid where it is clear that the servant leader in the organisation is on the top as well as on the bottom. According to Bartholomew (2006), the turned organisational structure fully corresponds to realisation of the philosophy of servant leadership in practice.

Covey (2002b) identified four key factors of servant leadership, namely leading by example, which includes personal integrity, the shaping and designing of the organisation's mission, vision and values, acting in accordance with them, integration of all employees into active exercise of the mission, vision and values, and the empowerment of employees. Based on the above-mentioned activities, the leader encourages employees to creativity and development, and thus, to the situation where they become servant leaders themselves (as Greenleaf already discussed).

Smith et al. (2004) define five characteristics of servant leadership, that is, respect for other people, the development of employees, development of the community, reflecting credibility and the involvement of employees in management (2004: 86). As positive effects of such leadership, the authors point to the more qualified and ethical employees, improved communication, better mutual relations and the creation of a common vision and clear goals.

Keith (2009) identified three fundamental characteristics of servant leadership, namely serving and aiding others in the pursuit of the organisation's mission, listening to employees and stakeholders for the purpose of identifying and meeting their needs and a concern for the continued development of employees.

In their review of the theory of servant leadership, Russell and Stone (2002) identified the characteristics that define this style of leadership. They divided these characteristics into two basic categories, that is, functional attributes and accompanying attributes. In the framework of functional attributes, they inserted the effective and practical characteristics of servant leadership, while the framework of accompanying attributes includes characteristics that supplement and enhance the attributes of the first framework. The authors point out that the latter attributes are not secondary to the former, but are complementary and sometimes even a necessary precondition of the functional attributes. The characteristics of the functional attributes are the abilities of vision, honesty, integrity, being trustworthy, leading by example, helpfulness, creativity, respect for others and empowerment. The accompanying attributes include characteristics such as good communication and listening, competence, visibility, influence, good governance, credibility, learning, encouraging others and delegating.

In addition, Russell and Stone (2002) believe that the servant leadership model has an impact on changes in organisations and society because it promotes both personal and organisational metamorphoses.

Liden et al. (2008) note that typical characteristics of a servant leader are listening, empathy, awareness, persuasion, abstractness, anticipation and commitment to both employee development and community development. Greenleaf (2002a) defined active listening as the first necessary response to any problem, while credibility is what enables a leader to apply changes through the use of persuasion and talking rather than forcing. When the servant leader listens to, sees and knows the situation then, according to Greenleaf, the leader is very close to the employees, which further reinforces mutual trust.

Using multivariate statistical methods, Liden et al. (2008) identified seven different dimensions of the servant leadership style, namely the conceptual skills, empowerment, helping employees in personal growth, putting employees in the foreground, ethical behaviour and acting, empathy and emotional support and care for the community. The authors included all seven dimensions in a questionnaire that was built for empirical research of servant leadership.

Given that we used their questionnaire in our research, the characteristics the authors found are discussed below.[37] Ethical leadership and behaviour, helping employees with personal growth and putting employees in the foreground are exceptions because we have already discussed them.

Conceptual skills

Conceptual skills denote the fact that the leader is capable of effectively thinking and solving complex problems and that they solve these problems with new and creative ideas (Liden et al. 2008). Greenleaf believed that a leader must be able to anticipate the future, wherein he must help himself with the experience gained in the past, combined with intuition. Otherwise, in Greenleaf's opinion, the leader is just a leader by title as he only reacts to current events.

Conceptuality also denotes how we understand a complex and abstract situation (Senge 2002). Carroll (2009) understands it as the ability to understand the broader picture because a leader should be able to understand both the actual situation as well as the abstract situation and visualise the future. Trompenaars and

Voerman (2010) believe the same, while Carroll (2009) adds that conceptual skills are what enables a leader to effectively think strategically.

According to Yukl (2002), conceptual and cognitive skills include analytical ability, logical thinking, designing concepts, inductive and deductive reasoning, foresight, intuition, prudence, creativity and the ability to cope with uncertain events. They are important for effective planning and organising work, solving problems and coordinating various activities. As a result, the leader must be familiar with the organisation and know how mutual activities intertwine and how change affects them.

Empowerment

Empowerment means ensuring the autonomy[38] of employees so they can independently decide, implement and monitor the progress of assigned tasks, although it is not appropriate for every organisation as it depends on the development stage the organisation is in (start of business, growth, maturity, decline) (Bass and Riggio 2006). Although empowerment is an important factor of good leadership (Russell 2001) and is typically positive, it can also have negative consequences when, for example, the goals of employees do not comply with the goals of the organisation and are in conflict with them (Bass and Riggio 2006).

Den Hartog and De Hoogh (2009) noted that leaders can empower employees directly by interacting, or indirectly when they provide opportunities for personal growth and success. Empowering employees allows the employees to obtain decision-making power (Schermerhorn 2008). This is understood by Kreitner (2004) as a process in which employees become fully-fledged partners in the decision-making process. Robbins and Langton (2003) see empowerment as a process in which leaders learn how to give up control over the employees and where employees learn how to take responsibility for their decisions and work. Casse and Claudel (2011) see this process as a process of giving and receiving in which autonomy in achieving organisational objectives and employee satisfaction are ensured. At the same time, Solomon (2004) noted that the consequence of empowering is a lower level of control over employees and a higher level of trust from the employees, wherein a higher level of confidence, which is a virtue, also means a higher level of risk.

In Greenleaf's concept of leadership, empowerment does not mean that the decision-making power is lost, but means the opposite (Shannon 1998). In this way, the employees become the leader's counterpart and become leaders themselves who actively implement the organisational mission (Russell and Stone 2002). In this connection, Schermerhorn (2008) notes that servant leaders empower their employees by ensuring that they have the necessary information, giving them responsibility, authority and power, and entrust them with self-management and decision-making.

Yukl (2002) noted that empowerment has a similar psychological effect like a high level of intrinsic motivation and a sense of self-efficacy, while its benefits are stronger loyalty, greater trust of employees, innovation, more creative initiatives, perseverance in problem-solving, optimism, satisfaction and lower employee fluctuation. On the other hand, this is also related to higher costs of personnel selection and training of employees, higher labour costs of more skilled employees and the risk of adopting incorrect decisions because of empowered employees. At the same time, Yukl notes that in addition to actual empowerment, there are other types of leader behaviour that promote employees' psychological feeling that they have been empowered by leaders (for example, the removal of bureaucratic obstacles, unnecessary controls, expressing confidence in employees, etc.)

Empowering employees is also important as it is through the delegation of powers and responsibilities to employees that leaders bring a vision to the situation and maintain its sustainability (Bennis and Nanus 2003).

We can look at empowerment from another angle, namely that when employees fully trust their leader, his decisions and follow him completely, they give him the right to concentrate all decision-making in his own hands (Greenleaf 2002a).

In the opinion of Trompenaars and Voerman (2010), empowerment is particularly effective in today's times when constant pressure is present in society, which demands to do more for less money and in the shortest time possible.

Empathy and emotional support

Empathy and emotional healing are understood in two ways in the context of servant leadership, that is, in relation to the employees and to the organisation.

In relation to the organisation, Greenleaf (2002a) understood emotional support in the sense of creating wholeness or completeness, namely when leaders help their employees achieve higher and nobler goals which they otherwise could not achieve on their own. Carroll (2009) understands this as a leader being able to transform and regenerate the organisation which, in turn, has a positive impact on the employees and other stakeholders.

In relation to employees, Greenleaf (2002a) understands empathy as putting oneself into the shoes of someone else, or as an imaginary projection of consciousness from one person to another. He is convinced that a servant leader should be empathic and should never turn his employees down, making the employees trust him more.

Bennis and Goldsmith (2010) understand empathy as consciously listening to someone else in the context of their own perceptions of a particular event, wherein attention is focused on this person rather than the listener. According to the authors, it is important that the listener does not give value judgements and that they have the feeling that they were heard. Barbuto and Wheeler (2006) state that this is precisely what creates a work environment in which employees can express both personal and business problems.

In connection to this, Yukl (2002) believes that if a servant leader wants to find out how to cater to the employees' needs in the best possible way, the leader must initially understand the employees. Therefore, the leader must first and foremost be able to listen, and thereby, get to know the employees' needs and aspirations. Carroll (2009) adds that empathy is necessary when leaders try to understand employees and establish a deeper relationship with them, which is exactly what a good leader does. In the context of leadership, Passmore (2010) understands empathy as an ability to understand 'the world' of others as if this were one's own world.

Empathy in leadership is also important for a leader in order for him to understand why employees behaved as they did. Consequently, it is easier for a leader to forgive the mistakes of the employees and they are more inclined to help the employees achieve their objectives (Lennick and Kiel 2009).

According to Greenleaf (2002a), leaders have a positive impact on themselves by implementing the abovementioned activities.

Care for the community

The seventh dimension of servant leadership is associated with the socially responsible behaviour of organisations and is consistent with the thinking of Aristotle who said that 'a good man shares his wealth only so that his friends have more: wealth unto them, nobleness to me – thus ensuring maximum value to oneself' (2002: 288). Rousseau also thought about responsible behaviour towards the community, namely that the subjects' 'duty to lay down the bill for their opinions to their sovereign, when the opinions are necessary for the community' (2001: 123). At the same time, Rousseau urged moral individuals to serve the interests of the community and urged them to abstain from serving their own private interests (Pribac 2001: 144).

To ensure care for the community, following the example of the leaders is of the utmost importance (Wayne et al. 1997, Lennick and Kiel 2009), especially at the start of the career path of each employee. Rousseau already knew this in figurative terms when he wrote that

> the people are like the individuals who constitute the people are; and the individuals are able to be taught only at a young age. When the habits are settled and prejudices rooted, it is a dangerous and futile venture, if one would be trying to change them.

> (Rousseau 2001: 46)

The best example of this type of behaviour, according to Greenleaf (2002a), is not the classic leader who is guided by the principles of the present hierarchy, but a leader who is first among equals (*primus inter pares*).

Greenleaf was also convinced that socially responsible behaviour, which is encouraged by servant leadership, starts with caring for one's own personal growth because a responsible man cares for himself as well as society. Lennick and Kiel (2009) agree with this and add that it is also a good indicator of integrity and an encouragement for everyone else to act in the same way.

In the light of this, Crossan and Mazutis (2008) believe that the organisation's care for the community today, where ethical behaviour is expected more and more, is simply indispensable.

Servant leadership in relation to other leadership models

Given that servant leadership falls within the framework of ethical leadership and that it intertwines, builds and differs from other leadership styles, the following section will deal with the differences in the relationship between servant leadership and other leadership models.

As Liden et al. (2008) note, servant leadership is an independent multidimensional construct, which significantly contributes to explaining the behaviour of employees in accordance with social norms, their in-role performance and their community-citizenship behaviour (2008: 175). At the same time, the authors recognise that servant leadership differs from traditional styles of leadership and offers more than the LMX and transformational leadership styles. The characteristics that distinguish it from other styles are the care for employees, establishing solid, long-term ties with employees, emphasising personal integrity. Aiming at the widest range of stakeholders outside the organisation, etc. Nandram and Vos (2010) agree with this and add that other styles of leadership are primarily focused on encouraging employees to achieve the goals of the organisation.

Page and Wong (2000) state that what distinguishes the servant leadership style from other styles of leadership is not the quality of the decisions taken, but how leaders show their responsibilities in practice and how they include everyone in the process of making decisions. Similarly, Spears (1998) believes that servant leadership in for-profit and non-profit organisations differs from the traditional autocratic and hierarchical model of leadership because it is focused on teamwork and care for the community. Jones-Burbridge (2012) adds the empowerment of employees to this.

Russell (2001), on the other hand, notes that the factors which differentiate servant leadership from other styles are the values of the leaders (for example, modesty and respect for others) and that the success and failure of servant leadership depends precisely on the personal values of leaders who practice this leadership style.

Sendjaya and Sarros (2002) and Ehrhart (2004) note that to some extent, Greenleaf's concept has similar features to Burns' concept of transformational leadership. Bartholomew (2006) believes that servant leadership is only a form or subgroup of transformational leadership. This is also why the authors find Burns' research highly relevant for servant leadership.[39]

At first glance, for Bass (1997), it seems that the servant leadership style overlaps with other models of leadership, especially the transformational model, where it is most consistent with its social dimension. Liden et al. (2008) concluded that the models are most consistent in two of the four dimensions of the transformational leadership model, namely in the idealised influence and intellectual stimulation. This means that servant leaders represent a model and an example, inspire employees with enthusiasm and actively encourage them to challenge and express different views in different situations. The coherence and affinity between the two was also found by Cerit (2010), that is, that between the factors of servant leadership's 'respect for employees', 'care for the development of employees' and the two factors of transformational leadership: 'individual care for the employees' and the 'intellectual stimulation of employees'.

In contrast, Smith et al. (2004) recognise a difference between the two models, namely the fact that transformational leadership puts a smaller emphasis on the emotional wellbeing of the employees and that it is more focused on the benefit of the organisation, while servant leadership has a greater focus on the individual. The difference is also seen in the fact that in the servant leadership model, the motivation for leading is based on the principle of equality between the leader and the employees, while in the transformational leadership model, it is based on achieving the organisational mission.

Building on the finding that servant leadership has most in common with the transformational leadership model, Graham (1991) highlights the difference between the models' two segments in which the servant leadership model supposedly exceeds and upgrades the transformational model:

1 In addition to caring for the development of employees and achieving organisational objectives, servant leaders are receptive to the needs of a broader range of stakeholders, including the wider social environment.
2 Servant leaders encourage employees to practice moral judgements and they are committed to their needs and interests, wherein the moral dimension of leadership is particularly emphasised.

At the same time, Graham (1991), Boyum (2006), Sendjaya et al. (2008), Parolini et al. (2009) and Sendjaya and Pekerti (2010) noted that the servant leadership style is chiefly focused on employees and not on the organisation and puts a greater emphasis on the needs of the employees, their development and autonomy, rather than on the delivery of results above expectations, which is the first principle in the transformational leadership model. Similarly, Dion (2012) states that servant leadership is more focused on caring for the employees, while the transformational leadership is more focused on getting the support of employees for achieving organisational objectives, wherein servant leaders reflect this through their practices and transformational leaders rely on their charismatic abilities.

Liden et al. (2008) add that leaders first focus on employees and only then on themselves, care for the community and care for spreading the servant leadership style among employees are all factors that are not integral parts of the transformational model. In their view, with regard to establishing good relations with employees, the servant leadership model is more similar to the LMX theory of leadership which, compared to the servant leadership style, does not put as much emphasis on caring for members of the group or team, their development into leaders and caring for the community (Liden et al. 2008: 163).

The servant leadership model was defined by Barbuto and Wheeler in relation to the transformational model and the LMX theory (2006: 305). They found that there are similarities and differences among all three leadership styles. The role of the servant leader is to serve their employees in order for them to become more autonomous, independent and wiser. The role of a transformational leader is to inspire employees to achieve organisational goals, while the role of a leader in the LMX theory is to build positive relationships between leaders and members of the group and their mutual exchange. Servant leadership therefore firstly wants to help and serve the employees, while transformational leadership firstly wants to lead. The LMX theory firstly wants to establish the right relationship between members and leaders. The moral dimension is clearly expressed in the servant leadership model, while in the other two models it is not so particularly exposed (Figure 2.10). The results of servant leadership manifest in employee satisfaction, their personal growth and taking on social responsibility. The results of transformational leadership manifest in higher employee effort in performing work, their satisfaction and the benefits of the organisation, while the results of the LMX model manifest in higher degrees of mutual trust and stronger motivation to work. On the group level, servant leadership is greatly focused on caring so as to meet the needs of all members, while on the organisational and social levels, servant leaders care for the sustainable social responsibility of the organisation. On the group level, transformational leaders seek to achieve organisational goals, while on the organisational and social levels they seek to ensure that the public supports the organisational goals. In the LMX model, on the group level, leaders care for the creation of various exchanges between the leader and the members, while on the organisational and societal levels, the model does not describe specific activities.

Figure 2.10 Leadership styles.

Source: Authors.

In addition, Smith et al. (2004) see the difference between the servant and transformational leadership models in the fact that servant leadership is more focused on the development of the spiritual culture of the organisation, while the transformational leadership model concentrates more on strengthening the dynamic culture. The authors believe that fast changing environments require transformational leadership, while servant leadership is more appropriate for more stable environments. Similarly, Schneider and Winnette (2011) noted that servant leadership is more suitable for leading non-profit voluntary organisations, particularly in terms of empowering the employees, their commitment to the organisation, employee satisfaction and their desire to stay in the organisation. In this regard, Bartholomew (2006) believes that Greenleaf's idea of the servant leader is based more on the moral dimension than on the spiritual dimension. Thus, the concept is believed to be a philosophical concept, although its recommendations and implications are highly practical and based on many years of practical experience.

A critical look at the concept of servant leadership

In addition to the above-mentioned and the positive qualities of servant leadership, researchers noted the shortcomings and weaknesses of the said style of leadership as presented below.

Northouse (2010) noted that the theory of servant leadership was based on Greenleaf's essay-type writing who, much like Burns, only described his own experiences and beliefs. Even though their thinking has over time proven to be correct, Northouse (2010), Spencer (2007) and Prosser (2010) are convinced of the need for empirical research in this area. Winston (2010) argued that, in addition to quantitative studies of servant leadership, which must continue, it is necessary to carry out qualitative studies to help understand the different components of the servant leadership style. The author points out that it is unclear whether the questionnaires, which were already made, measure servant leadership properly and independently as a stand-alone model, or if they measure other factors of other leadership models, such as authentic, transformational, etc.

Winston (2010) also provided criticism in the sense that what we know today about the servant leadership model is probably not just servant leadership. The author believes that the characteristics of servant leadership, like honesty, trust and hope, are all just as typical for other leadership styles such as transformational and authentic leadership. In contrast, Schermerhorn et al. (2008) wondered whether servant leadership, given its highly stressed concern for the employees, the organisation and society, is more its specific part of leadership rather than being a stand-alone leadership style.

Whetstone (2002) noted that servant leadership could be criticised because it is unrealistic, it encourages passivity, it is not useful in all circumstances and that its description of 'servant' has a negative connotation. Notwithstanding the foregoing, the author notes that servant leadership exists in practice. Yet the author sees a danger for servant leaders in the fact that, because of its openness, it may be subject to manipulation by employees.

Dierendonck and Nuijten (2011) see a disadvantage in the fact that there is still no generally accepted definition of servant leadership which, in their opinion, is the reason for the existence of different measurement instruments for measuring this style of leadership. Avolio et al. (2009) believe that these measurement instruments differ depending on the definitions and the definitions of various authors, which is seen as problematic.

Another problem lies in the fact there is no universal model of servant leadership like there is in the case of, for example, the transformational leadership model or the integrative theory of leadership. Walsh (2008) noted in its defence that a universal model of servant leadership cannot be established due to the differences among types of organisations.

Researching servant leadership

As already mentioned, research into the servant leadership model as an independent model is still in the early phases (Northouse 2010), and consequently, it is still not sufficiently studied and supported by empirical findings (Russell and Stone 2002).

Winston (2010: 180) noted that the exploration started with the conceptual article by Farling, Stone and Winston in 1999, in which regarding the fact that former contributions were merely descriptive in nature, the authors called for empirical research. Joseph and Winston (2005) and Dierendonck and Patterson (2010) noted that research on the servant leadership model has been on the rise since 1999; alternatively, as Vidaver-Cohen et al. (2010) and Reed et al. (2011) state, research into servant leadership and its impact on the organisation has only emerged in the last decade.[40, 41] Schneider and Winnette (2011) added that, in the meantime, the first reliable measurement instruments emerged in this field.

These measurement instruments included the instrument developed by Liden et al. (2008) that was used in our study. In preparing the questionnaire, the authors found that very few empirical studies had examined and measured servant leadership as an independent concept and that, before those, three measurement instruments and three research studies had met the criterion of validity. They were made by Page and Wong (2000), Ehrhart (2004) and Barbuto and Wheeler (2006). After them, servant leadership was studied by Sendjaya et al. (2008) as well as other authors. These measurement instruments and empirical findings are presented below.

Measurement instruments and findings

In formulating the questionnaire, Liden et al. (2008) included some contents from the measurement instruments made by Page and Wong (2000), Ehrhart (2004) and Barbuto and Wheeler (2006). As Dennis et al. (2010) found, 20 per cent of the contents were borrowed.[42] This was how the authors created a multidimensional questionnaire that consists of the above-mentioned seven different factors (conceptual/abstract skills, empowerment, helping employees with personal growth, putting employees in the foreground, ethical behaviour and acting, emotional support and creating value for the community) and 28 other variables. Each factor contains four variables and arguments, which are then assessed by those being questioned with the use of a seven-point Likert scale. The validity of the measurement instrument was confirmed by Liden et al. (2008) through the use of research and confirmatory factor analysis (2008: 173). At the same time, the authors found that all seven dimensions are correlated with each other, and that all seven dimensions are moderately to strongly correlated with the transformational leadership model (43 to 79) and the LMX theory of leadership (48 to 75). On this basis, the authors concluded that the factors of servant leadership are not over-saturated with transformational leadership or the LMX theory of leadership and that the correlations are not too high. They also found that all seven dimensions of leadership are significantly correlated with organisational affiliation and commitment, that servant leadership on the individual leader level uniquely contributes to understanding of the relationship between the organisation and the local community (society) and that servant leadership can benefit as a framework for understanding how leaders influence employees, the culture of the organisation and the broader social environment in which the entity operates (Liden et al. 2008).

Similarly, Dennis et al. (2010) found that the questionnaire of Liden et al. (2008) measures the characteristics of servant leadership on an individual level, which means in relation to the employees, organisation and the society/local community, which also includes the concept of altruism.

Page and Wong (2000) and Wong and Page (2003) developed a measurement instrument for the self-evaluation of leaders, namely the identification of positive and negative features and characteristics. It consists of 100 variables and 12 factors such as integrity, humility, courtesy, care for others, empowerment of employees, employee development, vision, setting goals, leadership, example, teamwork and employee participation in decision-making.

Based on the measurement instrument of Page and Wong (2000), Dennis et al. (2010) identified eight factors, which were honesty, credibility, responsibility, courage, vision, servility to others, strength and pride (vulnerability and modesty in the positive sense) and the development and empowerment of employees. Bartholomew (2006) identified seven factors of the servant leadership model in the measurement instrument of Wong and Page (2003), namely the empowerment and development of employees, servility to others, the accessibility and participation of employees in leadership, openness (vulnerability) and modesty, inspiration of employees, leadership with vision and courage, wherein integrity and credibility come to the forefront.

Wong and Page (2003) later developed a self-evaluation questionnaire for the servant leadership style, which is composed of 62 variables.

Ehrhart (2004) created a measurement instrument that contained seven dimensions of servant leadership, that is, the establishment of relationships with employees, the empowerment of employees, aiding employees in their personal growth and achieving success, ethical behaviour, conceptual skills of leaders, putting employees in the forefront and generating positive benefits for external stakeholders.

The author defined each of the seven dimensions with two variables, meaning a total of 14 variables, and in base determined a five-step grading scale in which employees can assess the conduct of their leaders.

Barbuto and Wheeler (2006) developed a questionnaire with 23 variables that measured the five dimensions of servant leadership (altruism, emotional healing, wisdom, persuasiveness and organisational stewardship). In addition to the positive link between servant leadership, transformational leadership and the LMX leadership theory, the authors empirically found a positive correlation between servant leadership and employee satisfaction, their above-average engagement in work and organisational performance.

Sendjaya et al. (2008) developed the servant leadership behaviour scale (SLBS) measurement instrument containing 35 variables that measure six dimensions of servant leadership (voluntary care for the employees and only secondly for oneself, authenticity and credibility, which includes integrity, treating employees as equal partners, moral responsibility, a transformative impact on the employees and an abstract understanding of the mission, including spirituality, which combines business and the mission). At the same time, the authors believe that their model of servant leadership is an upgrade of the transformational, authentic and spiritual models of leadership. Dennis et al. (2010), on the other hand, state that due to doubts about its inner validity (suspected multicollinearity), the questionnaire of Sendjaya et al. (2008) needs further testing and verification.

For the purpose of researching the links between servant leadership and employee trust in their leaders, Sendjaya and Pekerti (2010) used the SLBS measurement instrument developed by Sendjaya et al. (2008), and added variables that measured employee confidence and commitment to the leader. They found that servant leadership is an important predictor of trust in leaders, thereby indicating that they had upgraded the preliminary findings of Liden et al. (2008) in the fact that servant leadership contributes to strengthening trust in leaders (Sendjaya and Pekerti 2010: 658). They note that the leader's behaviour contributes to employee confidence in the leader: when they spread the organisational vision and help them easily identify with it, when they lead by example and when they respect values and encourage others to do the same, caring for the welfare of employees as well as when they encourage ethical behaviour of employees with the help of discussions about moral conduct (Figure 2.11).

Based on the measurement instruments that evaluate the servant leadership style and were developed by Liden et al. (2008), Barbuto and Wheeler (2006), Page and Wong (2000), Wong and Page (2003) and Ehrhart (2004), the authors Vidaver-Cohen et al. (2010) and Reed et al. (2011) developed a measurement instrument designed to assess the servant leadership of top leaders (executive servant leadership scale – ESLS). It consists of 25 variables and five dimensions, namely mutual support, care for the community, altruism, equality and integrity. The authors note that this is the first measurement instrument to be specifically focused on the behaviour of top executives.

POSITIVE EFFECTS OF SERVANT LEADERSHIP

- employee satisfaction (both life and job satisfaction), their above-average engagement in work and organisational performance
- employee trust in leaders and the organisation
- employee confidence in the leader
- higher motivation of employees
- caring for the welfare of others
- organisational commitment of employees
- employee perception of the importance of leadership values, such as integrity, competence and empathy
- better relations within the organisation
- stronger interconnectedness between goals, processes and team performance
- higher effectiveness in team work

Figure 2.11 Positive effects of servant leadership.
Source: Authors.

For the purposes of research into servant leadership, Chen et al. (2011) adapted the measurement instrument developed by Page and Wong (2000) with 12 factors, namely the new version included 48 of the 100 variables. They found that the spiritual values of servant leadership, as perceived in leaders by their employees, were statistically more significant than those in transactional leadership that contribute to the motivation of employees and their wellbeing.

Dierendonck and Nuijten (2011) developed a questionnaire to measure servant leadership – the servant leadership survey (SLS). It consists of 30 variables, which together form eight factors or dimensions, namely standing back, forgiveness, empowerment of employees, delegating accountability to employees, courage for taking responsibility, authenticity, humility and accepting the responsibility for the actions of the organisation (stewardship). The authors found that their questionnaire builds on the existing measurement instruments, which are generally all solely focused on working with people and do not include classical leadership functions such as giving directions. Because of this, the authors added another dimension to the questionnaire, namely delegating responsibility to employees, strengthening the courage for taking responsibility, and forgiving mistakes. The authors believe that forgiving the employees' errors is the one factor, in addition to servility towards employees and caring for their needs, which distinguishes servant leadership from transformational leadership.

Other relevant findings

Avolio et al. (2009) noted that the empirical findings in the field of servant leadership show a positive correlation between this leadership style and employee satisfaction, both life and job satisfaction, caring for the welfare of others and with organisational commitment (2009, 437).[43]

Joseph and Winston (2005) found a positive correlation between the employees' perception of the servant leadership style and their trust in their leaders and the organisation. With this, the authors confirm Greenleaf's (2002a) thesis that servant leadership is a prerequisite and an antecedent for trust in the leader and the organisation.

Washington et al. (2006) found a positive correlation between the employees' perception of the servant leadership style and their perception of the importance of selected leadership values, amongst which integrity, competence and empathy of the leaders were ranked high. They also found a positive correlation between gender and servant leadership, namely that women reflect the hospitable leadership style more strongly than their male counterparts.

Bartholomew (2006) found the positive effects of servant leadership on mutual relations within the organisation, while Cerit (2010) found a positive correlation and a positive impact of servant leadership on the organisational commitment of employees, namely factors such as the respect for employees, caring for the development of employees, caring for the development of the community, empowerment of employees and the authenticity of leaders.

In a study that used the measurement instrument of Liden et al. (2008), Hu and Liden (2011) found that servant leadership has a positive impact on the strength of the interconnectedness between goals, processes and team performance. They also found that servant leadership, in addition to clear objectives and processes, can serve as an important factor in the effectiveness of the team.

Notes

1 Možina et al. (2002) note that in Slovenia, the word 'management' translates as management, leadership, governance, conduct and directing.

2 As was noted by Greenleaf (2002a: 149), management and manipulation as terms both have a common origin in the word 'manus' (which translates into 'a hand'), as both denote a way of 'influence', with the difference that manipulation already has a fundamentally negative connotation.

3 Fairholm (1991) considers leadership to be one of the oldest professions.

4 The primary purpose of the initial study of management was focused on reducing the chaos in organisations and improve their efficiency and capacity (Northouse 2010), wherein a boom in its exploration occurred in the 1950s.

5 Kellerman (1984), for example, found that the term 'leader' or 'leadership' denote different things in different contexts (in the psychoanalytic theory, the role of the leader is represented by the father; in the field of social psychology, the leader represents someone with a strong personal influence; in politics, a man of status; in the field of organisational science, the leader and manager are often used alternately).

6 In favour of the virtues in leadership experience, Spinoza (2004) noted that in connection to solving conflicts within an organisation, emphasis must be placed on the importance of the leader's awareness that many conflicts in an organisation stem from the fact that people do not understand their thoughts properly or that they misinterpret the thoughts of others. Moreover, 'when they most eagerly argue, they think the same or they think about completely different things, so that when they see thoughts in other people as mistakes and absurdities, the said thoughts are neither mistakes nor absurdities' (Spinoza 2004: 178).

7 MacIntyre (1993) believed that Machiavelli was the first ethicist after the sophists, who argued for the evaluation of acts solely based on their consequences and not by the acts themselves.

8 In contrast to the contingent and the situational theory of leadership, the transformational theory does not concern itself with how a leader should act in a certain situation in order to be successful. Instead, the focus is on ideals, inspiration, innovation and individual care (Northouse 2010).

9 Yammarino et al. (2005) conclude that transformational leadership is a new chapter in the theory of leadership and that it stems from the early works of Burns, and later on, in the works and researches of Bass. Sosik (2006) added that in addition to the transformational style of leadership, a new momentum in the development of theory and practice of leadership was also influenced by the integrative model of leadership (the full range leadership model), which was developed by Bass and Avolio.

10 Given the fact that the researchers concluded that the servant leadership style has many features in common with the transformational leadership style, we introduced it in slightly more detail. More about their common features and differentiation can be found later on.

11 Burns (2010) formed the theory of transformational leadership on the basis of the study of state and political leaders.

12 Berlogar also notes that if transformational leadership was to be explained 'according to the Maslow hierarchy of needs, then we could say, that transformational leaders are counting on the needs of a higher order' (Berlogar 2000: 122).

13 Greenleaf wrote his first essay on the servant leadership style in 1969, while House published a book on charismatic leadership in 1976.

14 Bass (2002) believes that the conclusion suggests that the leader's intelligence, particularly social and emotional, contributes positively to the fact that employees perceive their leader as more transformational.

15 Yukl (2002) noted that the theories of charismatic leadership are under the influence of the ideas of Max Weber, who, in 1947, used the term in describing the personal impact of leaders on their employees.

16 The author notes that, in addition to this, various leadership styles are based on different ethical theories and approaches. This means, for example, that servant leadership is based on the deontological ethical theory (Kantian approach), the ethics of responsibility and the utilitarian ethical theory (Dion 2012).

17 Tavčar (2008: 129) believes that a leader can verify the morality of their own decisions by answering the question of how they would react if the same decision had been taken by someone else. Such a decision would impact the leader; the leader then answers whether he would have decided and acted in the same way, knowing that the consequences of such a decision would impact his family members or that his decision would be published in the media. The author considers an ethical decision to be one that brings the most benefits, is fair, acceptable to all concerned, respects fundamental human rights and has a certain duration.

18 Woiceshyn (2011) noted that Kohlberg's definition of ethical decision-making as a rational process, in which moral principles manifest when an individual thinks about moral dilemmas, provided him with a basis for empirical research in this area.

19 Brenner and Molander (1977) conducted a survey on a sample of managers in 1976, similar to the one carried out by Raymond C. Baumhart in 1961. They found that after 15 years, the managers were more cynical of the moral conduct of their peers and that the mere existence of ethical codes had no significant impact on business behaviour. According to the authors, the latter stems from the experience of the managers when they found themselves in ethical dilemmas or detected factors that strongly influenced their moral conduct.

20 Following the revelation of many scandals over the past decade related to economic crime, it is in this area of research of leadership that took a step forward. The first

article focused on this was published by Luthans and Avolio in 2003 (Northouse 2010: 215).

21 Dimovski et al. (2009) noted that research into the authentic leadership style has been the main challenge for the management of learning organisations since 2004.

22 Avolio and Gardner (2005) noted that the servant leadership style is, unlike the authentic leadership style, still insufficiently empirically explained.

23 The authors believe that the bridge between spirituality and religion is altruism and devotion to the interests of others. This is reflected in all great religions through the golden rule – do unto others as you would have them do unto you. At the same time, the author concludes that spirituality is necessary for every religion, while religion is not necessary for spirituality (Fry 2003).

24 Brown et al. (2005) developed a special measurement instrument for measuring the leader's ethical behaviour (ethical leadership scale – ELS), through which employees can assess the behaviour of their leaders.

25 Smith et al. (2004) add that Greenleaf did not provide a definition of servant leadership, but was focused on the behaviour of a servant leader and the influence of that behaviour on employees.

26 Greenleaf sent the first version of the essay in 1966 to about 200 people on influential leadership positions in various organisations across the United States (Boyum 2006).

27 Barbuto and Wheeler (2006) and Searle and Barbuto (2011) concluded that servant leadership, even though the concept is eight years older than the concept of transformational leadership, did not receive sufficient scientific and empirical attention during its initial period.

28 Greenleaf (2002a) saw the practical value of integrity in the beneficial performance of work rather than in education. He also argued that leaders are not easily made. The author added that a future leader, a competent person, is firstly enabled to make an organisational vision and to bring the organisational values to life. Help, encouraging and providing opportunities for personal growth follow after this.

29 In conjunction with this, Lennick and Kiel (2009) believe that it is hard to imagine someone who has integrity as well as a lack of responsibility towards others.

30 Whetstone (2002) noted that servant leadership is beneficial for a particular group, which also includes a member who is a servant leader. This is in stark contrast to the leadership style where the leader's primary concerns are power and his own wellbeing.

31 Lennick and Kiel (2009) are convinced that putting employees first, in the foreground, means investing in their development at the same time.

32 Authenticity was also discussed by Kant:

It is very nice to do people good for the love of them and due to favourable benevolence or if we are just for the love of order; however it is not a legal moral maxim of our behaviour, in accordance with our condition that we share as intelligent beings as humans, if we try, as volunteers, with proud arrogance to put ourselves beyond the idea of duty and if we try to do something independently of the commandments, as if we would not need any commandments.

(Kant 2003: 97)

33 In this connection, Lewis (2008) believes that servant leadership is only effective where it is genuine or authentic and not where the main objective is the desire for profit.

34 Yukl (2002) noted that genuine servant leaders defend what is good and right, even when it is not in the financial interest of the organisation and constantly oppose social injustice and inequality.

35 Sendjaya and Sarros (2002) understand 'stewardship' as a key feature of servant leadership, namely in terms of caring for the development of employees. Barbuto and Wheeler (2006) define 'stewardship' more broadly in the context of the organisation

(organisational stewardship), namely as care for the community in which the organisation operates, with the goal of receiving more investments than its own giveaway.

36 The authors identified Greenleaf as the 'grandfather' of the modern development of empowering in the leadership process (Page and Wong 2000).

37 The variables that determine each dimension or factor are presented in the empirical part.

38 With this, it differs from laissez-faire leadership where employee autonomy is taken for granted by default (Bass and Riggio 2006).

39 In reviews of several studies, the author found that the characteristics of transformational leadership also apply to servant leadership, while a reverse situation not does not necessarily mean the same (Bartholomew 2006).

40 In connection with this, Irving (2010) noted that servant leadership has mostly been studied in the USA and Europe so far. Cerit (2010) similarly added that the concept of servant leadership was pursued more in the developed Western world than in the East or in developing countries.

41 In Slovenia, prior to carrying out our research, servant leadership had not yet been scientifically investigated.

42 In a pilot study, the authors used a measurement instrument that contained nine factors and 85 variables. Five variables were taken directly from the instrument created by Page and Wong (2000), nine variables were taken directly from the instrument of Ehrhart (2004) and three variables were taken directly from the measurement instrument of Barbuto and Wheeler (2006) (Liden et al. 2008: 166).

43 The authors note that in the last 100 years, the leadership research was based on quantitative methods, whereas in recent years, qualitative research has been on the rise (Avolio et al. 2009).

3 The social significance of integrity and servant leadership

Given that both the personal integrity of leaders as well as the servant leadership style are focused on the wellbeing of employees, organisations, the environment and society in general, as we have already discussed in this book, we will briefly look at the development of the concept of social responsibility within for-profit and non-profit organisations, followed by a short peer review of both factors through the prism of their significance for society.[1]

Carroll (1999) and Carroll and Buchholtz (2000) noted that the concept of corporate social responsibility generally arose in the period since 1950, wherein in the last 30 years of the last century ever stronger public pressure was being put on the business of organisations (for example, employee rights, product safety, complaints of unethical conduct, neglect of the environment, lack of a concern for consumers, etc.). Carroll (2009) presented four categories of accountability important for leaders in all types of organisations, namely, for-profit, non-profit, government, education, etc. The first category is the successful implementation of the organisational mission, wherein the main purpose of for-profit organisations is the manufacturing and sale of products and services that provide benefits and profit. In the case of non-profit organisations, the organisational mission is the practice of activities for the targeted group. The second category is functioning in accordance with the law, the third category is care for the community and the fourth category is ethical behaviour and acting in accordance with a high level of integrity.

Similar to Carroll (1979), Wood (1991) divides social responsibility into four types, that is, economic, legal, ethical and discretionary (voluntary), or philanthropic as it was later named by Carroll (1991). Its primary purpose is to improve the quality of life (Carroll and Buchholtz 2000). The model of integrated social responsibility is shown in the following form of a pyramid, wherein philanthropy ranks at the top.

Carroll and Buchholtz (2000) subsequently identified social expectation concerning the various types of social responsibility of the organisation, namely, economic and legal social responsibility, the ethical type which includes the importance of high levels of leader and employee integrity, and philanthropic, which reflects altruism and in which servant leadership falls according to the philosophy and practice (Burkhardt and Spears 2002). Carroll and Buchholtz (2000) add that philanthropic social responsibility greatly influences employee morale.

Carroll and Buchholtz (2000), similar to Waddock et al. (2002), named the four types as comprehensive and complete social responsibility.

In relation to the above, Carroll (2009) noted that sometimes a sufficient criterion for a 'good leader' was simply effectiveness and efficiency, while today leaders are expected to behave ethically. The manager or leader cannot be merely focused on the goals and welfare of the organisation, but must also be focused on the stakeholders and the quality of the service (Bowie 1991). Waddock et al. (2002) added that the pressures of primary and secondary stakeholders, along with social and institutional pressures, reflected the basic social expectations, namely, integrity, respect, standards, transparency and accountability. It is common to all of them that they demand integrity. It is precisely organisational integrity that provides the maximum responsibility of the management. At the same time, Shahin and Zairi (2007) believed that social responsibility requires unconditional implementation of the 'social contract' between the organisations and the social environment. In doing so, organisations must be accountable to the long-term needs and demands aimed at optimisation of the positive impacts and minimisation of the negative consequences for the social environment. If this is to be achieved, the authors believe there must first be a change in the thinking and practices of leaders.

In conjunction with this, in the 1980s, Greenleaf (2002a) and Burns (2010) found that personal integrity, which is a fundamental component of servant leadership, is a key factor of social exchange. Further, servant leadership also includes altruism (Vidaver-Cohen et al. 2010, Reed et al. 2011). Both social exchange and altruism are extremely important in the context of the corporate social responsibility of the organisation. A genuine servant leader is undoubtedly socially responsible (Northouse 2010), which is reflected in how the leader cares for the privileged and disadvantaged ('have-nots'), who are treated as equal to stakeholders. In doing so, it should be noted that today's concept of social responsibility still ignores the individual responsibility of a single person as the bearer of social roles, for example, the leader, although individual justice and giving back what we have received was already discussed by Socrates in dialogue with other philosophers (Plato 1995). This confirms that the phenomenon of the social responsibility of organisations, companies and individuals is not new. There is only better awareness of the fact that we are not alone and that we live in interdependence with others (Watson 1991). For the author, this fact represents an enormous problem for anyone concerned with answering the question of 'how to act'. In so doing, Rousseau can lend a hand when he noted that 'because according to the social contract all citizens are equal, what everyone must do can be willed by everyone, while no one has the right to request something he would not do by himself' (2001: 91). In the context of leadership, this means that the leader can demand from employees only what he does himself, which, in turn, stresses the importance of leading by example.

According to Greenleaf (2002a), an individual who considers himself to be socially responsible must care for each institution he comes into contact with. He must establish a deeper relationship and more profound caring for the institution in which he is greatly involved. This is even more important when we know that organisations are weak and full of errors because of the weaknesses and mistakes of people who are in some way connected to the organisation. At the same time, a responsible individual is not destructive, but takes care of development wherein he understands this concern as his own mission (Greenleaf 1998). Therefore, according to Spencer (2007), servant leadership is not merely one of the possible leadership styles but it is increasingly becoming recognised for its functionality in relation to the others, which is the result of trust, sacrifice, motivation and inspiration. It is also effective in the case of solving dilemmas that arise in the process of the sustainable development of the organisation (Trompenaars and Woolliams 2009).

In a survey conducted in 1976, Brenner and Molander (1977) found that managers mostly answered the question of whether social responsibility is an ethical challenge for both the leader and the company in a positive manner. They also found that the managers felt the greatest social responsibility towards customers and only afterwards for the shareholders and employees, which was then mistakenly understood as a possible indicator of the fact that the centre of gravity was shifting from making profit to satisfying the needs of customers. Notwithstanding the above, ethical leadership is increasingly becoming a competitive advantage of a growing number of companies and organisations today (Karp 2003), where researchers have found a positive correlation between the socially responsible and ethical behaviour of leaders and a negative correlation between socially responsible and despotic leadership (De Hoogh and Den Hartog 2008).

Today, researchers agree that leaders have one of the most important roles in designing and implementing social responsibility in life (Waldman and Siegel 2008). Socially responsible leadership no longer merely means doing business and making profit because the responsibilities of organisations are greater (Kreitner 2004), namely, it is very important how the transaction is made, how the price is formed and how a product reaches its value (Karp 2003). Because of this, in today's complex social environment, leader integrity is increasingly important as a genuine will and the desire to take into account the overall role of their own business or the organisation in the environment in which it operates. Through the prism of personal and organisational integrity, the social responsibility of organisations towards external stakeholders denotes a responsibility whereby stakeholders are not to be harmed, but the opposite, they should be assured of some benefit and provided with added value (Lennick and Kiel 2009).

In relation to this, Aßlander et al. (2011) believe that today the need for responsible and fair leadership, ethical reflecting on leadership decisions and caring for sustainable development, which falls within the framework of ethics and consequently servant leadership, is stronger than ever.[2]

Notes

1 Bovens (1998) noted that a precise definition of social responsibility is often very difficult to attain. It basically reflects values that are not universal because they depend on the place, time and context, while originally it was meant to answer or defend someone (oneself, actions, etc.). The author divides responsibility into passive and active.

Passive responsibility is meant in terms of formal accountability for past behaviour, while active responsibility is meant in terms of a preventive factor against adverse situations and events in the present with the help of virtues. Both forms of responsibility are closely connected, wherein the moral acceptability of the passive form often depends on the capacity of the active form of responsibility. At the same time, the author believes that, of all forms of accountability, the most effective is the individual responsibility of the leader and everyone in the organisation, provided they have the possibility to act responsibly.

2 The concept of servant leadership is also in line with the philosophy of sustainable development in the fields of environment, health and social services, which must be included in the core of the business of organisations, without any compromise in favour of the cost or to the detriment of the quality of products or services (Laszlo and Zhexembayeva 2011).

4 How employees assess their leaders

As part of the study on the integrity of leaders and the servant leadership style, we conducted a survey in two different types of formal organisations, namely for-profit and non-profit. The acquired results were then, to a certain extent, also verified by the qualitative approach. Among for-profit organisations, we were able to carry out surveys in several Slovenian companies, while among non-profit organisations, we were able to conduct surveys in one state organisation that operates in the field of providing security.

The target (evaluation) group in all organisations were leaders at different organisational (hierarchical) levels. Their integrity and use of the servant leadership style was evaluated by their (subordinate) employees. In our research, we included representative samples of all employees in all of the participating organisations.

Our interest in the study was the influence of a leader's integrity on their leadership, specifically the servant leadership style, whereby we wanted to ascertain how integrity influences this leadership style. We also wished to determine how employees perceive the integrity of their leaders and the ethics of their behaviour. In addition, we sought to determine the extent to which, after the employees' evaluations, a servant leadership style is present in our environment, and if there is a difference in it in the context of for-profit and non-profit organisations. In doing so, we assumed that, judging from the nature of non-profit organisations, that such organisations would manifest more of the servant leadership style than their counterpart, the for-profit organisation.

Given that our goal was to determine the impact of integrity on the servant leadership style, we understood the perception of integrity as an independent variable, while we understood the perception of the servant leadership style as the dependent variable. In this way, our approach is consistent with the previous leadership studies where integrity was normally set as an independent variable of leadership or as a feature of good leaders (Palanski and Yammarino 2007: 172).[1]

Our empirical approach is also consistent with the opinion of Brown et al. (2005), which currently is necessary more than ever to consistently and systematically explore the ethical standpoint of leadership. The appearance of numerous immoral behaviours and actions in the business world on one hand, and the stronger interest in implementing ethical leadership on the other, have helped in striving towards such a goal (Brown and Trevino 2006). Our approach is also consistent with the findings of Bahovec (1993), who found that an ethical stance and its impact on others can be measured. The approach we take also coincides with the findings of Turner et al. (2002) in that the concepts of moral or ethical behaviour are used frequently, while there is relatively little research in that area. It was also confirmed by Simons (1999) and Parry and Proctor-Thomson (2002) that many organisations and leaders are in fact informed about the importance of integrity in business. This can also be clearly observed through formal statements and ethical codes; however, leaders do behave differently in practice. For this reason, there is a need for the research to move the focus from studying formal assessments to studying the actual behaviour of leaders. This is certainly not a new trend, as almost 30 years ago, Burns (1984) expressed a hope that researchers would continue to conduct more and more empirical studies of behaviour of leaders.

The chapter below deals with defining the research questions and presenting the initial research model. We prepared it on the bases of hypotheses, wherein it can be understood which authors influenced the research.[2]

How does integrity influence the servant leadership style?

How does integrity as a personal characteristic of the individual influence the servant leadership style and to what extent can the servant leadership style be understood with the use of integrity or which factors influence this leadership style? In our study, we wanted to find out how the employees perceive the integrity of their leaders and the presence of the servant leadership style in their organisations.

Based on our research question, we considered that servant leadership style is influenced by various factors, namely the leader's integrity, socio-demographic characteristics of the leader and the type of organisation being led by the leader:

1 We assumed that the higher the integrity of an individual leader, the more the leader practices the servant leadership style. The relationship is based on the arguments of various authors that personal integrity is an important positive factor in servant leadership (Page and Wong 2000, Covey 2002b, Greenleaf 2002a, Smith et al. 2004, Boyum 2006, Liden et al. 2008, McNenery 2008, Sendjaya et al. 2008, Lennick and Kiel 2009). Trevino et al. (2000) considered integrity to be the most important factor in ethical and servant leadership, while Russell (2001) and Russell and Stone (2002) see integrity as one of the most important leadership values. It is also based on the empirical findings of Washington et al. (2006), namely there is a positive correlation between the perception of employees of the servant leadership and their perception of leadership values, which includes leader integrity.

2 We also considered that the higher the leader's integrity, the more the leader is characterised by ethical behaviour and care for the community in which the organisation operates. This relation is based on the empirical findings of

Parry and Proctor-Thomson (2002), showing that the perception of the leader's integrity and the absence of unethical behaviour are positively correlated. It is also based on the findings of Peterson (2004) that both the perceived high level of the leader's integrity, as well as the strong belief of employees in universal moral principles, are positively correlated with ethical behaviour.

In addition, this relation is based on the finding that servant leadership falls within the framework of ethical leadership (Ehrhart 2004, Liden et al. 2008, Schermerhorn et al. 2008, Fry and Kriger 2009, Reed et al. 2011, Dierendonck and Nuijten 2011, Dion 2012). Ethical leadership is characterised by the fact it is based on the personal integrity of the leaders. Den Hartog and De Hoogh (2009) came to similar findings, namely that ethical leaders are characterised by integrity and making principled, fair and just decisions.

In formulating this relation, we also took the findings of Reed et al. (2011) into account, that is, that both the ethical behaviour of leaders, as well as their care for others, are integral parts of leadership. The findings of Greenleaf (2002a) and Burns (2010) were also considered, namely that personal integrity is a fundamental factor of social exchange. Greenleaf's (1998) belief that a genuine servant leader takes care of the social environment and the community in which the organisation operates was also taken into account.

3   We supposed that the higher the leader's integrity, the more the leader is characterised by caring for the interests of employees, helping others in personal growth and offering emotional support to employees. This relationship is based on the argument that a servant leader is firstly hospitable and servile and only secondly a leader (Greenleaf 2002a, 2002b, Northouse 2010), whereby integrity represents the foundation of social relations (Greenleaf 2002a, Lennick and Kiel 2009). In this context, Greenleaf (2002a) believed that a servant leader must be empathic and that such a leader should never turn employees down in any way. Other authors (Spears 1998, Page and Wong 2000, Yukl 2002, Fry 2003, Schermerhorn 2008, Carroll 2009, Lyons et al. 2009, Searle and Barbuto 2011) also consider that servant leaders put employees in first place.

In formulating this relationship, we also took account of the findings of Avolio et al. (2009), namely that the empirical findings indicate a positive correlation between servant leadership and a concern for the welfare of others.

4   We also assumed that the higher the leader's integrity, the more the leader is characterised by leaving employees to take responsibility for making important decisions and by informing the employees if something is not running properly. This relationship is based on the findings of Page and Wong (2000) and Boyum (2006), that is, on the fact that for servant leadership leader both integrity and employee empowerment are characteristics. The relationship is based on the findings of Schneider and Winnette (2011), namely that servant leadership in non-profit organisations is especially evident in the context of employee empowerment. By empowering employees, the employees gain

decision-making ability (Schermerhorn 2008) and become equal partners in the decision-making process (Kreitner 2004). In the concept of servant leadership, empowerment does not denote a loss of the leader's decision-making power, but it brings positive effects for both the employees and the organisation (Shannon 1998, Russell and Stone 2002).

At the same time, the relationship is based on the assumption that the leader's integrity influences the transparency of their relationships with employees, wherein the leader's sincerity is the key factor in genuine care for the personal growth of employees, as already advocated by Greenleaf (1998, 2002a, 2002b).

5   We supposed that the gender and age of the leader do not affect the servant leadership style. This assumption is based on the empirical findings of Bartholomew (2006) who did not find a statistically significant effect of gender on the servant leadership style. It is also based on the findings of Crane and Matten (2004), Brown et al. (2005) and Brown and Trevino (2006), namely that research studies do not confirm the effects of gender on the ethical behaviour of leaders.

Conversely, Robbins and Langton (2003) and Hoyt (2010) noted that empirical research on the leadership style only shows small differences between female and male leaders. Robbins and Langton (2003) noted that the major gap lies in the fact that male leaders are more prone to giving orders and controlling employees and formal authority, while female leaders are more prone to the democratic mode of leadership, with an emphasis on managing relationships, searching for consensus, empowering employees and strengthening the positive self-image of the employees, which is in fact consistent with servant leadership. Hoyt (2010) presents similar findings, namely that female leaders are more prone to a democratic and transformational style of leadership than male leaders.

The role of age is based on the findings of Crane and Matten (2004), namely that the research does not confirm the impact of age on ethical behaviour. It is also based on the findings of Bartholomew (2006) who did not find an impact of age on servant leadership.

6   Our basic thought was that the education of the leader and the leader's work and leadership experiences have a positive impact on the servant leadership style. The preposition is based on the findings of Crane and Matten (2004) showing that the research confirms the positive impact of education on ethical behaviour. Šter (1994) concluded similarly, namely that research confirms a positive correlation between people's skills and their positive attitude to values.

This assumed impact is also based on the findings of Crane and Matten (2004), revealing that the work experience of leaders has a positive impact on their ethical behaviour. The positive importance of experience was already emphasised by Aristotle, Rousseau and Greenleaf. We therefore agree with Aristotle's thought that young people can really become good professionals, while 'wisdom is only produced on a specific particular level, with which we only come to find through experience; a young person does not have experience, because experience only manifests over a longer period of time' (2002: 196). Therefore, according to Aristotle, anyone can properly judge only those things they are familiar with; this in turn means that properly assessing things applies only to experienced professionals (2002). From the above mentioned, Aristotle concluded that 'young people are not suitable for [a] lecture on political science, since they do not have real life experience yet; such experience is in fact the starting point and the subject of such discussions' (2002: 49).[3] The mind and wisdom develop over the years, which is the reason why, for Aristotle, it is necessary to 'regard arguments of the experienced elders and smart people, even if unproven, to be taken into account as evidence; such people have a sharpened and experienced eyesight, thus giving them the ability to see and observe efficiently' (2002: 201). In favour of such thinking, Rousseau added that 'the best and most natural system is the one where the wisest govern the many, if we can rely on them to rule in the favour of the many and not in their own' (2001: 68). The author added that old age was once respected (indicating the period of ancient Rome) because it denoted experience in business and calmness in consultations (Rousseau 1993: 74). Similarly, Greenleaf (2002a) stated that experienced (mature) people are the best in performing the most complex social functions that enhance justice and other important values.

7   We wanted to examine whether servant leadership is more typical of non-profit than for-profit organisations. The question is based on the findings of Smith et al. (2004) showing that servant leadership is more characteristic of non-profit organisations. In addition, Schneider and Winnette (2011) found that servant leadership is suitable for the management of non-profit and voluntary organisations, while Možina et al. (2002) believed that leaders of non-profit organisations, in comparison with the leaders of for-profit organisation, regard ethical values as most important.

8   We considered that there are no statistically significant differences between the leaders of non-profit and for-profit organisations in levels of personal integrity. The question bases itself on the findings of Lennick and Kiel (2009), namely that moral values are important in both for-profit and non-profit organisations and in all types and sizes of organisations. The similarities between for-profit and non-profit organisations were also researched by Greenleaf (2002a) and Sarros et al. (2011). Kellerman (2010) believes that the new millennium will show that leaders in the for-profit sector and leaders in state institutions share many more similarities than differences.

In addition, integrity is very often defined as a value in the mission statements of all types of organisations (Audi and Murphy 2006). The literature on leadership also ranks it among the general characteristics of good leadership (Goethals 2004), wherein it is particularly emphasised in the context of ethical and servant leadership (Howell and Avolio 1995, Bass and Steidlmeier 1999, Yukl 2002, Brown et al. 2005, Liden et al. 2008, Palanski and Yammarino 2009).

Initial model

The initial research model presents the expected effects which were examined in the study. As mentioned, we set integrity as an independent variable and servant leadership as the dependent variable. As an independent variable, we also set demographic information on the assessed leaders and the type of organisation (for-profit or non-profit) in which the leader works (Figure 4.1).

The survey was conducted on a sample of 1,164 respondents, namely 768 respondents employed in a non-profit organisation and 396 respondents employed in the for-profit sector in Slovenia. We will thereby acquire basic information on how employees perceive the integrity of their leaders and the servant leadership style. This is followed by a data analysis to determine the differences between non-profit and for-profit organisations and whether there are any differences in relation to individual socio-demographic characteristics. The analysis will be completed with a regression analysis where we tried to figure out which factors can serve us best when explaining servant leadership and the integrity of leaders.

The data are presented in text, tables and through pictures. For more detailed information, the reader can contact the authors.

Figure 4.1 The influence of integrity on the servant leadership style: the initial research model.

Source: Authors.

Notes

1 Moreover, integrity in philosophy, and also in leadership, can be understood as a construct on the individual level of a person (e.g. individual-level construct) (Palanski and Yammarino 2007: 172).
2 Because we were also interested in the perception of the personal integrity of leaders from both types of organisation, we added another hypothesis which states: 'Among leaders from the for-profit and non-profit organisations, no statistically significant differences exist in levels of personal integrity'.
3 Aristotle understood ethics as a practical discipline that needs to be implemented in real life, and associated it with political science (Gantar 2002).

5   The assessment of servant leadership and leader integrity through an employee perspective

From Table 5.1 and Table 5.2 it is possible to determine which questions define servant leadership and which determine the personal integrity of leaders. In the questionnaire on servant leadership a higher value denotes a better result, while in the questionnaire on integrity it is the opposite.

It is evident from Table 5.1 that on a seven-point scale, the respondents highly agree with the statements that their leaders are thoroughly familiar with the organisation and its objectives, the leaders share information when something is not going according to plan, they are capable of effective thinking for solving complex problems and they take time for personal talks with employees. Conversely, the lowest rated statements were that leaders mainly take care of the success of employees, they put employees' interests before their own, the leaders sacrifice their own interests to meet the needs of employees and that the career development of employees is a priority.

Table 5.2 shows that respondents most highly ranked statements that deal with their relationship to the organisation and the lowest ranked statements deal with their relations with the employees.

Thus, on a seven-point scale, the respondents agreed least with the statements that their leaders would treat them better if they belonged to another ethnic community, their leaders participated in activities that are harmful to the organisation, they would unduly appropriate the organisation's property and they would forge documents if such an act were useful to their work.

On the other hand, the respondents mostly agreed with the statement that their leaders pay special attention to certain favourite employees, but not to the respondent, that the leader would put the respondent at risk in order to protect himself, that the leader would lie to them and that the leader would understand employee mistakes as a personal attack on them.

The assessed leaders

In the third part of the questionnaire, we asked the respondents to indicate their leader's gender. They were also asked to estimate their approximate age, how much work and leadership experience they had and their leader's level of education.

Table 5.1 Rating of the servant leadership style from the employee perspective in non-profit and for-profit organisations together

	Rate your direct leader	M	SD
1	My manager can tell if something is going wrong	5.55	1.454
2	My manager gives me the responsibility to make important decisions about my job	4.90	1.563
3	My manager makes my career development a priority	3.55	1.716
4	My manager seems to care more about my success than his/her own	2.85	1.658
5	My manager holds high ethical standards	4.69	1.702
6	I would seek help from my manager if I had a personal problem	3.89	2.065
7	My manager emphasises the importance of giving back to the community	4.90	1.689
8	My manager is able to effectively think through complex problems	5.18	1.646
9	My manager encourages me to handle important work decisions on my own	4.73	1.674
10	My manager is interested in making sure that I achieve my career goals	3.97	1.826
11	My manager puts my best interests ahead of his/her own	2.96	1.621
12	My manager is always honest	4.81	1.815
13	My manager cares about my personal wellbeing	4.11	1.742
14	My manager is always interested in helping people in our community	4.78	1.624
15	My manager has a thorough understanding of our organisation and its goals	5.60	1.473
16	My manager gives me the freedom to handle difficult situations in the way that I feel is best	4.59	1.613
17	My manager provides me with work experiences that enable me to develop new skills	4.83	1.633
18	My manager sacrifices his/her own interests to meet my needs	3.07	1.645
19	My manager would not compromise ethical principles in order to achieve success	4.65	1.728
20	My manager takes time to talk to me on a personal level	5.12	1.753
21	My manager is involved in community activities	4.94	1.473
22	My manager can solve work problems with new or creative ideas	4.91	1.581
23	When I have to make an important decision at work, I do not have to consult my manager	4.00	1.702
24	My manager wants to know about my career goals	4.33	1.736
25	My manager does whatever she/he can to make my job easier	4.35	1.746
26	My manager values honesty more than profits	4.82	1.739
27	My manager can recognise when I am down without asking me	3.64	1.733
28	I am encouraged by my manager to volunteer in the community	4.02	1.790

1, I completely disagree; 2, I disagree; 3, I partially agree; 4, I neither agree nor disagree; 5, I partially agree; 6, I agree; 7, I completely agree; M, arithmetic mean; SD, standard deviation; N, 1,164.

Table 5.2 The assessment of leader integrity through the employee perspective in non-profit and for-profit organisations together

	Rate your direct leader	M	SD
1	Would use my mistakes to attack me personally	2.93	1.761
2	Always gets even	2.61	1.651
3	Gives special favours to certain 'pet' employees, but not to me	3.30	1.964
4	Would lie to me	3.07	1.851
5	Would risk me to protect himself/herself in work matters	3.10	1.809
6	Deliberately makes employees angry at each other	2.39	1.699
7	Is a hypocrite	2.09	1.421
8	Would use my performance appraisal to criticise me as a person	2.50	1.685
9	Has it in for me	2.12	1.450
10	Would blame me for his/her own mistake	2.44	1.630
11	Would falsify records if it would help his/her work situation	1.89	1.361
12	Lacks high morals	2.45	1.735
13	Makes fun of my mistakes instead of coaching me as to how to do my job better	2.05	1.423
14	Would deliberately exaggerate my mistakes to make me look bad when describing my performance to his/her superiors	2.29	1.626
15	Is vindictive	2.38	1.767
16	Would allow me to be blamed for his/her mistake	2.17	1.533
17	Avoids coaching me because (s)he wants me to fail	2.04	1.340
18	Would treat me better if I belonged to a different ethnic group	1.60	1.054
19	Would deliberately distort what I say	2.04	1.310
20	Deliberately fuels conflict among employees	2.21	1.543
21	Is evil	2.31	1.721
22	Would limit my training opportunities to prevent me from advancing	2.19	1.562
23	Would blackmail an employee if (s)he thought (s)he could get away with it	2.08	1.484
24	Enjoys turning down my requests	2.16	1.501
25	Would make trouble for me if I got on his/her bad side	2.83	1.892
26	Would take credit for my ideas	2.46	1.627
27	Would steal from the organisation	1.84	1.237
28	Would risk me to get back at someone else	2.11	1.397
29	Would engage in sabotage against the organisation	1.76	1.118
30	Would fire people just because (s)he does not like them if (s)he could get away with it	2.60	1.744
31	Would do things that violate organisational policy and then expect his/her subordinates to cover for him/her	2.07	1.393

1, I completely disagree; 2, I disagree; 3, I partially agree; 4, I neither agree nor disagree; 5, I partially agree; 6, I agree; 7, I completely agree; M, arithmetic mean; SD, standard deviation; N, 1,164.

The obtained data shows that among all leaders assessed in the non-profit and for-profit organisations, there were 83.6 per cent (971) males and 16.4 per cent (191) females. The average age of the leaders was 41.31 years, while the minimum age was 23 years and the maximum age was 60 years. Most, namely 20.7 per cent, of the assessed leaders were 40 years of age.

The work and leadership experience of the leaders was assessed by the respondents on a five-point scale, wherein 1 denoted that the leader is completely inexperienced and 5 denoted that the leader was very experienced. Based on the data, we may conclude that the respondents assessed 0.9 per cent or 10 leaders as completely inexperienced (grade 1) and 39 per cent or 454 leaders as very experienced (grade 5). Further, 4.6 per cent or 53 leaders were assessed with grade 2, 17.8 per cent or 207 leaders with grade 3 and 37.7 per cent or 439 leaders with grade 4.

In assessing their leader's work experience, the respondents assessed 1.3 per cent or 15 leaders as completely untrained (grade 1) and 31.7 per cent or 368 leaders as very experienced (grade 5). In addition, 9.6 per cent or 112 leaders were assessed with grade 2, 20.7 per cent or 240 leaders with grade 3 and 36.7 per cent or 427 leaders with grade 4.

In assessing their leader's education level, the respondents were asked to circle the highest level of education completed by their leader. The data obtained show that most leaders have a higher professional education (32.5 per cent or 376), while the least gained level of education was a doctorate (1.8 per cent or 21). A high school education was assessed for 8.7 per cent or 101 leaders, higher education for 9 per cent or 104 leaders, a university degree for 24.6 per cent or 284 leaders and a master's and/or specialisation for 23.4 per cent or 270 leaders. From the gathered data, we can conclude that most of the assessed leaders (57.1 per cent or 660) have a higher professional or university education.

The following shows the difference between the leaders assessed in the non-profit and for-profit organisations.

The difference between non-profit and for-profit organisations

The differences between non-profit and for-profit organisations in relation to the average values of the variables of both measurement instruments were assessed using a t-test. In order to facilitate and improve transparency, after a brief explanatory statement, we present them graphically, while the interested reader may contact the authors for more detailed information.

It is evident from Figure 5.1, which refers to servant leadership, that respondents from the for-profit organisations evaluated their leaders much better than respondents from the non-profit organisation. Conversely, the difference was found only in two situations, namely in the variables where the respondent is not required to have a consultation with the leader before taking an important decision, and where the leaders appreciate honesty more than other benefits or profit. In both cases, as well as with two other variables, that is, where the leader lets employees take responsibility in decision-making, and where employees would seek help from their leader in case of personal problems, a statistically significant

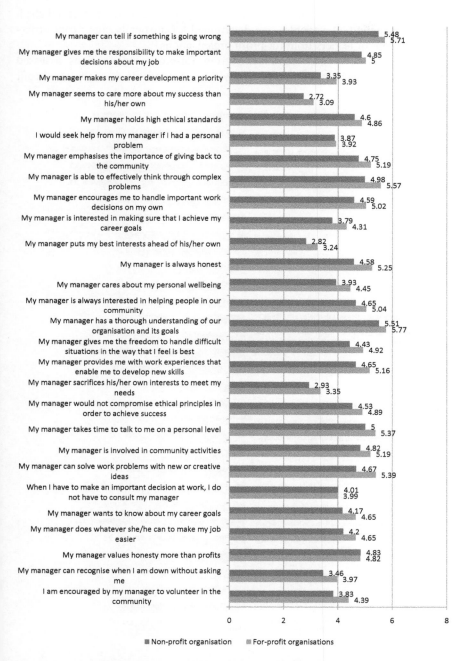

Figure 5.1 The differences in mean values of the variables in the questionnaire on servant leadership in for-profit organisations and the non-profit organisation.

Source: Authors.

difference between non-profit and for-profit organisations was not established. For the remaining 24 variables, we determined a statistically significant difference in favour of leaders from for-profit organisations.

Figure 5.2 shows that respondents from for-profit organisations assessed the integrity of their leaders more highly than respondents from the non-profit

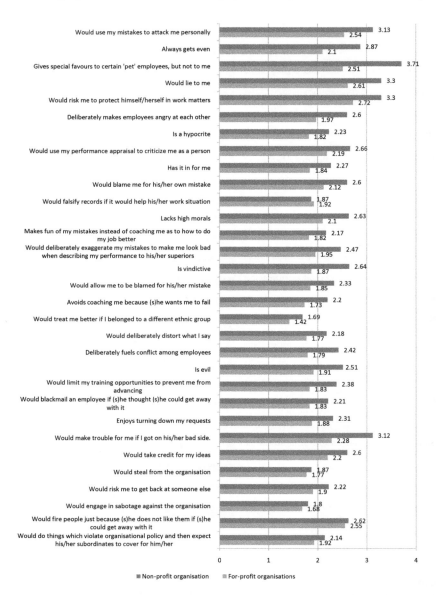

Figure 5.2 The differences in mean values of the variables in the questionnaire on leader integrity in for-profit organisations and the non-profit organisation.

Source: Authors.

organisations. Conversely, the difference was found only in one variable, namely when the leader would forge documents if the leader would benefit from doing so in his work, although the difference was not statistically significant.

In addition, statistically significant differences between both types of organisations were not found in only three variables: when the leader would unjustly appropriate the property of the organisation, when the leader would participate in activities harmful to the organisation and when a leader would break the employment relationship with someone the leader would not like if the leader could determine if such an act could be done.

Like with servant leadership, for the remaining 27 seven variables, we found that respondents from the for-profit organisations rated their leaders statistically higher than respondents from the non-profit organisation.

Differences among the assessed leaders[1]

We found that differences between the assessed leaders in both types of organisations exist, that is, in gender, age and education. Regarding gender, it was similar with the leaders as it was with the respondents, namely that in the for-profit organisations there are more female leaders than there are in the non-profit organisation. Thus, respondents in the for-profit organisations assessed that 61.4 per cent of their leaders were male (242) and 38.6 per cent female (152), while in the non-profit organisation, they assessed there were 94.9 per cent (729) male and 5.1 per cent (39) female leaders. The average age of the leaders in the non-profit organisation was 41.69 years, while in the for-profit organisations it was 40.58 years.

Unlike the demographic data of the respondents, we found that the leaders were on average better educated in the non-profit organisation than in the for-profit organisations; 0.3 per cent (2) of the assessed leaders in the non-profit organisation held a doctoral degree, 25.9 per cent (199) held a master's degree or a specialisation, 64.3 per cent (493) had a high or university education, 8.5 per cent (65) had a higher education, 1 per cent (8) held a secondary education. In the for-profit organisations, 4.9 per cent (19) of the assessed leaders held a doctoral degree, 18.3 per cent (71) had a master's degree or specialisation, 42.9 per cent (167) a high or university education, 10 per cent (39) a higher education and 23.9 per cent (93) had a secondary school education.

Differences were not found in work experience and leadership experience. The statistical data indeed showed that respondents from the for-profit organisations assessed their leaders as more experienced in work (4.16) and also as more experienced in leadership (3.94) than their non-profit counterparts (4.05 and 3.85).

Dimensions of servant leadership and leader integrity[2]

Servant leadership

On the basis of the factor analysis of the variables of the questionnaire on servant leadership, we confirmed the findings of Liden et al. (2008) and seven different factors, namely:

1 Conceptual skills.
2 Empowerment.
3 Helping employees with personal growth.
4 Putting employees first.
5 Ethical behaviour and conduct.
6 Emotional support.
7 Care for the community.[3]

We can conclude from the results that the respondents from both types of organisation ranked the conceptual skills of their leaders highest, while the worst ranked factor was 'putting the subordinates first' (see Table 5.3). We found that the inverted average value of the derivative variable of the factor 'index of integrity' is 5.69.[4]

Leader integrity

In the factor analysis of the variables in the questionnaire dealing with leader integrity (PLIS), given the findings of Craig and Gustafson (1998) showing that the questionnaire has a one-factor structure, we included all variables in the analysis, except for the previously eliminated one (no. 46).[5] We decided to name this factor as 'the integrity index'. The difference between the two factors is evident in the scree plot (Figure 5.3).

We thereby confirmed the findings of Craig and Gustafson (1998) by showing that the PLIS measurement instrument has a single-factor structure. The factor of the index integrity will be used in further data analysis.

Factors influencing the dimensions of servant leadership and integrity

In the final stage of the statistical processing of the data, we wanted to measure the intensity of the influence of the independent variables (the index of integrity;

Table 5.3 Dimensions of servant leadership for all leaders in for-profit and non-profit organisations

Dimensions	N	M	SD
Conceptual skills	1,160	5.312	1.306
Empowerment	1,160	4.556	1.351
Helping subordinates grow	1,160	4.165	1.501
Putting subordinates first	1,158	3.305	1.448
Ethical behaviour	1,160	4.744	1.526
Emotional healing	1,155	4.190	1.540
Creating value for the community	1,163	4.662	1.370
Index of integrity	1,108	5.693	1.270

1, I completely disagree; 2, I disagree; 3, I partially agree; 4, I neither agree nor disagree; 5, I partially agree; 6, I agree; 7, I completely agree; M, arithmetic mean; SD, standard deviation; N, 1,164.

Scree Plot

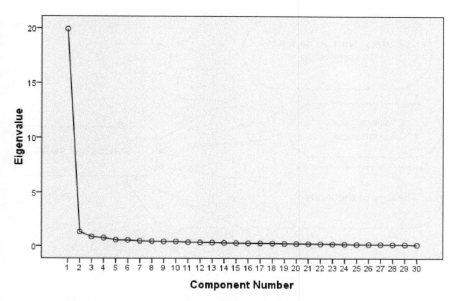

Figure 5.3 Factor analysis of the variables in the questionnaire on integrity.[6]
Source: Authors.

demographic data of the leaders – gender, age, work experience, leadership experience, education; demographic data of the respondents – gender, age, years of employment, education, continued education, managerial post; type of organisation – for-profit and non-profit) on the dependent variable (the seven factors of servant leadership). At the same time, we wanted to determine which of the independent variables can best be used to explain the individual elements of servant leadership.

As we are also interested in which independent demographic variables affect the index of integrity, we also used regression analysis for this purpose. In this case, we set the index of integrity as the dependent variable.[7],[8]

Influencing factors of servant leadership

The following pages show the factors of influence for all seven dimensions of servant leadership. Explanatory regression models are introduced to show these influences.

Based on the data, we may conclude that the greatest impact on the respondents' perception of the conceptual skills of their leaders is their perception of personal integrity in the leaders and that the latter is their most important predictor (Figure 5.4). This means that the higher the perception of the integrity of an

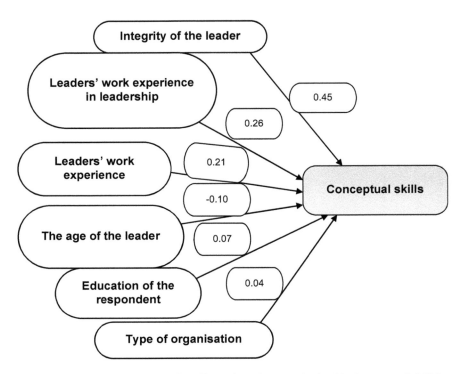

Figure 5.4 Factors affecting the first dimension of servant leadership (conceptual skills).
Source: Authors.

individual leader, the higher the perception of that leader's conceptual skills. The same applies to the assessment of the leadership experience and the work experience of the leaders, namely the greater they are, the higher is the respondent's perception of the conceptual skills. Regarding education, the data reveals that the higher a leader's education, the higher the respondents perceive that leader's conceptual skills. However, a positive perception of the leader's conceptual skills also depends on whether the assessed leaders and respondents come from a for-profit organisation.[9]

Regarding the age of the leader, which has a negative impact on the dependent variable, we can determine that the higher the age of the leader, the lower will be the respondents' perception of their leader's conceptual skills.

We can conclude that, the same as with the 'leader's conceptual skills', the biggest influence on the variable of 'empowerment' comes from the respondents' perception of their leader's personal integrity, which is consequently its most important predictor (Figure 5.5). This means that the higher the perception of the integrity of an individual leader, the higher is the perception of the empowerment the assessed leader employs in their leadership.

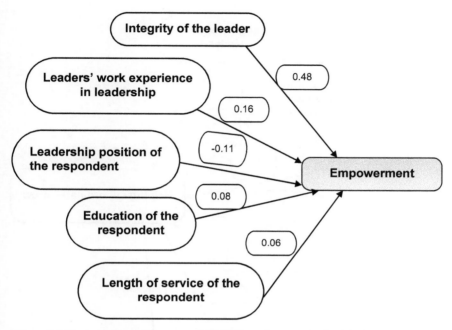

Figure 5.5 Factors affecting the second dimension of servant leadership (empowerment).
Source: Authors.

Regarding the assessment of the leaders' leadership experience, the data shows the higher the latter are, the higher is the respondents' perception of the empowerment used in the leader's leadership. Regarding the education of the respondent and their years of employment, the data reveals that the more the respondent is educated and the longer they were employed, the higher is their perception of empowerment.

For the independent variable 'the managerial post of the respondent', which is the only one in this model that is negatively connected to the dependent variable, we can conclude with the help of the data analysis that a respondent who is a leader has a statistically significantly higher perception of empowerment than a respondent who is not a leader.[10]

We may conclude that the biggest influence on the variable 'helping employees with personal growth' comes from the respondents' perception of the personal integrity of the leaders, which means that the latter is the most important predictor (Figure 5.6). From this, we can conclude that the higher the perception of the integrity of an individual leader, the higher the perception of the leader's help offered to employees regarding their own personal growth.

Regarding the assessments of the work experience of the leaders and their leadership experience, the data shows that the higher they are, according to the respondent, the higher is their perception of the help that the leader offers to the employees regarding their own personal growth.

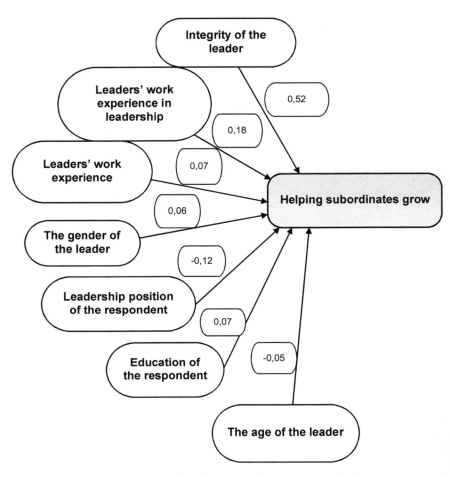

Figure 5.6 Factors affecting the third dimension of servant leadership (helping employees with personal growth).

Source: Authors.

The dependent variable is also influenced by the gender of the leader whereby, with the help of data analysis, we can conclude that female leaders, given the respondents' perception, offer employees more help in their personal growth than their male counterparts.[11]

The education of the respondent has a positive effect, which means that the more the respondent is educated, the higher is their perception of the leader's help, while regarding the age of the respondent, we can conclude that it is negatively connected to the dependent variable (it has a negative impact on it). This means that the older the respondent is, the lower is their perception of the help that the leader provides in the employee's personal growth.

For the independent variable 'managerial post of the respondent', which connects negatively with the dependent variable, we may conclude that a respondent who is also a leader, in comparison with a respondent who is not a leader, has a statistically significantly higher perception of the help offered by their leader regarding personal growth.[12]

We can conclude that the respondents' perception of the leader's personal integrity has the largest impact on the variable 'putting employees first', which means that the perception of personal integrity is the most important predictor (Figure 5.7). Here we may conclude that the higher the perception of an individual leader's integrity, the higher is the leader's perceived behaviour in terms of the leader putting employees first.

Based on the assessment of the leaders' work experience, we can conclude that the greater the work experience according to the respondent, the higher is their perception of their leader's behaviour with regard to the leader putting employees first.

The gender of the leader also impacts the dependent variable. With the help of the data analysis, we may conclude that female leaders, according to the perception of the respondents, put their employees first more than their male counterparts.[13]

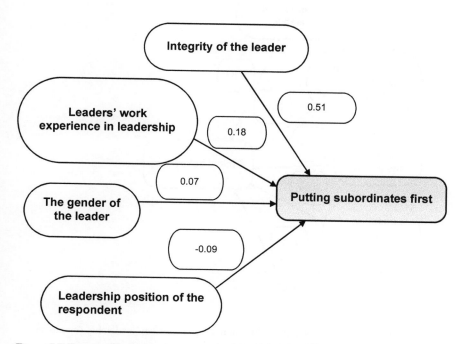

Figure 5.7 Factors affecting the fourth dimension of servant leadership (putting the employees first).

Source: Authors.

For the independent variable 'managerial post of the respondent', which connects negatively with the dependent variable in this model, we can conclude that a respondent who is a leader, in comparison with a respondent who is not a leader, has a statistically significantly higher perception of the leader's behaviour in terms of putting employees first.[14]

Based on the data we can conclude that the perception of the respondents of the personal integrity of leaders has the largest impact on the dependent variable 'ethical behaviour and conduct', which, in turn, means that the perception of personal integrity in the leader is also its most important predictor. Consequently, the higher perception of the leader's personal integrity, the higher the respondent's perception of the leader's ethics of their behaviour and conduct (Figure 5.8).

The assessment of the leader's work experience shows that the greater the work experience, according to the respondents, the higher the respondent's perception of their ethical behaviour and conduct. Conversely, the age of the leader is negatively connected to the dependent variable, which, in turn, means that the older the leader is, the higher will be the respondent's perception of the leader's ethical behaviour and conduct.

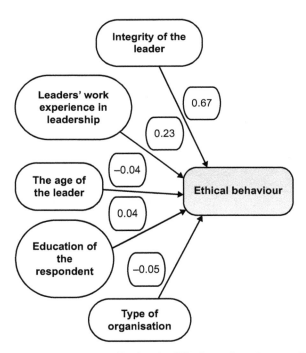

Figure 5.8 Factors affecting the fifth dimension of servant leadership (on ethical behaviour and conduct).

Source: Authors.

A positive perception of the ethical behaviour and conduct of leaders also depends on whether the assessed leaders come from a for-profit organisation.[15] Regarding the education of the respondent, the data show that the higher the respondent's education, the higher is the respondent's perception of the ethical behaviour and conduct of their leader.

We can conclude that the respondents' perception of the leader's personal integrity has the greatest impact on the dependent variable (emotional support), which, in turn, means it is also the most important predictor (Figure 5.9). Consequently, the higher the perception of the leader's integrity, the higher is the

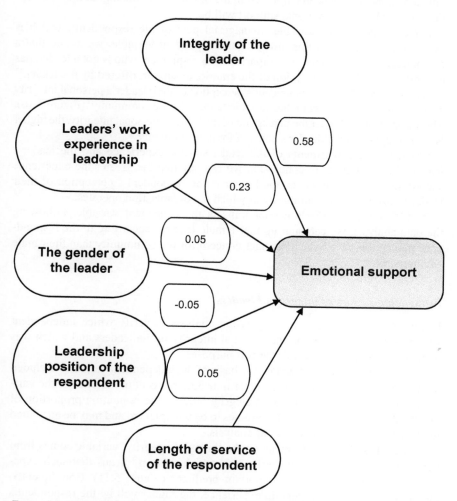

Figure 5.9 Factors affecting the sixth dimension of servant leadership (emotional support).

Source: Authors.

perception of the emotional support they provide to the staff. In addition, we may conclude that the higher the leadership experience of the leader according to the respondents, the higher is a respondent's perception of the emotional support the leader offers to the employees.

The leader's gender also impacts the dependent variable. Following the data analysis, we can convincingly say that female leaders, according to the perception of the respondents, offer more emotional support to their employees than their male counterparts.[16]

Regarding the respondents' years of employment, the data shows that the more time a respondent has been employed in the organisation, the higher their perception of their leader's emotional support will be.

For the independent variable 'managerial post of the respondent', which is negatively connected in this model to the dependent variable, we assure that a respondent who is a leader, in comparison to a respondent who is not a leader, has a significantly higher perception of the emotional support offered by the leader.[17]

We can conclude that a respondent's perception of their leader's personal integrity also has the largest impact on the variable 'caring for the community' (Figure 5.10). This means that the higher the perception of the leader's personal integrity, the higher is the perception of that leader's concern for the community.

Based on the assessments of the leader's work experience and the leader's leadership experience, In conclusion we can say that the greater the experience according to the respondents, the higher is the respondent's perception of their leader's caring for the community in which the organisation operates.

In addition, the leader's gender impacts the dependent variable. Following the data analysis, we can sum up that female leaders, according to the respondents' perception, also have a stronger concern for the community than their male counterparts.[18]

Influencing factors of integrity of leaders

Finally, we would like to use regression analysis to verify which independent variables have an impact on the personal integrity of the leaders and which was treated as a dependent variable for this purpose.

It is clear from Table 5.4 that on the basis of the independent variables included in the regression analysis, we can determine 33.5 per cent of variance or the variability of the dependent variable 'integrity index'. The remaining proportion of the variability (to 100 per cent) continues to be unexplained and may be attributed to other factors not included in our analysis.

We note that the largest impact on the 'index of integrity' variable comes from the leadership experience of the leaders, which, in turn, means that such experience is the variable's most important predictor (Figure 5.11). Consequently, the more a leader has leadership experience, the higher will be the respondent's perception of their leader's integrity. The same goes for the assessment of the leader's work experience, namely that the greater the leader's work experience

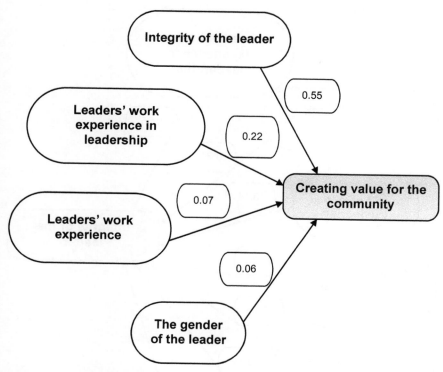

Figure 5.10 Factors affecting the seventh dimension of servant leadership (caring for the community).

Source: Authors.

Table 5.4 Variance and the level of significance of the regression model: 'index of integrity'

Regression model number 8	R	R^2	Adjusted R^2	F	p
Index of integrity	0.583	0.339	0.335	77.036	0.000

$p \leq 0.05$.

in the respondent's perception, the higher will be the respondent's perception of their leader's integrity.

The length of both a respondent's employment and education also has a positive impact, meaning that the longer a respondent has been employed and the higher the respondent's education, the higher is the respondent's perception of their leader's integrity.

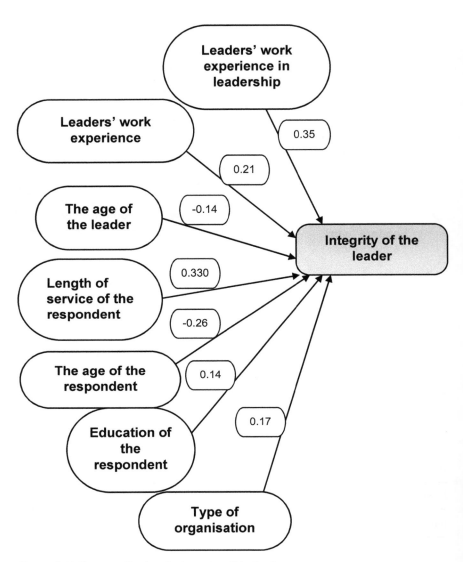

Figure 5.11 Factors affecting the integrity of the leader.

Source: Authors.

On the other hand, the age of the leader as well as the age of the respondent are negatively connected to the dependent variable. This means that the older the leader and the respondent are, the lower is the respondent's perception of their leader's integrity.

In addition to the above, we can see that, in our case, a positive perception of the leader's integrity also depends on whether the assessed leaders and respondents come from a for-profit organisation.[19]

Qualitative assessment

After completing the research, every participating organisation was offered feedback in the form of a direct presentation of the results, which would also include a comparison of the organisation with other organisations.[20] Our offer was accepted by the non-profit organisation as well as nine other for-profit organisations; five of them came from the field of engineering and four from the field of tourism. The non-profit organisation, two engineering organisations and two tourist organisations requested a direct presentation of the results, while the other five only requested the information in written format. The direct presentations were always attended by all executives and leaders from each organisation. We presented the latter with statistical data using tables and graphs and participated in the following substantive discussion.

In the discussions with the leaders, we found that all of them stressed the positive role and importance of ethics and high levels of personal integrity in leading organisations. We also found they are aware of the importance of good relations with the employees and their personal growth, while at the same time they recognise that they should devote more time to this segment of leadership. We did not find any substantive and 'motivational' differences between the leaders of the non-profit organisation and the leaders of the for-profit organisations. The largest difference noticed in the discussion was between the leaders of the non-profit organisation and the leaders of the for-profit organisations on one hand, and the leaders of the organisations in the field of tourism. The latter highlighted a problem, namely the poor commitment and motivation of the employees for work and a lack of employee loyalty of those in charge of organising the company. According to the leaders, the biggest cause of this is the employees' low job security and poor education. The leaders from the non-profit organisation and the other for-profit organisations did not emphasise this problem.

The leaders of those organisations where a direct presentation of the results was asked for rated the feedback and the discussion as useful and practical.

Reflection on identified impacts

The discussion is structured in thematic clusters that were addressed in order to improve their transparency. Thus, we will first deal with the demographic data of the respondents and the assessed leaders. After that, we will discuss the results that were connected with servant leadership, leader integrity, the impact of integrity on servant leadership, the impact of the leaders' demographic details on their integrity and the impact of the respondents' demographic details on both studied phenomena.

The discussion is followed by a presentation and explanation of the final model that was developed on the basis of all the findings.

Demographic data of assessed leaders

At the outset, on the basis of the information on the course of the research and the results of it, we can conclude that we covered a sufficiently large sample of employees in the non-profit organisation and all of the for-profit organisations so that the data can be generalised to the entire population of participating organisations.

Given the differences in the respondents' demographic data, it is worth noting that the percentage of women surveyed from for-profit organisations (47.9 per cent) was significantly higher than the percentage of women surveyed in the non-profit organisation, whereby both figures reflect the actual situation. We believe that the reason for this difference is primarily the content of the work as employees in the non-profit organisation work in the field of providing security, which is more distinctive and appealing to males. For the employees from the for-profit organisations, working in the fields of engineering and tourism, the gender representation is more proportionate. The next difference lies in the educational structure, namely the employees from the for-profit organisations are somewhat better and more highly educated than those in the non-profit organisation, which is contributed to by the fact that half of them come from the engineering field where employees are relatively highly educated. Conversely, in this connection, we found that at the time of conducting the research, a number of employees from the non-profit organisation were in the process of further education (25.1 per cent), slightly more than the employees in the for-profit organisations (23.3 per cent). In our view, this confirms our general thesis that the education level of employees, especially with the advent of a new generation of employees, is gradually increasing. The findings also apply to the non-profit organisation operating in the field of providing security.

It is also worth mentioning the difference in the higher average number of years of employment in the non-profit organisation (15.04/13.09) and the higher average number of years in the for-profit organisation (13.58/9.33). We believe the main reason for this is the difference in the long period of full-time study required before being able to become employed in the for-profit organisations, especially those in the field of development engineering. The second reason for this, in our opinion, is the difference in job security, which is still higher in the non-profit, state organisation.

In addition, it should be noted that almost a quarter of the respondents from the for-profit sector performed tasks in managerial positions (24.7 per cent), while in the non-profit organisation, the share of participating leaders was smaller than 10 per cent (9.2 per cent). We believe that the higher and better results for the leaders assessed in the for-profit organisations are connected to this fact, which complicates the objectivity and simultaneously increases the risk of a biased assessment. Leaders are less sensitive in assessing their own leaders in comparison to their co-workers who are not leaders themselves (Simons 2002). This is particularly the case when it comes to assessing the integrity of the leaders.

Based on the differences among the demographical data of the assessed leaders, we may conclude that more female leaders were assessed in the for-profit organisations (38.6 per cent) than in the non-profit organisation (5.1 per cent). According to our estimates, the reason for this is the same as the differences among the respondents, namely primarily in the content of the work or profession which is, again, more appealing to men in the non-profit organisation. At the same time, our findings confirm the findings of other authors, namely that the number of female leaders in leading positions is generally lower than the number of men in leading positions (Kanjuo Mrčela 1996).

On the other hand, contrary to the respondents, we found that the leaders assessed in the non-profit organisation are, on average, better educated than the leaders assessed in the for-profit organisations. The reason for this is due to the poor education of the leaders of the tourist organisations versus the leaders from the engineering organisations since they, are in fact, separate from the leaders of the tourist organisations, better educated than the leaders of the non-profit organisation.

Servant leadership

Regarding the servant leadership style, we found that the employees evaluated the conceptual skills of their leaders best and rated their willingness to firstly take care of the employees the worst. The finding is true for the leaders in the non-profit organisation as well as in the for-profit organisations.

Putting employees first, when seen from the perspective of the worst rated factors against the best rated factor, follows the factors of helping employees with their personal growth, emotional support, empowerment, caring for the community, ethical behaviour and conduct and conceptual skills, which are, as already stated, the best rated factor of servant leadership. The order is, despite the statistically significant differences in all seven factors, the same in the non-profit organisation as it is in the for-profit organisations. There is only one exception in helping the employees with their personal growth and emotional support which are 'mutually exchanged'. In the non-profit organisation, the emotional support is ranked third from the bottom, while it is ranked second from the bottom in the for-profit organisations. Regarding the leader's help with the employees' personal growth, it is the other way around. Each of the seven factors of servant leadership is significantly positively connected among themselves with a risk level of $p=0.00$.

We can conclude from the above that in both the non-profit organisation and the for-profit organisations, which were studied in the survey, the concern for the employees was in last place. Although the average values of the worst ranked factors are higher than 3 and 4, we believe that servant leadership, which excels in putting employees in first place, is not particularly present. Similarly, in a somewhat different context, with the help of semi-structured interviews with leaders from both types of organisations, Arnold and Loughlin (2010) found that leaders in the context of the individual caring for the employees are more inclined to support employees in decision-making rather than being concerned for the employees' personal growth.

In our opinion, the reason for that is multi-faceted, having both a human and cultural nature, and is also linked to the individual organisational culture. This is confirmed by the results of the GLOBE study from 2004, where it was found that in Slovenia, it is a general characteristic of leaders to express power, their high autonomy and their independent decision-making, specifically, more than inspiration, a collective attitude and taking care of the personal needs of employees (Northouse 2010).

In contrast, we found that the employees perceive the ethical behaviour and conduct of their leaders and their leaders' caring for the community relatively well, right after the highest perception of the conceptual skills of their leaders. Thus, for this segment of servant leadership (ethics of leaders and their caring for the community), unlike putting the employees first, we can confirm that in our environment it is relatively well present. Empowering employees, emotional support and helping employees with their personal growth came right after this factor of leadership and before the factor of putting the employees first.

In determining the differences between non-profit and for-profit organisations, we found a statistically significant difference in all seven factors of servant leadership in favour of the leaders in the for-profit organisations. Thus, contrary to our expectations, we found that servant leadership is statistically significantly less present in the non-profit organisation than in the for-profit organisations. In doing so, we found that the reason for this probably does not lie in the differences between the non-profit and for-profit organisations (Drucker 2001, 2004, 2005) but mainly in the organisational structure of the studied state, non-profit organisation from the field of providing security. This one falls within the framework of large hierarchical organisations with a mechanical bureaucracy, which does not apply to any of the participating for-profit organisations. Therefore, below an attempt will be made to explain the obtained results with the help of the findings of Weber and Mintzberg and a few other authors.

According to Mintzberg (1979), for the studied non-profit organisation with a machine bureaucracy, it is typical to have formalised and standardised work processes, centralisation, technocracies, high specialisation and large operational units. The author adds that such a structure, which reflects a clear and authoritative hierarchy and specific communication channels, was first defined by Max Weber. The latter found that a bureaucratic organisation is based on rules, skills, written and impersonal acts in dealing with people (Weber 2009). Možina et al. (2002) noted in this connection that Weber saw in bureaucracy, a way of managing, although he also saw in it as a lever for the ethical behaviour of organisations in the prevention of unwanted behaviour. Conversely, the authors mentioned a critical aspect of the state bureaucracy, namely its inefficiency and the finding that individuals work in such an environment because of the rules rather than because of service users. Even Schermerhorn (2008) notes that today the term bureaucracy is often accompanied with a negative connotation, whereby the reasons for this include stiffness and the employees' apathy.

On the other side, Pagon (2003b) notes that the traditional bureaucratic model of the organisation, to which our non-profit organisation belongs, is characterised by a one track career path system. This means that an employee starts working in the lowest workplace and then gradually progresses up the hierarchy. From the point of view of modernisation, the author advocates the introduction of a multiple-track career system based on relevant qualifications, experience and skills, as the author believes that it is not necessary for a good leader to start at the bottom of the hierarchy.

Northouse (2010) contends that the solution lies in shifting from a bureaucratic mindset towards a more flexible structure based more on mutual cooperation among the employees. Through this, instead of merely following their leaders, the employees increasingly become their co-workers in achieving the organisational goals. This is also supported by the conclusions of Lustig et al. (2010) based on their empirical findings, where they found that leaders in the for-profit sector put more emphasis on trust than leaders in the non-profit, public sector. The latter are more inclined to supervision and compliance with the rules, are less flexible and more long-term-oriented, making it more difficult for them to accept change. The reason for this probably lies in the reasons described above.

The solution to remedy such a situation lies in a professional bureaucracy which, unlike a mechanical bureaucracy, allows employees to perform work more independently (Mintzberg 1979). A professional bureaucracy is characterised by a bureaucracy without centralisation and where the work of the employees is based on knowledge and skills, wherein the standards are determined by professional associations outside each particular organisation.[21] Unlike a mechanical bureaucracy, which is based on an organisational hierarchy and authority, a professional bureaucracy emphasises authority of a professional nature and the power of expertise.

Building on the above, we may conclude that if the studied non-profit organisation focused more on a professional bureaucracy, based on the power of knowledge, it would probably be easier for servant leadership and leader integrity to manifest.

Leader integrity

Given the results concerning leader integrity, we may conclude that the respondents rated it relatively highly as the average value of the index of integrity is 5.69 on a seven-point scale. In so doing, the employees rated personal integrity the highest in the context of their fair attitude to the organisation and the lowest in the context of fair and objective relations of the leader towards the employees and in taking responsibility for their own behaviour. At the same time, between the leaders of the for-profit and non-profit organisations, there are statistically significant differences in favour of the leaders from the for-profit organisations, but only in the relation of the leaders towards their employees. In the relationship between the leaders towards the organisations they lead, statistically significant differences were not found. In our opinion, the causes for this are similar to those for servant leadership and can be traced back to the negative impact the bureaucratic hierarchical structure has on the employees' work. On one hand, the results show a fairly high level of leader integrity through the prism of fairness in the relationship towards the organisation, while on the other hand, there is a *large gap between the declarative values and the actual behaviour in relation to the employees*. Leaders who act in this way and, for example, blame employees for their own mistakes, as we have found with the questionnaire on integrity, can be described as quasi or pseudo leaders (Bass and Steidlmeier 1999). In this context, and in line with the content of the PLIS questionnaire, which was used in the research, we believe that the management of employees in which the leader's integrity shows also means that those leaders accept the risks stemming from the upright posture and principled conduct. At the same time, the leader speaks the truth, which has a significant impact on the effectiveness of their leadership and employee loyalty, and does not act in an opportune way; instead, the leader defends what is right, even though such behaviour will be detrimental (Lennick and Kiel 2009). All this contributes to greater confidence in the leader, while on the other hand, the loss of confidence is consequently also associated with a loss of reputation and respect.

The employees assessed the personal integrity of the leaders, or the absence of the leader's unethical behaviour (Craig and Gustafson 1998), on average, even better than the ethical aspect of servant leadership. Unfortunately, this does not necessarily mean the presence of exemplary ethical behaviour (Palanski and Yammarino 2007), although integrity by itself contains a moral ideal and not just a moral minimum. The established index of integrity in the non-profit organisation (5.5) and the for-profit organisations (6) is relatively high and indicates that the employees have a good opinion about the integrity of their leaders. It should be reiterated that the PLIS measurement instrument, which was used in our research, mostly measures the subjective perception of the employees and one aspect of integrity and not, for example, the consistency between the spoken words and actions of the leaders (Simons 1999, 2002). It is based on the utilitarian concept and evaluation of leaders regarding their behaviour according to established rules, which provide the greatest good for the greatest number of people (Craig and Gustafson 1998).

Moreover, the finding that the majority of the studied organisations consider the integrity of their leaders to be positive is very important as personal integrity provides organisational integrity and vice versa (Solomon 1992). In addition, a good organisational policy strengthens and promotes integrity, which is consistent with Aristotle's approach to business ethics (Solomon 2004). Although this factor was not assessed in our study, we believe that in all the organisations that agreed to participate they were at least aware of the importance of integrity. This manifests in the fact that more than half of the participating organisations sought our feedback in the form of data analysis, while a quarter of the participants even requested a direct presentation with a discussion. Conversely, it is significant that the cooperation with us was renounced by organisations, which themselves were publicly regarded as being socially responsible with a strong concern for their employees. That is, according to our estimates, important from the perspective of setting an example for the employees since, as already stated by Kohlberg (in Brown et al. 2005: 117), the majority of employees are inspired by the ethical conduct of their leaders and other significant individuals. In doing so, personal integrity undoubtedly has a very important role.

In addition, the findings are important from the perspective of the moral development of the leader because leaders at the highest level of moral development act under the influence of universal ethical principles such as fairness, equality and so on. (Burns 2010). In our view, this means that the higher the leader's integrity, the higher that leader is on the scale of moral development and is therefore more susceptible to universal ethical principles, which are specific to the third level of moral development according to Kohlberg (1975). At the same time, such a leader is less susceptible to the influence of others, including his superiors (Peterson 2004), which, in our opinion, is also very important.

In connection with the leaders' integrity, we want to specifically emphasise the argument that leaders would behave better with their employees if they belonged to another ethnic or national group. We found that employees from both types of organisations at least agreed exactly with this statement which, in our opinion, points to a relatively insignificant problem and a good situation in our cultural environment.[22]

The impact of integrity on servant leadership

With the analysis of the impact of integrity on the servant leadership style we found that it has a positive impact on all seven dimensions of the servant leadership style. The greatest impact can be observed on the ethical behaviour and conduct of the leader and the smallest impact on their conceptual skills. This seems logical as personal integrity is a virtue, a prerequisite and a foundation of ethical conduct.

It also seems logical to us that the leader's integrity is more connected to the emotional support offered to employees, caring for the community, helping employees in their personal growth and putting employees first rather than by empowering them. All four dimensions or dimensions of the servant leadership style are in fact directly (personally) connected with the way people are treated, while empowerment, like conceptual skills, even though it means the raising of new servant leaders, is more related to the way of leading an organisation and performing tasks.

On the basis of the results, we can conclude that the higher the leader's integrity, the more the leader is susceptible to ethical behaviour and conduct, caring for the community in which the organisation operates, fair and objective treatment of employees and the greatest good for the greatest number of people (the utilitarian aspect); however, it is still also relatively close to altruism and care for others. All of the above is included in the characteristics of the servant leadership style, which, in turn, means we can also defend the thesis that the higher the leader's integrity, the more the leader assumes the servant leadership style and that personal integrity impacts the servant leadership style. This was also confirmed in our study. In addition, with the help of our analysis, we also identified other impacts on the servant leadership that will be discussed below. Prior to this, we want to first repeat and emphasise that by confirming that personal integrity positively impacts servant leadership, the aim of our study was achieved. With this, we were also able to confirm and upgrade the findings of Washington et al. (2006), who found a positive correlation between employees' perception about the importance of certain leadership values among which, in addition to competence and empathy, integrity was ranked.

The impact of the leaders' demographic factors on the servant leadership style

In addition to personal integrity, we found that the socio-demographic characteristics of the leaders, such as gender, age, work and leadership experience, also impact servant leadership. An impact of education was not found. We also found an impact of the organisation from which the leader comes. The findings related to the leader's gender, age, education and the type of organisation represent something new for us as we were not expecting them. Regarding the gender of the leaders, we found that female leaders are more prone to putting employees first, helping employees in their personal growth, caring for the community and are more emphatic than their male counterparts.

Washington et al. (2006) similarly found that female leaders reflected the servant leadership style to a greater extent than their male counterparts. The same is with Arnold and Loughlin (2010), who found that female leaders preferred to sacrifice their own interests for the benefit of employee development than their male counterparts. This is in fact very much in the spirit of the philosophy of the servant leadership style.

In addition, with the help of the PLIS questionnaire, Peterson (2004) found that female leaders are less susceptible to unethical behaviour than their male counterparts. Kanjuo Mrčela (1996) argued that leadership in the new millennium will be increasingly based on attributes that are socially identified as feminine (for example, emotional support and empathy). Mrčela rejects the division between the male and female leadership styles and sees a trend in the withdrawal of 'rigid, hierarchically oriented leadership styles in favour of participative styles, with a fundamental concern for human values and the quality of working life'.

Given the above, we believe that female leaders will in any case be at least as susceptible to the servant leadership style as their male counterparts, which is obviously not true in reverse. We believe that the future research will provide a clearer answer.

In relation to the demographic variable of the age of the leaders, contrary to our expectations, we found a negative impact, namely on the conceptual skills and ethical behaviour and conduct of the leaders. This means that the employees perceive better conceptual skills and more ethical behaviour in their younger leaders. We believe the reason for this is associated with the inter-generational differences in knowledge about leadership, the relationship towards leadership and the excessive criticism of the younger generations aimed at the older and more experienced generations. In Slovenia, this is even more pronounced due to the transition from one social system (socialism) to another (capitalism) in the early 1990s. This impact is not connected with the leader's education level, which will be outlined below.

Notwithstanding the foregoing, we believe that in different circumstances, the age of the leaders can have a positive impact on servant leadership. This will be discussed later on. The same applies to the work and leadership experience, for which we found that, as opposed to the age of the leaders, they have a positive impact on servant leadership. In doing so, we also found that the leadership experience of the leaders impacts all seven dimensions of servant leadership, while the leader's work experience impacts their conceptual skills, helping employees in their personal growth and caring for the community. As mentioned, the positive impact of work experience was already seen as a prerequisite for the development of wisdom by Aristotle, Rousseau, Greenleaf and others.

For the education of the leaders we found, contrary to our predictions, that education does not affect any of the seven dimensions of servant leadership. Apparently, the attitude of the leaders towards their employees, caring for the community and the ethical behaviour and conduct of the leaders are more associated with the leader's integrity, their moral development, their work and leadership experience and their inner feeling for a fellow human, as well as the leader's gender, than education.

Regarding the impact of the type of organisation on servant leadership, we found that it is relevant in relation to two dimensions of servant leadership, namely the leaders' conceptual skills and the leaders' ethical behaviour and conduct. In both cases, the impact is statistically more significant in the for-profit organisations, which was something we did not expect. We believe that, besides the negative impact of the mechanical bureaucratic structure on the employees' work, we also need to take into account the specifics of the work (providing security, development in engineering and tourism), making it hard to discuss such an impact in general as the difference between for-profit and non-profit organisations.

The impact of the demographic factors on the leaders' integrity

The results show that the leadership experience of the leaders and their work experience both have the largest impact on the personal integrity of the leaders as well. This confirms the general thesis that one strengthens one's own integrity throughout one's life, which is similar to wisdom, which increases proportionally to the accumulation of life experiences. As already mentioned in connection to servant leadership, where we also found a positive impact of work and leadership experience of the leaders, the discussion has been going on from the time of Ancient Greece and Aristotle.

Conversely, the age of the leader, similar in the case of servant leadership, also has a negative impact on personal integrity. In other words, the older the leader is, the worse the respondents' perception of the leader's integrity. We believe the reasons for this are the same as with servant leadership and that they are linked to the cultural environment and the social situation in Slovenia. Otherwise, given the identified positive impact of leadership and work experience of the leaders in relation to the wisdom and life experiences, the old age of the leaders should have been a positive predictor of both integrity and servant leadership.

At the same time, we found that the magnitude of the leader's personal integrity impacts the fact whether the leader is employed in a non-profit or for-profit organisation. In 27 of the 31 variables of the PLIS questionnaire, we found statistically significant differences between the leaders from both sectors, namely always in the favour of the leaders from for-profit organisations. We believe the reasons for this primarily relate to the impact of the mechanical bureaucracy on the work of the employees.

The impact of the demographic factors of the respondents

In our research, we also found impacts of individual demographic variables of the respondents or employees on their perception of the servant leadership, namely age, education, years of employment and their position in the organisation. Regarding the age of the respondents, we found a negative impact, which means that the older the employee, the more critical they are in assessing the offered help the leader provides for their personal growth or that they detect such help worse than their younger colleagues. We believe it is not necessary for this information to reflect the passivity of the leaders, but it can also reflect the indifference or insensitivity of older employees regarding this type of their leader's help, which in turn affects their assessment.

Regarding the education of the employees, we found the exact opposite of what we found concerning the education of the leaders; namely, in this case, it has a positive impact on the perception of conceptual skills, empowerment, helping employees in their personal growth and the ethical behaviour and conduct of the leaders. In our opinion, this might, on one hand, indicate a better understanding of the function of leadership from the perspective of the educated employees, while on the other, it can indicate their greater independence and autonomy from their leaders in carrying out their work. In any case, the findings show that encouraging employees to engage in further education and invest in their education is certainly beneficial for the organisation.

A positive impact on the perception of empowerment and the emotional support of the leaders was also found with the number of years of the employees' employment in the organisation. This shows that the length of employment has a positive impact on the relationship between the employees and their leaders. For those workers who have been employed for a longer periods of time, the leaders are more prone to giving them greater autonomy in performing tasks, and they are more disposed to establishing a more personal relationship with them than with employees who have only been in the organisation for a short time.

In relation to the demographic characteristics of the employees, we also found that their perception of servant leadership is impacted by whether they work in a managerial post or not. The results show that employees who are themselves leaders better perceive their own leaders from the perspectives of empowerment, helping employees in their personal growth, putting the employees first and the emotional support for the employees who are not leaders. As previously mentioned, this shows lower criticality and a lack of objectivity or, as Simons (2002) notes, this suggests the leaders are less sensitive in assessing their leaders than their co-workers who are not leaders.

To sum up, employees or respondents can be divided into two categories. The first includes those who are more critical of the leader's conduct, namely older employees, those who are not leaders themselves and employees who are less educated. The second category includes younger employees, those who are leaders themselves, those who are better educated and those who have been employed for longer periods of time. Given that the latter category, which is less critical of the leader's conduct, includes employees who are leaders themselves, this fact certainly affects the objectivity of their assessments or the reduced sensitivity in their evaluations of their leaders (Simons 2002).

A similar impact of the respondents' demographic factors, rather than the perception of servant leadership, comes from respondents' perception of the leader's integrity. Here too we found an impact of age, education and years of employment. Age has a negative effect, which means that the older the employee, the more critical they are of their leader's integrity, while education and years of employment both have a positive impact. Consequently, older employees who are less educated assess their leader's integrity lower than older employees who are more educated.

Final model

Based on all of the theoretical and empirical findings, along with the opinions and views treated in the debate, we have created the ultimate and final model (Figure 5.12). With this model we wish to present those factors that, in our estimate, affect the servant guidance and integrity of leaders and the direction of those influences. According to this, we studied the impact of integrity, socio-demographic data and the type of organisation in the servant leadership style, the latter being placed in the centre of the model.

As can be seen from the discussion thus far, servant leadership is influenced by various factors. It is via such factors that we can affirm that the personal integrity of the leader, leadership experience and work experience in general have a positive impact on servant leadership. The personal integrity of the leader, together with leadership experience, has the greatest impact on all factors of servant leadership studied in this book. This means that the concern for the strengthening of personal integrity and the moral development of leaders, including harvesting leadership work experience, is vital for the success and development of an organisation

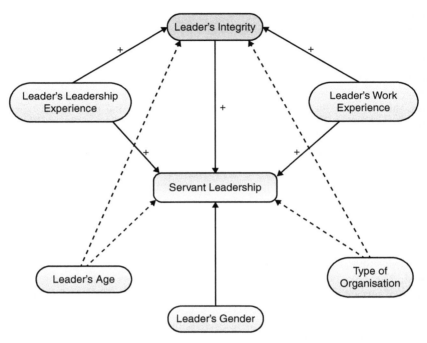

Figure 5.12 The influence of integrity on the servant leadership style: the final model.
Source: Authors.

coupled with staff satisfaction and that of other stakeholders. The same concern applies to strengthening the personal integrity and moral development of employees who are not managers. It is from among them that new leaders emerge and, when building up their experience, a very important role is played by the example set by their leaders. It is therefore even more important that leaders recognise the importance of their own integrity, not only in the context of the absence of the unethical behaviour and practices we have examined in our study. It is equally important for their words and deeds to be consistent, which should reflect the values they promote and are part of the mission and organisational strategies. At the same time, their actions must reflect as many virtues as possible if we want the employees to have a good example of what type of conduct is required. All of this has an impact on the integrity of leaders that is consequently also reflected in the intensity of the organisational integrity, which ultimately affects the sustainable development of an organisation.

As already mentioned, the work and leadership experience of leaders is also useful at keeping a positive impact in terms of conceptual skills. This is especially understandable because both knowledge and wisdom demand plenty of time and experience. It is also understandable in all the other factors of servant leadership; the ability to empower employees, employee care, placing employees in the spotlight, emotional support, ethical behaviour and showing concern for the community. All of these factors are prerequisites for a leader to operate outwardly and focus on others. There are many more prerequisites for this and we have, along with the above mentioned, only touched on a few, namely, altruism, human nature, moral development and so on. This all means that man's personality must primarily be tuned so that moral conduct and a concern for others are a genuine way of motivation. Second, maturity is yet another precondition for this, as it is only then that the role of a leader can work in a servant way. The cornerstone of this is, of course, that through moral behaviour and conduct, integrity is strengthened and, likewise, other virtues pursuant to this may be strengthened. Therefore, both the work and leadership experience of leaders is of the utmost importance in relation to both servant leadership and personal integrity.

As evident from our discussion, the gender of leaders also influences servant leadership. We found that among all factors of servant leadership, where the concern for both employees and the wider community is at the forefront, women as leaders are more susceptible to this factor. In conceptual skills, empowerment and ethical behaviour among leaders of both genders, no significant differences were identified. Accordingly, the role of female leaders of organisations that care for employees and their development and are, furthermore, aware of their responsibility to society and the community where the organisation is located, is likewise very important.

The survey results did not confirm our assumptions that servant leadership is more typical of non-profit than for-profit organisations. We will therefore reconsider our initial mental construct. We established that servant leadership depends more on various factors, with organisational structure being at the top of the list (e.g. bureaucracy, hierarchy and so on), followed by the type of organisation itself. Moreover, it is also surely affected by the performance criteria and values that every organisation sets for itself. One of them is definitely customer satisfaction, which is especially important for for-profit organisations as it ultimately affects their very existence. This leads to the fact that the leadership of an organisation, with the aim to satisfy both customers and service users, must primarily make a positive impact on employees who provide those services. This form of management style is transferred, although in a spurious way, through the employees to the customers, and consequently, affects the economic performance of an organisation. In the case of non-profit organisations, as we discovered in our case, the declarative mission and written values alone do not suffice. In addition, with an appropriate organisational structure, preferably one that is not a rigid, mechanical bureaucracy, it is also necessary to establish performance criteria. Then, most importantly, these criteria have to be taken into account and consistently measured in a suitable manner. In so doing, we note that a large hierarchical organisation that functions according to the principles of a mechanistic bureaucracy apparently does not offer the most appropriate environment for developing servant leadership or strengthening the integrity of both leaders and employees. This is also evidenced by our empirical results. Therefore, we believe that if due to various circumstances, an organisation requires the existence of a mechanistic bureaucratic structure, this can be applied to all the lessons learned in the field of personnel management and we should consider replacing the rigid mechanistic bureaucracy, at least in certain segments, with a more flexible organisational structure. It can be said that professional bureaucracy and adhocracy amount to more than a mechanistic bureaucracy based on the knowledge and skills of employees and, hence, certainly provides a better environment for developing social skills. Even better than that, and according to our estimates, is the fact that the organisational environment focusing on the mission of an organisation also subordinates the rest to the mission. Moreover, in our assessment, there can only be an organisational environment where managers and employees at the centre of the very mission primarily show a concern for others, while their behaviour is based on their undisputed personal integrity and moral conduct.

The last factor included in our study and in our assessment of the impact on servant leadership is important: the age of the leader. Unlike work and managerial experience that positively affect both the servant leadership and the integrity of the leaders, with the age of a leader this is clearly not the case. In our view, it depends on various circumstances. This means that it cannot be predicted. In our case, we established a negative effect of the age of leaders based on their conceptual skills and ethical behaviour and conduct. As already stated, the reason for such findings is chiefly attributed to both intergenerational differences in their knowledge of conduct as well as excessive criticism (younger versus older). The outcome of this score is certainly affected by the choice of the studied organisations as we believe that with education, health, culture, marketing, advertising and so on, one could arrive at a different result.

Based on the above, we estimate that our study has an applied value and great practical potential. It reflects the interplay between theory and practice, with an emphasis on the personal integrity and moral conduct of leaders and their concern for employees. The importance of what has been written was, to some extent, confirmed by means of the qualitative approach and talks with the leaders of the participating organisations.

With our study we want to support and encourage the view that all efforts should be concentrated on the correct selection of leaders and their career development, regardless of the type or structure of organisation.

Summary

Despite the previously mentioned limitation, based on the analysis of this study's results, we can conclude that the goals of the study were achieved, and thus, to a certain extent, with the help of specific insights from the field of psychology, we have contributed to the development of both fields, namely ethics as well as the field of management.

Based on the analysis of the primary and secondary theoretical resources with which we have examined and compared the theoretical concepts from Ancient Greece to the present day and assessed the similarities and differences between the two areas of research, we have managed to use the empirical approach in analysing the degree of influence of the leader's personal integrity on the servant leadership style in the non-profit organisation and in the for-profit organisation and at the same time in confirming such an influence. According to the available information, research oriented in such a way has not been previously conducted before. We have thereby also contributed to development of the field of empirical research of integrity in relation to leadership, where Vicchio (1997), Craig and Gustafson (1998), Palanski and Yammarino (2007, 2009), Carroll (2009) and Northouse (2010) identified a lack of empirical research.

A new contribution to the development of science is also represented by the results of the employees' perception of their leaders as well as the finding that the servant leadership style is present among the leaders of the for-profit and non-profit organisations. Contrary to our predictions, we found that servant leadership is more present in the for-profit organisations than in their non-profit counterpart. Our understandings of the reasons for this were shown in the previous discussion. In short, we can summarise that, according to our estimates, the main reasons for this are connected to the impact of the mechanical bureaucratic structure of the large non-profit organisation has on the leadership and the relationship to the employees, the type of job (providing security, development engineering and tourism) and the structure of our sample of respondents. The respondents from the for-profit sector were on average better educated than the respondents from the non-profit organisation while, in addition, more leaders were included among the respondents from the for-profit organisations than their non-profit counterpart, which certainly affects the results. We also found that female leaders show servant leadership traits considerably more than their male counterparts. Although the results are also a consequence of the statistical factors and not solely the actually observed differences between sectors, they are certainly useful when it comes to the design of policies in the field of human resource management. This is especially true where leadership, which is based on values, social responsibility, caring for employees, a flexible organisation and so on, is preferred. To this end, we have formed a final model on the basis of our own findings. We believe that, given its applied nature, the study represents a practical contribution to the theory of ethics and management, namely in the fields of personal integrity and the servant leadership style.

At the same time, our contribution also lies in the fact that we simultaneously explored the ethical aspect of leadership, as also advocated by several authors (Burns 1984, Simons 1999, Turner et al. 2002, Parry and Proctor-Thomson 2002, Brown et al. 2005, Spencer 2007, Northouse 2010, Winston 2010, Prosser 2010). We did not regard ethical leadership as an independent concept of leadership, but as Reed et al. (2011) and Dion (2012) viewed it, as a basis for the common theoretical framework of servant leadership, transformational leadership, authentic leadership and spiritual leadership. The mentioned leadership styles are based on the personal integrity of leaders, values, ethical behaviour and leading by example as well as caring for others.

With all that, like those who advocate the interweaving of theory and practice, we followed the recommendations of Avolio (2010), in the fact that such interlacing or participation is essential for effective leadership research today.

Notes

1 With the help of a t-test, we assessed the statistically significant differences between the demographic data of the assessed leaders in the non-profit and for-profit organisations.
2 A factor analysis of variables of both measurement instruments was used to verify the findings of Liden et al. (2008) showing that the questionnaire that measures servant leadership (servant leadership measure) consists of a seven-factor structure, as well as the findings of Craig and Gustafson (1998) indicating that the questionnaire that measures the personal integrity of leaders (PLIS) is one-dimensional or that it has a single-factor structure. Given the model, we set the factors of servant leadership as the dependent variables and the factor of integrity as an independent variable. Which variables represent a specific factor can be accurately seen in the next section.
3 These factors were used in assessing and analysing the correlations and in the regression analysis.
4 The result represents a reversed average value of the derived variables. This, for example, means that the original value of the derived variable on a seven-level scale is 2.307 instead of 5.693.
5 As the data are very extensive in this part, we do not present them here; instead, the interested reader can obtain them from the authors.
6 Likewise, we found that all extracted communalities are greater than 0.3 (the minimum is 571), and that the same applies to all factor weights (the minimum is 696), which fully belong to the first factor, 'the index integrity'.
7 For the involvement of an individual variable, we took the degree of probability of $p < 0.05$ into account.
8 The data in the stage of explaining the variance of all seven factors of servant leadership (dependent variable) and the data on whether the regression models as a whole are statistically significant, are all shown in the Appendix. Thereafter follows a presentation of the assessments of the regression coefficients for each regression model separately. These data are shown in the form of explanatory models, namely, starting from the initial research model provided (see Figure 4.1). At the very end, we present the data of the regression analysis with the index of integrity as a dependent variable. Detailed data from the regression analysis are shown in the Appendix, that is, the level of explained variance of the dependent variables, the statistical significance of the regression model and the assessment of the regression coefficients, which are specifically marked in the text.
9 The perception of conceptual competencies is statistically significantly higher in for-profit organisations ($F=13.018$; $p=0.000$).
10 The perception of empowerment is statistically significantly higher among respondents who are leaders ($F=7.683$; $p=0.000$).
11 ($F=1.908$; $p=0.002$).
12 The perception of helping employees with personal growth is statistically significantly higher among respondents who are leaders ($F=13.275$; $p=0.000$).
13 ($F=2.970$; $p=0.000$).
14 The perception of putting the employees first is statistically significantly higher among respondents who are leaders ($F=0.772$; $p=0.000$).
15 The perception of ethical behaviour and conduct is statistically significantly higher in for-profit organisations ($F=11.557$; $p=0.000$).
16 ($F=0.004$; $p=0.007$).

17 The perception of emotional support is statistically significantly higher among respondents who are leaders (F=11.891; p=0.000).

18 (F=0.007; p=0.000).

19 The perception of integrity is statistically significantly higher in for-profit organisations (F=46.710; p=0.000).

20 The comparison was made by comparing an individual for-profit organisation with the remaining selected profit organisations from the same sector (for example, a tourist organisation in relation to the other tourist organisations). The non-profit organisation was compared with the rest of the for-profit organisations combined.

21 Such a case is a medical chamber.

22 This does not apply to the USA, where the questionnaire had been carried out. It concerns the same variable, which was, due to the excessive deviation in its kurtosis, excluded from the multivariate data analysis.

6   Conclusion

Based on our findings, we may conclude that we have found the importance of personal integrity for the process of leadership while exploring the importance, philosophy and effects of servant leadership. We found that personal integrity has a significantly positive impact on the servant leadership style. Our goal, which is connected to raising awareness about the importance of personal integrity and the significance of caring for others, especially in the context of leadership, can be considered as a lifelong project. We can also understand it as an answer to the question of what we ourselves can do to improve the situation in the field of leadership, which Greenleaf described as one of the easiest issues, yet he himself found to be extremely difficult to answer (2002a: 29). The answer, in addition to establishing an objective, also requires a vision and a dream because every great achievement is born from big dreams (Greenleaf 1998, 2002a).

We also tried to point to the importance of ethical behaviour and integrity through a historical overview of considerations and findings of global philosophical authorities that discussed whether it is sufficient for ethical behaviour to merely hold knowledge (Socrates, Plato) or whether it is necessary to also behave in a certain way (Aristotle), or whether ethical behaviour is based on reason (Descartes, Spinoza, Kant) and so on. By dealing with virtue ethics, virtues and justice as the most perfect virtue (Aristotle 2002), we attempted to show the foundation of personal integrity, which is influenced by other moral rules such as the categorical imperative (Kant 2003). Conversely, we emphasised ethical leadership as good and desired leadership, as well as the servant leadership style, whereby the significance of good deeds and serving others was already stressed by Socrates and Aristotle. With the broader examination of both studied concepts, we wished to show the similarities and differences between the various factors and thereby place personal integrity and servant leadership within the whole and within two areas – business ethics and personnel management.

Previous findings clearly show that the leader's personal integrity and good leadership go hand in hand, that they are not in conflict and that in the long run, leadership cannot be successful without integrity. This confirms our thesis that the higher the individual's integrity, the better the individual is as a leader. It should be noted that the findings do not suggest that leaders should only employ one particular leadership style. The findings show that leadership styles intertwine and differ and oppose each other in individual segments. In our case, this means that servant leadership is most related to transformational leadership while still including elements from the LMX theory, authentic and spiritual leadership styles. On the other hand, personal integrity is extremely important for both the servant and transformational leadership styles. This is all the more true because both leadership styles fall within the scope of ethical leadership, which emphasises the moral aspect of leadership, which today represents what society wants and needs. At the same time, servant leadership is important in terms of the individual's moral development (Kohlberg 1975) because a leader with a high level of integrity, who acts with their own moral conscience and understands the benefits of others in the first place, has a feeling for the universal ethical principles ranks at the highest level – the post-conventional level of moral development.

In relation to personal integrity, we must understand that it represents perfection and an ideal to which man strives, and that due to human nature, man can only approximately come close to it. Regarding this, we fully agree with Moore who says that 'with ideals, we think about the state of something, which would be absolutely perfect' (2000: 255). Therefore, it is important to maintain realistic expectations and be aware that the higher the leader's integrity, the better the example that is set for the leader's employees with regard to how to act. In this respect, Kirkpatrick and Locke (1991) are convinced that an organisation gets from its employees the same type of behaviour the organisation advocates. At the same time, it is necessary to be aware that in the field of ethical behaviour and conduct in accordance with a high level of integrity any type of coercive practice is ineffective. Two things here are most important, that is, personal knowledge about what is right and the usefulness of a type of behaviour as well as one's own will, which Socrates already emphasised by saying that 'the soul will not hold any enforced doctrine' (Plato 2002, 396). It is similar with ethical codes, mission statements, strategies and other documents that set the desired values, namely that they must be lived in practice or otherwise they are worthless.

With the help of individual findings from the field of psychology, we tried to take a step towards the field of research on integrity and virtue ethics as well as the servant and ethical leadership style, which are today seen as necessary (Burns 1984, Craig and Gustafson 1998, Simons 1999, Turner et al. 2002, Parry and Proctor-Thomson 2002, Brown et al. 2005, Spencer 2007, Palanski and Yammarino 2007, 2009, Carroll 2009, Northouse, 2010, Prosser 2010, Winston 2010).

We found that the higher the leader's integrity in the perception of employees, the more the leader will express ethical behaviour and conduct, emotional support for employees, care for the community, helping employees with personal growth, putting employees first, empowerment and conceptual skills. All of these are dimensions of servant leadership, leading us to conclude that the higher the leader's integrity, the more the leader will practice servant leadership. We simultaneously also found that servant leadership is positively impacted by the work and leadership experience of the leader and that in comparison with their male counterparts, female leaders are more susceptible to the four dimensions of servant leadership, namely, helping employees with their personal growth, putting the employees first, emotional support and caring for the community. Conversely, our findings support the findings of Washington et al. (2006), that is, that female leaders reflect the servant leadership style to a greater extent than male leaders. Our findings also support the findings of Robbins and Langton (2003), showing that female leaders are more prone to managing relations and strengthening the self-image of the employees, and also support the findings of Arnold and Loughlin (2010), revealing that female leaders are more prone to sacrificing their own interest for the benefit of employee development. Our findings also coincide with the findings of Kanjuo Mrčela (1996), namely that leadership in the new millennium will be increasingly based on the attributes that are deemed to be feminine (for example emotional, support and caring for relations).

In addition to the positive impacts found in our study, we identified the negative impact of the age of leaders on their conceptual skills and their ethical behaviour and conduct. This surprised us because, according to the findings of other researchers (Crane and Matten 2004, Bartholomew 2006), we had not expected age to have an impact on the servant leadership style. On the other hand, we were also surprised because the detected negative impact is not consistent with the found positive impact of the work and leadership experience on leadership, as was already discussed by Aristotle. It seems that the reason for this lies in the specific cultural contexts that we already mentioned in the discussion.

We were also surprised by the finding that the education of the leader does not affect the leader's leadership. We had expected the very opposite as such an impact was observed by other authors (Šter 1994, Crane and Matten 2004); clearly, other influences such as leader integrity, their work and leadership experience as well as their gender are more important.

Given the fact that throughout history it has been shown that the future and destiny of mankind depends largely on its morality and the power of it (Šter 1994), we can see the significance of personal integrity in a wider context. Unfortunately, George and Sims (2007) noted that due to the unethical behaviour of many leaders in recent years, and their primary focus on their self-interest, trust in leadership is at its lowest level in the last 50 years. According to our estimates, the solution to this situation is certainly the systematic strengthening of personal and organisational integrity and ethical behaviour, which is focused on care for the employees as well as other stakeholders. That is because, as Waddock (2007) notes, tomorrow's leaders will not only be confronted with the requirement for effective work in complex and varied business environments, but also with an increasingly expressed requirement for transparent and responsible behaviour. To this end, we formed a final applied model, with the positive impact of personal integrity on servant (ethical) leadership at the centre.

In this regard, it again seems important to emphasise Aristotle's finding that virtue 'manifests because of the same reasons which in turn also strengthens it (and if these reasons change) and vice versa' (2002: 80). This also applies to personal integrity with which man is not born, rather, it is similar to all the other virtues, it is obtained through learning and practice (Crane and Matten 2004). Behaving in accordance with integrity is anything but easy, although Aristotle already noted that 'no human activity is as consistent as those made in accordance with virtue ... such acts do not disintegrate into oblivion' (2002: 66–7).

Before we conclude, we would like to highlight a few considerations of Spinoza, Socrates and Plato who analogously reflect on the subject matter and further confirm our thinking. Thus, for example, Spinoza noted that

> even if the road to everything is steep, it can be found. However, what is found so infrequently must really be difficult. How should it also happen, for all to ignore the well-being if it were easily accessible and available without much effort? Everything good is as difficult as it is rare.
>
> (Spinoza 2004: 359)

Socrates speculated that 'the sharp sight of the intellect begins only when the sight of the eye begins to lose its power' (Plato 2002: 218), while Plato noted that

> to sum it all up in one word, natural intelligence and a good memory are equally powerless to aid someone who has not an inborn affinity with the subject [of moral goodness]. Without such endowments there is not the slightest possibility [of really *doing* philosophy]. Hence, all those with no natural aptitude for and affinity with justice and all the other noble ideals, though in the study of other matters they may be both intelligent and retentive—all those too who have affinity [with justice and moral ideals] but are stupid and unretentive—such will never any of them grasp the most complete truths in regard to moral concepts.
>
> (Plato 1961, 2002: 32, 2004: 1659)

The reflections of the three authors reflect our deepest beliefs and, however idealistic our thoughts and ideas may sound, we believe the concept we have studied, with the proper understanding and realistic expectations, and considering all situational, cultural and social constraints, is usable anywhere, anytime. This is ultimately proven by our and findings of different authors. As an example, Whetstone (2001) noted that the perfect virtuous leader is in reality merely an unattainable ideal, yet it serves as a good model that leaders can try to achieve. The fact that perfection is not life-like was already understood by Aristotle (2002), who for this purpose saw the best solution in the middle, between too much and too little, between excesses and shortages. In this way, the real striving for an upright posture, principality and a high level of personal integrity comes to the fore, which positively influences inner satisfaction. Again, this was already known by the Ancient Greeks, who related virtues with happiness (Kant 2003). At the same time, such behaviour is very important from the perspective of leading by example, which in both servant leadership as well as in leading with integrity is certainly the most effective way of how employees and co-workers learn to behave in the desired way.

The results regarding leader integrity show that the respondents rated it relatively highly, as the average value of the index of integrity is 5.69 on a seven-point scale. In doing so, the employees rated personal integrity the highest in the context of their fair attitude to the organisation and the lowest in the context of the leader's fair and objective relations towards the employees and in taking responsibility for their own behaviour. At the same time, among the leaders of the for-profit and non-profit organisations, there are statistically significant differences in favour of the leaders from the for-profit organisations, but only in the relationship of the leaders towards their employees. In the relationship of the leaders towards the organisations they lead, statistically significant differences were not found. In our opinion, the causes of this are similar to those in servant leadership and can be traced back to the negative impact a bureaucratic hierarchical structure has on employees' work. On one hand, the results reveal a fairly high level of leader integrity through the prism of fairness in the relationship towards the organisation while, on the other hand, a large gap between the declarative values and the actual behaviour in relation to the employees.[1] Leaders who act in this way and, for example, blame employees for their own mistakes, as we found in the questionnaire on integrity, can be described as quasi or pseudo leaders (Bass and Steidlmeier 1999). In this context, and in line with the content of the PLIS questionnaire that was used in the research, we believe that the management of employees in which the leader's integrity shows also means that the leader accepts the risks stemming from the upright posture and principled conduct. At the same time, the leader speaks the truth, which has a significant impact on the effectiveness of their leadership and employee loyalty, and does not act in an opportune way, but instead, the leader defends what is right, even though such behaviour will be detrimental (Lennick and Kiel 2009). All of this contributes to greater confidence in the leader while, on the other hand, the loss of confidence is consequently also associated with a loss of reputation and respect.

Note

1 This is also affected by the human resource management and socio-demographic factors of leaders.

Appendix

Description of the method and the sample

Process

For participation in our survey in 2010, we proposed to cooperate with one large Slovenian state non-profit organisation in the field of providing security and 33 other Slovenian for-profit organisations and companies (hereinafter for-profit organisations). Our proposals were answered positively by the non-profit organisation and 16 small and medium-sized for-profit organisations. Eight of these fall within the category of tourism and eight within the category of engineering. Given that the non-profit organisation is in the category of large organisations with several thousand employees, we wanted to obtain a similar large for-profit organisation. After several unsuccessful attempts, we decided to invite smaller profit organisations, while limiting ourselves to the above-mentioned areas of tourism and engineering. The reason for this decision is multi-faceted. After we received confirmation of the participation of the large non-profit organisation, we continued our search further only in the for-profit sector. As already stated, we wanted to determine the differences between a large non-profit based organisation and a large for-profit organisation, namely starting with the typology of Blau and Scott (2003) and based on the findings of Drucker (2001, 2004, 2005). After we had failed to identify a large for-profit organisation to participate, we gained one small organisation from the field of tourism and one medium organisation from the field of engineering. This was followed by our decision to continue our search only in the tourism and engineering for-profit fields. In this way, we tried to obtain evenly structured data for the comparison. The search for cooperating for-profit organisations was stopped when we had obtained eight small or medium organisations from both sectors. The decision to stop the search was contributed to by the fact that six months had passed between the first and the last survey in the for-profit sector.

The fact that 16 small and medium-sized for-profit organisations from two different profit sectors and only one large non-profit organisation participated in our survey certainly affects the relevance of the comparison of the data obtained. Particularly unreliable was the comparison between the non-profit organisation and the one for-profit organisation. To avoid this, and to still be in line with the research questions, we compared the data only in summary form. This means the data obtained via the survey in the non-profit organisation was later compared to the pooled data we obtained through the surveys of all for-profit organisations together.

The process of the research unravelled in a way whereby all participating organisations provided the data on the number of employees on the basis of which we calculated the representativeness of the samples. Given that in the for-profit organisations the number of employees did not exceed 130 per organisation, we decided to invite all employees into the survey. In total, we personally distributed 1,819 printed questionnaires (980 in the non-profit organisation and 839 in the for-profit organisations), which was accompanied by a cover letter and an envelope. In the letter, we explained the purpose of the survey to the participants and asked them to participate. At the same time, we asked them to assess only one person throughout the questionnaire, namely their direct supervisor or leader. The completed questionnaire was then placed in the attached envelope and submitted to a pre-agreed location. All respondents were guaranteed anonymity and confidentiality of the practices with the acquired data. In this way, we took full account of the recommendations of Kaiser and Hogan (2010) and wanted to obtain a minimum number of socially desirable responses (Peterson 2004).

In total, the survey questionnaire was completed and returned by 1,256 respondents, 42 of whom we excluded due to a lack of completed sections. From the 1,214 fully completed questionnaires we excluded another 50 (altogether 92 or 7.32 per cent of all returned questionnaires) due to the presumption they contained only socially desirable answers or because they only contained extremes – highest or lowest values of the variables.

In analysing the data, we took 1,164 questionnaires into account, representing 63.99 per cent of all returned questionnaires of all employees who were asked to participate.

Measurement instrument

In our research, to measure the desired variables, we used two quantitative measurement instruments – questionnaires.

For the measurement of the perception of the leader's personal integrity, we used the perceived leader integrity scale (PLIS) questionnaire developed by Craig and Gustafson (1998), which is based on the utilitarian theory of ethics. It is made for the purpose of evaluating the perception of integrity and the moral behaviour of the leaders, namely in such a way that employees evaluate the behaviour of their leaders. The evaluation focuses on the consistency of the behaviour with the rules, which ensures the greatest good for the greatest number of people.

With the factor analysis, we found the same as Craig and Gustafson (1998) found, namely, that the survey is one-dimensional. In the original questionnaire, which consists of 31 variables of affirmative forms and negative stances, the respondents answered by using a four-point Likert scale (Datta 2005, Baker and Craig 2006). For our purposes, we used a seven-point Likert scale, which provides better results (Peterson 2004) and also because we wanted to standardise the measurement scale for both measurement instruments. In this way, we calculated the inverted value of the variables and thereby ensured the same direction on the seven-point scale, where a higher value means a better result.

To measure servant leadership, we used the servant leadership measure developed by Liden et al. (2008). The questionnaire was designed to explore servant leadership as an autonomous and independent model of leadership. It consists of seven dimensions (conceptual – abstract skills, empowerment, helping employees with personal growth, emotional support, caring for the community), which were confirmed in the same way as Liden et al. (2008) did, namely with factor analysis. An interested leader may request the results from the authors. Each factor contains four variables, which means a total of 28 variables were assessed by the respondents using the seven-point Likert scale.

Before using the questionnaires, we obtained the two authors' written consents, namely from Robert C. Liden on 26 November 2008, and from Craig S. Bartholomew on 15 June 2009. The questionnaires were combined into a single questionnaire and we added our own questions about the sociodemographic data of the evaluated leaders and respondents.

The socio-demographic data of the leaders contain information about their gender, age, work experience, leadership experience and education. We wanted to determine whether these variables have any influence of the leadership and leader integrity. As already noted, we assumed that the gender and age of the leader would not affect the servant leadership and that servant leadership is more reserved for educated leaders.

We added the demographic data of the respondents (data on gender, age, working age, years of employment and education) to the data on the leaders. We also asked the respondents whether they perform tasks in a managerial post and whether they are involved in education as part of acquiring a higher level of education.

The questionnaire designed for the needs of the survey includes 72 variables. It consists of five parts where the first part contains 28 variables on leadership, the second part contains 31 variables on the personal integrity of the leaders, the third part contains five variables on the demographic data of the evaluated leaders, the fourth part includes eight variables on the demographic data of the respondents and the fifth part is dedicated to voluntary commenting.

The original questionnaires were initially translated from the English language into Slovenian with the help of a professional translator. After that, they were translated back into English by a second professional translator, thus ensuring the correctness of the translation. When translating, we focused on the importance of the same understanding of the content in another cultural environment (Datta 2005). We were also aware of the problem and risk of a possible different interpretation of the measurement instrument (Yukl 2002), which was created and used in the United States. A test of the external validity was carried out so that we let the questionnaire be read by everyone who later helped in collecting data and asked them about their opinion on every single variable. We found that the contents of both questionnaires were properly understood in our cultural environment. The questionnaire and its internal consistency were first checked in a pilot study.

In our study, we used the method of determining the employees' perception of the leadership and behaviour of their leaders. We did not use the self-assessment method, thus avoiding the influence of the self-image when leaders assess themselves unrealistically and more positively than their colleagues and employees would (Berlogar 2000). This same method, where employees and colleagues assess the ethical behaviour of their leaders, is also advocated by Becker (1998), Craig and Gustafson (1998), Simons (1999), Parry and Proctor-Thomson (2002), Brown et al. (2005), Brown and Trevino (2006), Sarros and Cooper (2006), Kaiser and Hogan (2010). Brown and Trevino (2006) and Kaiser and Hogan (2010) add that employees are the best source of information because they can observe their leaders directly when they are working with people and when they are engaged in decision-making.

Testing the measurement instrument: the pilot study

Once we had confirmed the external validity of the questionnaire and found that it is properly understood in our cultural context, we conducted a pilot study in November 2009. We carried the pilot study on a sample of 50 respondents in one of the inner units of the state non-profit organisation in which we carried out our main survey later in the first half of 2010.

When conducting the pilot study, we took account of the same criteria as were included when implementing our main survey. We added a cover letter and an envelope to the questionnaire. In the letter, we explained the purpose of the survey and asked them to participate. At the same time, we asked them to assess only one person in their questionnaire, namely their direct supervisor or leader. After completing the questionnaire, the respondents placed the questionnaire in the envelope and submitted the envelope to a pre-agreed location. All respondents were guaranteed anonymity and confidentiality of the practices with the acquired data.

With the pilot study, we confirmed the reliability of the measurement instrument because the coefficient of internal consistency (Cronbach's alpha) for the questionnaire on leadership amounted to 0.962, while the questionnaire on integrity amounted to 0.974.

The data gathered in the pilot study were later merged with the data gained in the main survey. This means they are included in the set of respondents from the non-profit organisation.

The reliability of the questionnaires

The calculated coefficient of internal consistency (Cronbach's alpha) for the used set of variables from number 1 to 28, which are focused on measuring the presence of the servant leadership style (servant leadership measure), amounts to 0.972 in our study. For the set of variables from numbers 29 to 59, which are focused on measuring the personal integrity of leaders (perceived leader integrity scale – PLIS), the internal consistency coefficient amounts to 0.982.

By examining the correlation coefficients between each variable and the other covered variables (corrected item-total correlation), we found that all variables are highly correlated with the whole (greater value than 0.3), which confirms the reliability of the measurement instruments or questionnaires. Even with the review of the value of Cronbach's alpha, in the event that an individual variable is not included in the analysis (Cronbach's alpha if item deleted), we found that all values revolve around a common α 0.972 and α 0.982. In the case of variable number 23, we found a slightly higher value (0.973), but because the difference is not significant, and because the value represents a high level of reliability, we decided that the variable would not be excluded from further analysis.

Based on those results, we also found that both questionnaires are highly reliable.

Asymmetry and kurtosis

By analysing the set of variables from number 1 to 28, which measure the presence of servant leadership, we found they distribute normally in a ratio between −3 and 3.

By analysing variables from numbers 29 to 59, which measure the perception of the personal integrity of the leaders, we found that all variables except number 46 (the leader would treat me better if I belonged to another ethnic/national minority) and number 55 (my leader would appropriate the property of the organisation), are distributed normally in the ratio between −3 and 3. For variables 55 and 57, due to the minimal deviation from kurtosis (3.443 and 3.436), we decided to keep them for further analysis. For variable number 46, due to the large deviation from flatness kurtosis (6.418), we decided to dismiss it from the multivariate data analysis.

Pearson's correlation coefficient between variables and multicollinearity

In order to check the possible existence of multicollinearity, we calculated and examined the correlations between variables in both measurement instruments. In this stage of the analysis, we were alert to weak correlations ($r<0.1$) as well as correlations ($r>0.9$) (Field 2006) that were too strong.

Based on the correlations between the variables of the questionnaire on leadership we found that they correspond to the above-mentioned criteria. The highest determined correlation ($r=0.819$) was between variables 11 (leader sets the main interests of the employees before their own) and 18 (the leader sacrifices their own interests in order to satisfy the needs of employees).

In correlations between variables of the questionnaire on leader integrity, we also found that they are appropriate. The highest determined correlation ($r=0.826$) between variables 41 (the leader is making fun out of the employees' mistakes instead of advising them how to do a better job) and 42 (the leader deliberately stressed the employee's mistakes in front of the leader's own superiors, so that the employee looked bad) and 34 (the leader deliberately strengthened the conflicts between employees) and 48 (the leader deliberately causes anger among employees), namely r=0.811.

Given the above mentioned, we decided that in the factor analysis to keep all variables except number 46 (the leader would treat me better if I belonged to another ethnic/national minority), which was eliminated at a preliminary stage.

Descriptive statistics of the determined factors and calculation of the inverted value of the variables and the index of integrity

Based on the factor analysis of the variables through which we confirmed the existence of seven factors in the questionnaire on leadership and the one-factor structure of the questionnaire on integrity, we calculated the variables that constitute individual factors and their mutual correlation. In order to provide a uniform application of the measurement scale 1 to 7 for both measurement instruments, we first calculated the inverted value of all related variables, and second, the calculation of the variable (factor) 'index of integrity'. According to the original form of the questionnaire on integrity, a lower value denotes a better result, while in the questionnaire on leadership, a lower value denotes a poorer result and a higher result a better result of leader behaviour.

With the help of inverted values of the variables, we standardised the measurement scale, whereby the value of 1 denotes complete disagreement and the worst rating, while the value of 7 denotes complete agreement and the best result, which we already found when calculating the average values of the individual variables.

Correlation between factors and the index of integrity

Below, we first want to check the correlation between the independent variable (the index of integrity) and the dependent variables (factors of leadership).

With the help of Pearson's coefficient of correlation, we found a strong and positive statistically significant correlation between the factors of servant leadership and 'the index of integrity' ($r \geq 0.571$; $p=0.000$). A positive and statistically significant correlation was also observed among the factors of servant leadership.

The difference in mean values between factors and the index of integrity in the non-profit and for-profit organisations

The difference between the independent and dependent variables was calculated by using a t-test where we were interested in the general difference between the non-profit and for-profit organisations.

We found that statistically significant differences exist between the mean values of all factors of servant leadership and the mean values of the index of integrity. It is evident from the data that the respondents from the for-profit sector assessed all dimensions of servant leadership (all seven factors) and leader integrity better than the respondents from the non-profit organisation. The interested reader can obtain more information about the t-test from the authors.

Table A.1 Variance and the level of significance in the evaluated regression models

Factors/regression models	R	R²	Adjusted R²	F	p
1. Conceptual skills	0.803	0.644	0.642	316.293	0.000
2. Empowerment	0.622	0.387	0.384	132.814	0.000
3. Helping subordinates grow	0.724	0.524	0.521	164.833	0.000
4. Putting subordinates first	0.644	0.415	0.413	185.847	0.000
5. Ethical behaviour	0.810	0.656	0.654	398.844	0.000
6. Emotional healing	0.738	0.544	0.542	249.199	0.000
7. Creating value for the community	0.747	0.558	0.556	332.427	0.000

$p \leq 0.05$.

Regression analysis

We used a linear regression analysis that enables a choice between various methods of integrating the independent variables in the regression model. For our purposes, we first conducted the analysis with the enter method and then with the stepwise method. At the end, we decided to take into account the information obtained with the stepwise method, which on the basis of statistical criteria progressively includes and excludes independent variables according to their statistical significance. This continues until it selects a combination of variables that has the most impact on the dependent variable. We also decided on this method because the individual influence on the selection of a statistically significant variables is minimal as it allows a researcher in an initial stage to decide which of the independent variables will be tested by the model (Field 2006). The same stepwise method was used by Dierendonck and Nuijten (2011) in researching servant leadership in the context of identifying the strongest predictors.

We can conclude from Table A.1 that, on the basis of the independent variables that were included in the regression analysis, we can explain 64.2 per cent of variance or the variability of the 'conceptual skills', 38.4 per cent of variability of the dependent variable 'empowerment', 52.1 per cent of variability of the dependent variable 'helping employees in their personal growth', 41.3 per cent of variability of the dependent variable 'putting employees first', 65.4 per cent of the variability of the dependent variable 'ethical behaviour and conduct', 54.2 per cent of the variability of the dependent variable 'emotional support' and 55.6 per cent of the variability of the dependent variable 'caring for the community'. The remaining percentage of variability (up to 100 per cent) remained unexplained, which may be attributed to other factors that were not included in our analysis.

In Table A.1 we can also observe the F-value for each model and that all seven evaluated regression models are statistically significant ($p < 0.001$). Because of this, we can reject with a low level of risk the null hypothesis that all regression coefficients are equal to 0 and find that all regression models as a whole are statistically significant.

References

12Manage. 2009. Bilthoven: The Netherlands. Available from: www.12manage.com; accessed 30 May 2016.

Adair, John. 1997. *Effective Leadership Masterclass – What every manager can learn from the great leaders*. London: Pan Books.

Adair, John. 2002. *Inspiring Leadership*. London: Thorogood.

Adair, John. 2004. *The John Adair Handbook of Management and Leadership*. London: Thorogood.

Agamben, Giorgio. 2004. *Homo Sacer – Suverena Oblast in Golo Življenje*. Ljubljana: Študentska Založba.

Ahn, Mark J., Larry W. Ettner and Amanda Loupin. 2012. 'Values v. traits – based approaches to leadership: insights from an analysis of the Aeneid'. *Leadership and Organization Development Journal* 33(2): 112–30.

Alban-Metcalfe, Juliette and Glenn Mead. 2010. 'Coaching for transactional and transformational leadership'. In *Leadership Coaching: Working with Leaders to Develop Elite Performance*, ed. Jonathan Passmore. London: Kogan Page, pp. 211–28.

Andolšek, Stane. 1996. *Uvod v zgodovino socioloških teorij*. Ljubljana: Zavod Republike Slovenije za Šolstvo.

Andrews, Martha C., Thomas Baker and Tammy G. Hunt. 2011. 'Values and person – organization fit: Does moral intensity strengthen outcomes?' *Leadership and Organization Development Journal* 32(1): 5–19.

Aristotle. 2002. *Nikomahova Etika*. Ljubljana: Slovenska matica.

Arnold, Kara A. and Catherine Loughlin. 2010. 'Individually considerate transformational leadership behaviour and self sacrifice'. *Leadership and Organization Development Journal* 31(8): 670–86.

Audi, Robert and Patrick E. Murphy. 2006. 'The many faces of integrity'. *Business Ethics Quarterly* 16(1): 3–21.

Audi, Robert. 2008. 'The marketing of human images as a challenge to ethical leadership'. In *Leadership and Business Ethics*, ed. Gabriel Flynn. Dublin: Springer, pp. 197–210.

Avolio, Bruce J. 2005. *Leadership Development in Balance – Made/Born*. New Jersey: Lawrence Erlbaum Associates.

Avolio, Bruce J. 2010. 'Pursuing authentic leadership development'. In *Handbook of Leadership Theory and Practice*, ed. Nitin Nohria and Rakesh Khurana. Boston: Harvard Business School Publishing, pp. 739–68.

Avolio, Bruce J. and Bernard M. Bass. 2002. *Developing Potential Across a Full Range of Leadership*. New Jersey: Lawrence Erlbaum Associates.

Avolio, Bruce J. and William L. Gardner. 2005. 'Authentic leadership development: getting to the root of positive forms of leadership'. *The Leadership Quarterly* 16(3): 315–38.

Avolio, Bruce J., Fred O. Walumbwa and Todd J. Weber. 2009. 'Leadership: current theories, research, and future directions'. *Annual Review of Psychology* 60: 421–49.

Aßlander, Michael, John Filos and Byron Kaldis. 2011. 'Foreword: Pathos for ethics, business excellence, leadership and quest for sustainability'. *Journal of Business Ethics* 100(1): 1–2.

Badaracco, Joseph L. and Richard R. Ellsworth. 1992. 'Leadership, integrity and conflict'. *Management Decision* 30(6): 29–34.

Badiou, Alain. 1996. *Etika*. Ljubljana: Društvo za teoretsko psihoanalizo.

Bahovec, D. Eva. 1993. *Razprava o izvoru in temeljih neenakosti med Ljudmi – Uredniške opombe in spremna študija.* Ljubljana: Študentska organizacija Univerze v Ljubljani.

Baker, Becca and S. Bartholomew Craig. 2006. 'When actions speak louder than words: the relative importance of leader behaviors in predicting global impressions of integrity'. In *Leadership, It's All Relative: Applying Relative Importance Statistics to Leadership.* Atlanta: Academy of Management.

Barbuto, John E. Jr. and Daniel W. Wheeler. 2006. 'Scale development and construct clarification of servant leadership'. *Group and Organization Management* 31(3): 300–26.

Barbuto, John E. Jr. 2007. 'Becoming a Servant Leader: Do You Have What It Takes?' University of Nebraska – Lincoln Extension. Available from: http://extensionpublications.unl.edu/assets/pdf/g1481.pdf; accessed 30 May 2016.

Barker, Richard A. 2006. 'The nature of leadership'. In *Leadership Perspectives*, ed. Alan Hooper. Hampshire: Ashgate, pp. 343–68.

Barnes, Jonathan. 1999. *Aristotel.* Šentilj: Aristej.

Bartholomew, C. Sandra. 2006. *The Influence of Gender, Age, and Locus of Control on Servant Leader Behavior among Group Leaders at The Culinary Institute of America.* Minnesota: Walden University.

Bass, M. Bernard. 1990. *Bass and Stogdill's Handbook of Leadership: Theory, Research, and Managerial Applications*, 3rd edn. New York: Free Press.

Bass, M. Bernard. 1997. 'Does the transactional – transformational leadership paradigm transcend organizational and national boundaries?' *American Psychologist* 52(2): 130–9.

Bass, M. Bernard. 2002. 'Cognitive, social, and emotional intelligence of transformational leaders'. In *Multiple Intelligences and Leadership*, ed. Ronald E. Riggio and Susan E. Murphy and Francis J. Pirozzolo. New Jersey: Lawrence Erlbaum Associates, pp. 105–17.

Bass, M. Bernard and Paul Steidlmeier. 1999. 'Ethics, character, and authentic transformational leadership behavior'. *The Leadership Quarterly* 10(2): 181–217.

Bass, M. Bernard and Ronald E. Riggio. 2006. *Transformational Leadership*, 2nd edn. New Jersey: Lawrence Erlbaum Associates.

Batson, C. Daniel, Elizabeth R. Thompson, Greg Seuferling, Heather Whitney and Jon A. Strongman. 1999. 'Moral hypocrisy: appearing moral to oneself without being so'. *Journal of Personality and Social Psychology* 77(3): 525–37.

Batson, C. Daniel, Elizabeth Collins and Adam A. Powell. 2006. 'Doing business after the fall: the virtue of moral hypocrisy'. *Journal of Business Ethics* 66(4): 321–35.

Becker, E. Thomas. 1998. 'Integrity in organizations: beyond honesty and conscientiousness'. *Academy of Management Review* 23(1): 154–61.

Bennis, Warren. 2002. 'Become a tomorrow leader'. In *Focus on Leadership: Servant-Leadership for the Twenty-First Century*, ed. Larry C. Spears and Michele Lawrence. New York: John Wiley & Sons, pp. 100–9.

Bennis, Warren G. and Burt Nanus. 2003. *Leaders: The Strategies for Taking Charge*. New York: Harper Business Essentials.

Bennis, Warren and Joan Goldsmith. 2010. 'Maintaining trust through integrity'. In *The Jossey-Bass Reader on Nonprofit and Public Leadership*, ed. James L. Perry. San Francisco: Jossey-Bass, pp. 293–304.

Berlogar, Janko. 2000. *Managerska Etika ali Svetost Preživetja*. Ljubljana: Fakulteta za družbene vede.

Berlogar, Janko. 2006. *Osebni in Družbeni Vidiki Komuniciranja v Javni Upravi*. Ljubaljana: Fakulteta za upravo.

Blackburn, Simon. 2008. *Dictionary of Philosophy*. New York: Oxford University Press.

Blanchard, Ken. 2002. 'The heart of servant-leadership – foreword'. In *Focus on Leadership: Servant-Leadership for the Twenty-First Century*, ed. Larry C. Spears and Michele Lawrence. New York: John Wiley & Sons, pp. ix–xii.

Blau, Peter M. and Richard W. Scott. 2003. *Formal Organizations: A Comparative Approach*. Stanford: Stanford University Press.

Bovens, Mark. 1998. *The Quest for Responsibility: Accountability and Citizenship in Complex Organisations*. Cambridge: Cambridge University Press.

Bowie, Norman E. 1991. 'Challenging the egoistic paradigm'. *Business Ethics Quarterly* 1(1): 1–21.

Boyum, Ginny. 2006. 'The Historical and Philosophical Influences on Greenleaf's Concept of Servant Leadership: Setting the Stage for Scientific Theory Building'. Servant Leadership Research Roundtable. Available from: www.regent.edu/acad/global/publications/sl_proceedings/2006/boyum.pdf; accessed 30 May 2016.

Bracher, James F. 2008. 'Integrity Arch'. Available from: www.brachercenter.com/integrityarch.html; accessed 30 May 2016.

Bratož, Rajko. 2003. *Grška zgodovina*. Ljubljana: Zveza zgodovinskih društev Slovenije.

Brenner, Steven N. and Earl A. Molander. 1977. 'Is the ethics of business changing?' *Harvard Business Review* 55(January/February): 57–71.

Brewer's Dictionary of Phrase and Fable, 15th edn. 1995. London: Cassell Publishers.

Brown, E. Michael and Linda K. Trevino. 2006. 'Ethical leadership: a review and future directions'. *The Leadership Quarterly* 17(6): 595–616.

Brown, E. Michael, Linda K. Trevino and David A. Harrison. 2005. 'Ethical leadership: a social learning perspective for construct development and testing'. *Organizational Behavior and Human Decision Processes* 97(2): 117–34.

Brown, Marvin T. 2006. 'Corporate integrity and public interest: a relational approach to business ethics and leadership'. *Journal of Business Ethics* 66(1): 11–8.

Burkhardt, John and Larry C. Spears. 2002. 'Servant-leadership and philanthropic institutions'. In *Focus on Leadership: Servant-Leadership for the Twenty-First Century*, ed. Larry C. Spears and Michele Lawrence. New York: John Wiley & Sons, pp. 222–43.

Burns, James MacGregor. 1984. *Leadership: Multidisciplinary Perspectives – Foreword*. New Jersey: Prentice-Hall, Inc.

Burns, James MacGregor. 2010. *Leadership*. New York: HarperCollins Publishers.

Caldwell, Cam, Linda A. Hayes, Ranjan Karri and Patricia Bernal. 2008. 'Ethical stewardship – implications for leadership and trust'. *Journal of Business Ethics* 78(1–2): 153–64.

Caldwell, Cam, Linda A. Hayes and Do Tien Long. 2010. 'Leadership, trustworthiness, and ethical stewardship'. *Journal of Business Ethics* 96(4): 497–512.

Cambridge Advanced Learner's Dictionary. 2003. Cambridge: Cambridge University Press.

Carroll, Archie B. 1979. 'A three-dimensional conceptual model of corporate perform-ance'. *Academy of Management Review* 4(4): 497–505.

Carroll, Archie B. 1991. 'The pyramid of corporate social responsibility: toward the moral management of organizational stakeholders'. *Business Horizons* 34(4): 39–48.

Carroll, Archie B. 1999. 'Corporate social responsibility: evolution of a definitional con-struct'. *Business and Society* 38(3): 268–95.

Carroll, Archie B. 2009. *Business Ethics*. New York: Routledge.

Carroll, Archie B. and Ann K. Buchholtz. 2000. *Business and Society: Ethics and Stakeholder Management*, 4th edn. Nashville: South-Western College Publishing.

Carver, John. 2002. 'The unique double servant-leadership role of the board chair'. In *Focus on Leadership: Servant-Leadership for the Twenty-First Century*, ed. Larry C. Spears and Michele Lawrence. New York: John Wiley & Sons, pp. 188–209.

Casse, Pierre and Paul Claudel. 2011. 'Leadership styles: a powerful model'. *Training Journal* January 2011: 46–51.

Cerit, Yusuf. 2010. 'The effects of servant leadership on teachers' organizational commit-ment in primary schools in Turkey'. *International Journal of Leadership in Education* 13(3): 301–17.

Chen, Chin-Yi, Chun-Hsi Vivian Chen and Chun-I Li. 2011. 'The influence of leader's spiritual values of servant leadership on employee motivational autonomy and eudae-monic well-being'. *Journal of Religion and Health* 52(2): 418–38.

Ciulla, Joanne B. 2004. 'Ethics and leadership effectiveness'. In *The Nature of Leadership*, ed. John Antonakis, Anna T. Cianciolo and Robert J. Sternberg. Thousand Oaks: Sage Publications, pp. 302–27.

Cloud, Henry. 2009. *Integrity*. New York: HarperCollins Publishers.

Cohen, William A. 2010. *Heroic Leadership: Leading with Integrity and Honor*. San Francisco: Jossey-Bass.

Comte-Sponville, Andre. 2002. *Mala razprava o velikih vrlinah*. Ljubljana: Vale-Novak.

Cotterell, Arthur, Roger Lowe and Ian Shaw. 2006. *Leadership Lessons from the Ancient World: How Learning from the Past Can Win You the Future*. Chichester: John Wiley & Sons.

Covey, Stephen R. 2002a. *Servant Leadership: A Journey into the Nature of Legitimate Power and Greatness - Foreword*. New Jersey: Paulist Press.

Covey, Stephen R. 2002b. 'Servant-leadership and community leadership in the twenty-first century'. In *Focus on Leadership: Servant-Leadership for the Twenty-First Century*, ed. Larry C. Spears and Michele Lawrence. New York: John Wiley & Sons, pp. 26–33.

Covey, Stephen R. 2004. *The 7 Habits of Highly Effective People*. New York: Free Press.

Covey, Stephen R. 2006. 'Servant Leadership – Use your voice to serve others'. *Leadership Excellence* 23(12): 5–6.

Craig, S. Bartholomew and Sigrid B. Gustafson. 1998. 'Perceived leader integrity scale: an instrument for assessing employee perceptions of leader integrity'. *The Leadership Quarterly* 9(2): 127–45.

Crain, William C. 1985. 'Kohlberg's stages of moral development'. In *Theories of Development: Concepts and Applications*, 2nd edn, ed. William C. Crain. Englewood Cliffs: Prentice-Hall, pp. 118–36.

Crane, Andrew and Dirk Matten. 2004. *Business Ethics*. New York: Oxford University Press.

Crossan, Mary and Daina Mazutis. 2008. 'Transcendent leadership'. *Business Horizons* 51(2): 131–9.

Crossman, Joanna. 2010. 'Conceptualising spiritual leadership in secular organizational contexts and its relation to transformational, servant and environmental leadership'. *Leadership and Organization Development Journal* 31(7–8): 596–608.

Datta, Anasuya. 2005. *Measurement Equivalence of English and Spanis Versions of the Perceived Leader Integrity Scale*. Carolina: North Carolina State University.

De George, Richard T. 2001. 'When integrity is not enough'. In *The Leader's Imperative – Ethics, Integrity, and Responsibility*, ed. J. Carol Ficarrotta. Indiana: Purdue University Press, pp. 213–27.

De Hoogh, Annebel H.B. and Deanne N. Den Hartog. 2008. 'Ethical and despotic leadership, relationships with leader's social responsibility, top management team effectiveness and subordinates' optimism: a multi-method study'. *The Leadership Quarterly* 19(3): 297–311.

Den Hartog, Deanne N. and Annebel H.B. De Hoogh. 2009. 'Empowering behaviour and leader fairness and integrity: studying perceptions of ethical leader behaviour from a levels-of-analysis perspective'. *European Journal of Work and Organizational Psychology* 18(2): 199–230.

Dennis, Robert S., Linda Kinzler-Norheim and Mihai Bocarnea. 2010. 'Servant leadership theory: development of the servant leadership assessment instrument'. In *Servant Leadership: Developments in Theory and Research*, eds. Dirk van Dierendonck and Kathleen Patterson. New York: Palgrave Macmillan, pp. 169–79.

DePree, Max. 2002. 'Servant-leadership: three things necessary'. In *Focus on Leadership: Servant-Leadership for the Twenty-First Century*, eds. Larry C. Spears and Michele Lawrence. New York: John Wiley & Sons, pp. 88–97.

Descartes, Rene. 1957. *Razprava o Metodi – Kako pravilno voditi razum ter v znanostih iskati resnico*. Ljubljana: Slovenska matica.

Dictionary of the Slovenian Language. 2001. Ljubljana: DZS.

Dienhart, John. 2005. 'Moral development'. In *The Blackwell Encyclopedia of Management*, 2nd edn, eds. Patricia H. Werhane and R. Edward Freeman. Oxford: Blackwell Publishing Ltd, pp. 354–6.

Dierendonck, Dirk and Kathleen Patterson. 2010. 'Servant leadership: an introduction'. In *Servant Leadership: Developments in Theory and Research*, eds. Dirk van Dierendonck and Kathleen Patterson. New York: Palgrave Macmillan, pp. 3–10.

Dierendonck, Dirk and Inge Nuijten. 2011. 'The servant leadership survey: development and validation of a multidimensional measure'. *Journal of Business and Psychology* 26(3): 249–67.

Dimovski, Vlado, Sandra Penger and Judita Peterlin. 2009. *Avtentično Vodenje v Učeči se Organizaciji*. Ljubljana: Planet GV.

Dineen, Brian R., Roy J. Lewicki and Edward C. Tomlinson. 2006. 'Supervisory guidance and behavioral integrity: relationship with employee citizenship and deviant behavior'. *Journal of Applied Psychology* 91(3): 622–35.

Dion, Michel. 2012. 'Are ethical theories relevant for ethical leadership?' *Leadership and Organization Development Journal* 33(1): 4–24.

Drucker, Peter F. 2001. *Managerski izzivi v 21. stoletju*. Ljubljana: GV Založba.

Drucker, Peter F. 2004. *O managementu*. Ljubljana: GV Založba.

Drucker, Peter F. 2005. *Managing the Nonprofit Organization: Practices and Principles*. New York: Collins Business.

Ehrhart, Mark G. 2004. 'Leadership and procedural justice climate as antecedents of unit-level organizational citizenship behavior'. *Personnel Psychology* 57(1): 61–94.

Fairholm, Gilbert W. 1991. *Values Leadership – Toward a New Philosophy of Leadership*. New York: Praeger Publishers.

Ferrell, O. C., John Fraedrich and Linda Ferrell. 2011. *Business Ethics: Ethical Decision Making and Cases*, 8th edn. Mason: South-Western Cengage Learning.

Field, Andy. 2006. *Discovering Statistics Using SPSS*, 2nd edn. London: Sage Publications.

Fitsimmons, Gary. 2008. 'The foundational standard: integrity'. *The Bottom Line: Managing Library Finances* 21(1): 24–6.

Flynn, Gabriel. 2008. 'The virtuous manager: a vision for leadership in business'. In *Leadership and Business Ethics*, ed. Gabriel Flynn. Dublin: Springer, pp. 39–56.

Fowler, Henry Watson. 2009. *A Dictionary of Modern English Usage*. New York: Oxford University Press.

Fry, Louis W. 2003. 'Toward a theory of spiritual leadership'. *The Leadership Quarterly* 14(6): 693–727.

Fry, Louis and Mark Kriger. 2009. 'Towards a theory of being-centered leadership: multiple levels of being as context for effective leadership'. *Human Relations* 62(11): 1667–96.

Gantar, Kajetan. 2002. *Nikomahova etika – Uvodna beseda in slovar*. Ljubljana: Slovenska matica.

Gavin, Joanne H., James Campbell Quick, Cary L. Cooper and Jonathan D. Quick. 2003. 'A spirit of personal integrity: the role of character in executive health'. *Organizational Dynamics* 32(2): 165–79.

George, Bill and Peter Sims. 2007. *True North: Discover Your Authentic Leadership*. New York: John Wiley & Sons, Inc.

Girodo, Michel. 2003. 'Ocenjevanje tveganega vedenja in strateški sistemi: nova orodja za preprečevanje korupcije ter krepitev integritete'. In *Etika, integriteta in človekove pravice z vidika policijske dejavnosti*, eds. Milan Pagon, Gorazd Meško and Branko Lobnikar. Ljubljana: Visoka policijsko-varnostna šola, pp. 205–23.

Goethals, George R., Georgia J. Sorenson and James MacGregor Burns. 2004. *Encyclopedia of Leadership*. Thousand Oaks: Sage Publications, Inc.

Graham, Jill W. 1991. 'Servant leadership in organizations: Inspirational and moral'. *The Leadership Quarterly* 2(2): 105–19.

Graham, Jill W. 1995. 'Leadership, moral development, and citizenship behavior'. *Business Ethics Quarterly* 5(1): 43–54.

Grant, Patricia. 2011. 'An Aristotelian approach to sustainable business'. *Corporate Governance* 11(1): 4–14.

Greenleaf, Robert K. 1998. *The Power of Servant Leadership*. San Francisco: Berrett-Koehler Publishers, Inc.

Greenleaf, Robert K. 2002a. *Servant Leadership: A Journey into the Nature of Legitimate Power and Greatness*. New Jersey: Paulist Press.

Greenleaf, Robert K. 2002b. 'Essentials of servant-leadership'. In *Focus on Leadership: Servant-Leadership for the Twenty-First Century*, eds. Larry C. Spears and Michele Lawrence. New York: John Wiley & Sons, pp. 18–25.

Griffin, Ricky W. 2002. *Management*. Boston: Houghton Mifflin Company.

Grob, Leonard. 1984. 'Leadership: the Socratic model'. In *Leadership: Multidisciplinary Perspectives*, ed. Barbara Kellerman. New Jersey: Prentice-Hall, Inc., pp. 263–80.

Harman, Gilbert. 1999. 'Moral philosophy meets social psychology: virtue ethics and the fundamental attribution error'. *Proceedings of the Aristotelian Society*. Available from: www.princeton.edu/~harman/Papers/Virtue.html; accessed 30 May 2016.

Hartman, Edwin M. 2008. 'Socratic questions and Aristotelian answers: a virtue-based approach to business ethics'. In *Leadership and Business Ethics*, ed. Gabriel Flynn. Dublin: Springer, pp. 81–101.

Heineman, Benjamin W. Jr. 2008. *High Performance with High Integrity*. Boston: Harvard Business Press.

Hendry, John. 2013. *Management. A Very Short Introduction*. Oxford: Oxford University Press.

Henry, Bob. 2008. 'Servant-leadership: a CEO's perspective'. In *Servant – Leadership: Bringing the Spirit of Work to Work*, eds. Ralph Lewis and John Noble. Gloucestershire: Management Books 2000 Ltd, pp. 70–83.

Hesse, Herman. 2007. *The Journey to the East*. London: Peter Owen Publishers.

House, Robert J. 1976. *A 1976 'Theory of Charismatic Leadership'*. Working Paper Series 76-06. Toronto: University of Toronto. Available from: http://files.eric.ed.gov/fulltext/ED133827.pdf; accessed 30 May 2016.

Howard, Anthony. 2010. 'Perspectives on practice: a new global ethic'. *Journal of Management Development* 29(5): 506–17.

Howell, Jane M and Bruce J. Avolio. 1995. 'Charismatic leadership: submission or liberation?' *Business Quarterly* 60(1): 62–70.

Hoyt, Crystal L. 2010. 'Women and leadership'. In *Leadership: Theory and Practice*, 5th edn, ed. Peter G. Northouse. London: Sage Publications, pp. 301–33.

Hu, Jia and Robert C. Liden. 2011. 'Antecedents of team potency and team effectiveness: an examination of goal and process clarity and servant leadership'. *Journal of Applied Psychology* 96(4): 851–62.

Huberts, Leo W. J. C., Muel Kaptein and Karin Lasthuizen. 2007. 'A study of the impact of three leadership styles on integrity violations committed by police officers'. *Policing: An International Journal of Police Strategies and Management* 30(4): 587–607.

Huberts, Leo W. J. C., Jeroen Maesschalck and Carole L. Jurkiewicz. 2008. 'Global perspectives on good governance policies and research'. In *Ethics and Integrity of Governance: Perspectives Across Frontiers*, eds. Leo W.J.C. Huberts, Jeroen Maesschalck and Carole L. Jurkiewicz. Cheltenham: Edward Elgar Publishing, pp. 239–64.

Hunt, Sonja M. 1984. 'The role of leadership in the construction of reality'. In *Leadership: Multidisciplinary Perspectives*, ed. Barbara Kellerman. New Jersey: Prentice-Hall, Inc., pp. 157–78.

Irving, Justin A. 2010. 'Cross-cultural perspectives on servant leadership'. In *Servant Leadership: Developments in Theory and Research*, eds. Dirk van Dierendonck and Kathleen Patterson. New York: Palgrave Macmillan, pp. 118–29.

Jelovac, Dejan. 1997. *Poslovna etika*. Ljubljana: Študentska Organizacija Univerze.

Jerman, Frane. 1992. *Filozofija*. Ljubljana: Državna Založba Slovenije.

Jones-Burbridge, Jo Ann. 2012. 'Servant leadership'. *Corrections Today* 73(6): 45–7.

Johnson, Craig E. 2007. 'Best practices in ethical leadership'. In *The Practice of Leadership: Developing the Next Generation of Leaders*, eds. Jay A. Conger and Ronald E. Riggio. San Francisco: Jossey-Bass, pp. 150–71.

Joseph, Errol E. and Bruce E. Winston. 2005. 'A correlation of servant leadership, leader trust, and organizational trust'. *Leadership and Organization Development Journal* 26(1): 6–22.

Kaiser, Robert B. and Robert Hogan. 2010. 'How to (and how not to) assess the integrity of managers'. *Consulting Psychology Journal: Practice and Research* 62(4): 216–34.

Kampanakis, Joseph. 2000. 'Police organizational culture and policemen's integrity'. In *Policing in Central and Eastern Europe: Ethics, Integrity and Human Rights*, ed. Milan Pagon. Ljubljana: College of Police and Security Studies, pp. 497–506.

Kanjuo Mrčela, Aleksandra. 1996. *Ženske v Menedžmentu*. Ljubljana: ČZP Enotnost.

Kant, Immanuel. 2003. *Kritika praktičnega uma*. Ljubljana: Društvo za teoretsko psihoanalizo.

Kant, Immanuel. 2005. *Utemeljitev metafizike nravi*. Ljubljana: Založba ZRC, ZRC SAZU.

Karp, Tom. 2003. 'Socially responsible leadership'. *Foresight* 5(2): 15–23.

Keith, Kent. M. 2009. 'Servant leaders: observe three basic principles'. *Leadership Excellence* 26(5): 18–9.

Kellerman, Barbara. 1984. *Leadership: Multidisciplinary Perspectives: Introductory Remarks*. New Jersey: Prentice-Hall, Inc.

Kellerman, Barbara. 2010. 'Ties that bind'. In *The Jossey-Bass Reader on Nonprofit and Public Leadership*, ed. James L. Perry. San Francisco: Jossey-Bass, pp. 594–622.

Keohane, Nannerl O. 2010. *Thinking about Leadership*. New Jersey: Princeton University Press.

Kirkpatrick, Shelley A. and Edwin A. Locke. 1991. 'Leadership: do traits matter?' *Academy of Management Executive* 5(2): 48–60.

Kocijančič, Gorazd. 2002. *Platon: Izbrani dialogi in odlomki – Uvod in Spremna beseda*. Ljubljana: Mladinska knjiga.

Kocijančič, Gorazd. 2004. *Platon: Zbrana dela - II. knjiga*. Celje: Mohorjeva družba.

Koehn, Daryl. 2005a. 'Integrity as a business asset'. *Journal of Business Ethics* 58(1–3): 125–36.

Koehn, Daryl. 2005b. 'Virtue ethics'. In *The Blackwell Encyclopedia of Management*, 2nd edn, eds. Patricia H. Werhane and R. Edward Freeman. Oxford: Blackwell Publishing Ltd., pp. 535–8.

Kohlberg, Lawrence. 1975. 'The cognitive-developmental approach to moral education'. *The Phi Delta Kappan* 56(10): 670–7.

Kotter, John P. 1990. *A Force for Change: How Leadership differs from Management*. New York: Free Press.

Kreitner, Robert. 2004. *Management*, 9th edn. Boston: Houghton Mifflin Company.

Kunzmann, Peter, Franz-Peter Burkard and Franz Wiedmann. 1997. *DTV Atlas Filozofije*. Ljubljana: DZS.

Laabs, Carolyn. 2011. 'Perceptions of moral integrity: contradictions in need of explanation'. *Nursing Ethics* 18(3): 431–40.

Laszlo, Chris and Nadya Zhexembayeva. 2011. *Embedded Sustainability – The Next Big Competitive Advantage*. Sheffield: Greenleaf Publishing.

Lennick, Doug and Fred Kiel. 2009. *Moral Intelligence*. New Jersey: Wharton School Publishing.

Lennick, Doug and Fred Kiel. 2011. 'Moral leadership'. *Leadership Excellence* 28(11): 17.

Lennick, Doug and Fred Kiel. 2012. 'Moral leadership by example'. *Baseline* 115: 13.

Lewis, Ralph. 2008. 'Serving organisations'. In *Servant-Leadership: Bringing the Spirit of Work to Work*, eds. Ralph Lewis and John Noble. Gloucestershire: Management Books 2000 Ltd, pp. 38–54.

Lewis, Ralph and John Noble. 2008. *Servant-Leadership: Bringing the Spirit of Work to Work*. Gloucestershire: Management Books 2000 Ltd.

Liden, Robert C., Sandy J. Wayne, Hao Zhao and David Henderson. 2008. 'Servant leadership: development of a multidimensional measure and multi-level assessment'. *The Leadership Quarterly* 19(2): 161–77.

Locander, B. William and David L. Luechauer. 2006. 'Trading Places: how do you practice servant-leadership in an exchange-driven world?' *Marketing Management* 15(3): 43–5.

Lustig, Patricia, John Reynolds, Gill Ringland and Richard Walsh. 2010. 'Leadership in the public sector – the next decade'. *The International Journal of Leadership in Public Services* 6(1): 34–44.

Luthans, Fred, Carolyn M. Youssef and Bruce J. Avolio. 2007. *Psychological Capital: Developing the Human Competitive Edge*. New York: Oxford University Press.

Lyons, Nick, Vish Kini and Prit Chahal. 2009. 'Servants and leaders'. *Education for Primary Care* 20(5): 338–9.

McFall, Lynne. 1987. 'Integrity'. *Ethics* 98(1): 5–20.

MacIntyre, Alasdair. 1993. *Kratka zgodovina etike*. Ljubljana: Znanstveno in publicistično središče.

MacIntyre, Alasdair. 2006. *Odvisne racionalne živali: Zakaj potrebujemo vrline*. Ljubljana: Študentska založba.

McNenery, Terri. 2008. 'Reflections: servant-leadership and you'. In *Servant-Leadership: Bringing the Spirit of Work to Work*, eds. Ralph Lewis and John Noble. Gloucestershire: Management Books 2000 Ltd, pp. 200–11.

Manz, C. Charles and Henry P. Sims Jr. 1987. 'Leading workers to lead themselves: the external leadership of self-managing work teams'. *Administrative Science Quarterly* 32(1): 106–28.

Maxwell, John C. 2007. *Ni takšne stvari kot 'poslovna' etika*. Velenje: IPAK.

Mayer, C. Roger, James H. Davis and David F. Schoorman. 1995. 'An integrative model of organizational trust'. *Academy of Management Review* 20(3): 709–34.

Merriam-Webster's Collegiate Encyclopedia. 2000. Springfield: Merriam-Webster.

Mesner-Andolšek, Dana. 1995a. *Organizacijska kultura, zbirka Manager*. Ljubljana: Gospodarski vestnik.

Mesner-Andolšek, Dana. 1995b. *Vpliv kulture na organizacijsko strukturo*. Ljubljana: Fakulteta za družbene vede.

Messick, David M. 2005. 'Psychology and business ethics'. In *The Blackwell Encyclopedia of Management*, 2nd edn, eds. Patricia H. Werhane and R. Edward Freeman. Oxford: Blackwell Publishing Ltd, pp. 440–43.

Miller, Mike. 2003. 'Servant leadership inspires followers'. *Credit Union Magazine* September 2003: 20–1.

Mintz, Steven M. 1996. 'Aristotelian virtue and business ethics education'. *Journal of Business Ethics* 15(8): 827–38.

Mintzberg, Henry. 1979. *The Structuring of Organizations*. Englewood Cliffs: Prentice-Hall.

Miščević, Nenad. 1993. *Kratka zgodovina etike: Na prizorišču sodobne etike*. Ljubljana: Znanstveno in publicistično središče.

Moore, George Edward. 2000. *Principia Etika*. Ljubljana: Študentska založba.

Morrison, Allen. 2001. 'Integrity and global leadership'. *Journal of Business Ethics* 31(1): 65–76.

Možina, Stane, Rudi Rozman, Miroslav Glas, Mitja Tavčar, Danijel Pučko, Janko Kralj, Štefan Ivanko, Bogdan Lipičnik, Jože Gričar, Metka Tekavčič, Vlado Dimovski and Bogomir Kovač. 2002. *Management – Nova znanja za uspeh*. Radovljica: Didakta.

Mumford, Michael D., Whitney B. Helton, Brian P. Decker, Mary Shane Connelly and Judith R. Van Doorn. 2003. 'Values and beliefs related to ethical decisions'. *Teaching Business Ethics* 7(2): 139–70.

Musek, Janek. 1993. 'Duhovna kriza, vrednote in psihologija'. *Psihološka Obzorja* 2(3/4): 123–41.

Nandram, Sharda S. and Jan Vos. 2010. 'The spiritual features of servant-leadership'. In *Spirituality and Business*, eds. Sharda S. Nandram and Margot Esther Borden. Berlin: Springer, pp. 233–44.

Nietzsche, Friederich. 1988. *Onstran dobrega in zlega*. Ljubljana: Slovenska matica.

Noble, John. 2008. 'Principles and practicalities'. In *Servant-Leadership: Bringing the Spirit of Work to Work*, eds. Ralph Lewis and John Noble. Gloucestershire: Management Books 2000 Ltd, pp. 25–37.

Northouse, Peter G. 2010. *Leadership: Theory and Practice*, 5th edn. London: Sage Publications.

Ones, Deniz S., Chockalingam Viswesvaran and Frank L. Schmidt. 2003. 'Personality and absenteeism: a meta-analysis of integrity tests'. *European Journal of Personality* 17(S1): 19–38.

Oxford Advanced Learner's Dictionary. 1989a. Oxford: Oxford University Press.

Oxford Collocations Dictionary. 2009. Oxford: Oxford University Press.

Oxford Concise English Dictionary, 11th edn. 2004. Oxford: Oxford University Press.

Oxford English Dictionary, 2nd edn. 1989b. Oxford: Clarendon Press.

Page, Don and Paul T. P. Wong. 2000. 'A Conceptual Framework for Measuring Servant-Leadership'. Available from: www.twu.ca/academics/graduate/leadership/servant-leadership/conceptual-framework.pdf; accessed 30 May 2016.

Pagon, Milan. 2000. 'Policijska etika kot zvrst uporabne etike'. *Varstvoslovje* 2(2): 158–67.

Pagon, Milan. 2003a. 'Policijska etika in integriteta'. In *Etika, integriteta in človekove pravice z vidika policijske dejavnosti*, eds. Milan Pagon, Gorazd Meško and Branko Lobnikar. Ljubljana: Visoka policijsko-varnostna šola, pp. 11–26.

Pagon, Milan. 2003b. 'The need for a paradigm shift in police leadership'. In *Police Leadership in the Twenty-first Century*, eds. Robert Adlam and Peter Villiers. Winchester: Waterside Press, pp. 157–68.

Pagon, Milan, Sanja Kutnjak Ivkovich and Branko Lobnikar. 2000. 'Police integrity and attitudes toward police corruption: a comparison between the police and the public'. In *Policing in Central and Eastern Europe: Ethics, Integrity and Human Rights*, ed. Milan Pagon. Ljubljana: College of Police and Security Studies, pp. 383–96.

Paine, Lynn Sharp. 2005. 'Integrity'. In *The Blackwell Encyclopedia of Management*, 2nd edn, eds. Patricia H. Werhane and R. Edward Freeman. Oxford: Blackwell Publishing Ltd, pp. 247–9.

Painter-Morland, Mollie. 2008. *Business Ethics as Practice: Ethics as the Everyday Business of Business*. Cambridge: Cambridge University Press.

Palanski, E. Michael and Francis J. Yammarino. 2007. 'Integrity and leadership: clearing the conceptual confusion'. *European Management Journal* 25(3): 171–84.

Palanski, E. Michael and Francis J. Yammarino. 2009. 'Integrity and leadership: a multi-level conceptual framework'. *The Leadership Quarterly* 20(3): 405–20.

Palanski, E. Michael and Francis J. Yammarino. 2011. 'Impact of behavioral integrity on follower job performance: a three-study examination'. *The Leadership Quarterly* 22(4): 765–86.

Palanski, E. Michael and Gretchen R. Vogelgesang. 2011. 'Virtuous creativity: the effects of leader behavioural integrity on follower creative thinking and risk taking'. *Canadian Journal of Administrative Sciences* 28(3): 259–69.

Palmer, Donald. 2007. *Ali središče drži? Uvod v zahodno filozofijo.* Ljubljana: Državna založba Slovenije.

Parolini, Jeanine, Kathleen Patterson and Bruce Winston. 2009. 'Distinguishing between transformational and servant leadership'. *Leadership and Organizational Development Journal* 30(3): 274–91.

Parry, W. Ken and Sarah B. Proctor-Thomson. 2002. 'Perceived integrity of transformational leaders in organizational settings'. *Journal of Business Ethics* 35(2): 75–96.

Passmore, Johathan. 2010. 'Leadership coaching'. In *Leadership Coaching: Working with Leaders to Develop Elite Performance*, ed. Jonathan Passmore. London: Kogan Page, pp. 5–16.

Peete, David. 2005. 'Needed: servant-leaders'. *Nursing Homes: Long Term Care Management* 54(7): 8.

Peterson, Christopher and Martin E. Seligman. 2004. *Character Strengths and Virtues: A Handbook and Classification.* Oxford: Oxford University Press.

Peterson, Dane. 2004. 'Perceived leader integrity and ethical intentions of subordinates'. *The Leadership and Organization Development Journal* 25(1): 7–23.

Petrick, Joseph A. and John F. Quinn. 2000. 'The integrity capacity construct and moral progress in business'. *Journal of Business Ethics* 23(1): 3–18.

Plato. 1961. *Plato: The Collected Dialogues*, eds. Edith Hamilton and Huntington Cairns. Princeton: Princeton University Press.

Plato. 1995. *Država.* Ljubljana: Založba Mihelač.

Plato. 2002. *Platon: Izbrani dialogi in Odlomki.* Ljubljana: Mladinska knjiga.

Plato. 2003. *Poslednji dnevi Sokrata.* Ljubljana: Slovenska matica.

Plato. 2004. *Platon: Zbrana Dela - I. Knjiga.* Celje: Mohorjeva družba.

Plato. 2005. *The Symposium.* London: Penguin Books Ltd.

Posner, Barry Z. 2001. 'What does it mean to act with integrity?' *Teaching Business Ethics* 5(4): 461–73.

Pribac, Igor. 2001. *Družbena pogodba – Spremna beseda.* Ljubljana: Krtina – Knjižna zbirka Temeljna dela.

Price, Terry L. 2003. 'The ethics of authentic transformational leadership'. *The Leadership Quarterly* 14(1): 67–81.

Prosser, Stephen. 2010. 'Opportunities and tensions of servant leadership'. In *Servant Leadership: Developments in Theory and Research*, eds. Dirk van Dierendonck and Kathleen Patterson. New York: Palgrave Macmillan, pp. 25–38.

Raeper, William and Linda Smith. 1995. *Vodnik po idejah – Religija in filozofija v preteklosti in danes.* Ljubljana: Založništvo Jutro.

Ramsey, Robert D. 2003. 'What is a "servant leader"?' *Supervision* 64(11): 3–5.

Reave, Laura. 2005. 'Spiritual values and practices related to leadership effectiveness'. *The Leadership Quarterly* 16(5): 655–87.

Reed, Lora L., Deborah Vidaver-Cohen and Scott R. Colwell. 2011. 'A new scale to measure executive servant leadership: development, analysis, and implications for research'. *Journal of Business Ethics* 101(3): 415–34.

Rickards, Tudor and Murray Clark. 2006. *Dilemmas of Leadership.* New York: Routledge.

Riggio, Ronald E. and Francis J. Pirozzolo. 2002. 'Multiple intelligences and leadership: implications for leadership research and training'. In *Multiple Intelligences and Leadership*, eds. Ronald E. Riggio, Susan E. Murphy and Francis J. Pirozzolo. New Jersey: Lawrence Erlbaum Associates, pp. 242–51.

Riggio, Ronald E. and Jay A. Conger. 2007. 'Getting it right – the practice of leadership'. In *The Practice of Leadership – Developing the Next Generation of Leaders*, eds. Jay A. Conger and Ronald E. Riggio. San Francisco: Jossey-Bass, pp. 331–44.

Riha, Rado. 2005. *Utemeljitev metafizike nravi – Uvodna študija*. Ljubljana: Založba ZRC, ZRC SAZU.

Robbins, Stephen P. and Nancy Langton. 2003. *Organizational Behaviour: Concepts, Controversies, Applications*, 3rd Canadian edn. Toronto: Pearson Education Canada Inc.

Rousseau, Jean-Jacques. 1993. *Razprava o izvoru in temeljih neenakosti med ljudmi*. Ljubljana: Študentska organizacija Univerze v Ljubljani.

Rousseau, Jean-Jacques. 2001. *Družbena Pogodba*. Ljubljana: Krtina-Knjižna zbirka Temeljna dela.

Rowe, Jimmy and Charles Kellam. 2011. 'Ethics and moral development: core ingredients of a compliance culture'. *Home Health Care Management and Practice* 23(1): 55–9.

Russell, Robert F. 2001. 'The role of values in servant leadership'. *Leadership and Organization Development Journal* 22(2): 76–83.

Russell, Robert F. and A. Gregory Stone. 2002. 'A review of servant leadership attributes: developing a practical model'. *Leadership and Organization Development Journal* 23(3): 145–57.

Šajković, Radmila. 2004. *Etika – Uvodna študija*. Ljubljana: Slovenska matica.

Sarros, James C. and Brian K. Cooper. 2006. 'Building character: a leadership essential'. *Journal of Business and Psychology* 21(1): 1–22.

Sarros, James C., Brian K. Cooper and Joseph C. Santora. 2011. 'Leadership vision, organizational culture, and support for innovation in not-for-profit and for-profit organizations'. *Leadership and Organization Development Journal* 32(3): 291–309.

Schafer, Joseph A. 2010. 'Effective leaders and leadership in policing: traits, assessment, development, and expansion'. *Policing: An International Journal of Police Strategies and Management* 33(4): 644–63.

Schermerhorn, John R. Jr. 2008. *Management*. Hoboken: John Wiley & Sons, Inc.

Schermerhorn, John R. Jr., James G. Hunt, Richard N. Osborn and Mary Uhl-Bien. 2008. *Organizational Behavior*, 11th edn. Hoboken: John Wiley & Sons, Inc.

Schneider, Sherry K. and George M. Winnette. 2011. 'Servant leadership versus transformational leadership in voluntary service organizations'. *Leadership and Organization Development Journal* 32(1): 60–77.

Schumann, L. Paul. 2001. 'A moral principles framework for human resource management ethics'. *Human Resource Management Review* 11(1–2): 93–111.

Schuyler, Kathryn Goldman. 2010. 'Increasing leadership integrity through mind training and embodied learning'. *Consulting Psychology Journal: Practice and Research* 62(1): 21–38.

Searle, Travis P. and John E. Barbuto Jr. 2011. 'Servant leadership, hope, and organizational virtuousness: a framework exploring positive micro and macro behaviors and performance impact'. *Journal of Leadership and Organizational Studies* 18(1): 107–17.

Sendjaya, Sen and James C. Sarros. 2002. 'Servant leadership: its origin, development, and application in organizations'. *Journal of Leadership and Organization Studies* 9(2): 57–64.

Sendjaya, Sen and Andre Pekerti. 2010. 'Servant leadership as antecedent of trust in organizations'. *Leadership and Organization Development Journal* 31(7–8): 643–63.

Sendjaya, Sen, James C. Sarros and Joseph C. Santora. 2008. 'Defining and measuring servant leadership behaviour in organizations'. *Journal of Management Studies* 45(2): 402–24.

Senge, Peter M. 2002. *Servant Leadership: A Journey into the Nature of Legitimate Power and Greatness – Afterword*. New Jersey: Paulist Press.

Shahin, Arash and Mohamed Zairi. 2007. 'Corporate governance as a critical element for driving excellence in corporate social responsibility'. *International Journal of Quality and Reliability Management* 24(7): 753–70.

Shannon, James P. 1998. *The Power of Servant Leadership – Afterword*. San Francisco: Berrett-Koehler Publishers, Inc.

Simons, L. Tony. 1999. 'Behavioral integrity as a critical ingredient for transformational leadership'. *Journal of Organizational Change Management* 12(2): 89–104.

Simons, L. Tony. 2002. 'Behavioral integrity: the perceived alignment between managers' word and deeds as a research focus'. *Organization Science* 13(1): 18–35.

Smith, Brien N., Ray V. Montagno and Tatiana N. Kuzmenko. 2004. 'Transformational and servant leadership: content and contextual comparisons'. *Journal of Leadership and Organizational Studies* 10(4): 80–91.

Smith, Jonathan and Andrew F. Malcolm. 2010. 'Spirituality, leadership and values in the NHS'. *The International Journal of Leadership in Public Services* 6(2): 39–53.

Solomon, Robert C. 1992. 'Corporate roles, personal virtues: an Aristotelean approach to business ethics'. *Business Ethics Quarterly* 2(3): 317–39.

Solomon, Robert C. 2004. 'Aristotle, ethics and business organizations'. *Organization Studies* 25(6): 1021–43.

Sosik, John. J. 2006. 'Full range leadership: model, research, extensions and training'. In *Inspiring Leaders*, eds. Ronald J. Burke and Cary L. Cooper. New York: Routledge, pp. 33–66.

Sovre, Anton. 2003. *Poslednji dnevi Sokrata – Predgovor in uvod*. Ljubljana: Slovenska matica.

Spears, Larry C. 1998. *The Power of Servant Leadership – Preface and Introduction*. San Francisco: Berrett-Koehler Publishers, Inc.

Spears, Larry C. 2002. 'Tracing the past, present and future of servant-leadership'. In *Focus on Leadership: Servant-Leadership for the Twenty-First Century*, eds. Larry C. Spears and Michele Lawrence. New York: John Wiley & Sons, pp. 1–16.

Spears, Larry C. 2009. 'Servant Leadership'. *Leadership Excellence* 26(5): 20.

Spears, Larry C. 2010. 'Practicing servant-leadership'. In *The Jossey-Bass Reader on Nonprofit and Public Leadership*, ed. James L. Perry. San Francisco: Jossey-Bass, pp. 116–23.

Spencer, J. Louis. 2007. 'The New Frontier of Servant Leadership'. Servant Leadership Research Roundtable. Available from: www.regent.edu/acad/global/publications/sl_proceedings/2007/spencer.pdf; accessed 30 May 2016.

Spinoza, De Brauch. 2004. *Etika*. Ljubljana: Slovenska matica.

Šter, Jože. 1994. *Kaj je moralno*. Ljubljana: Davean.

Strahovnik, Vojko. 2004. 'Uvod v vrlinsko epistemologijo'. *Analiza* 8(3): 101–18.

Strahovnik, Vojko. 2010. *Profesionalna Etika za Slovensko Vojsko*. Kranj: Fakulteta za državne in evropske študije.

Strahovnik, Vojko. 2012. 'Spoznavne vrline, integriteta in etika javne uprave'. In *Javna etika in integriteta: Odgovornost za skupne vrednote*, ed. Bećir Kečanović. Ljubljana: Komisija za preprečevanje korupcije, pp. 127–37.

Šumi, Robert. 2006. *Krepitev integritete policistov*. Ljubljana: Fakulteta za varnostne vede.

Šumi, Robert. 2007. 'Krepitev integritete policistov – Model dobre prakse'. *Varstvoslovje* 9(3–4): 186–95.

Šumi, Robert and Branko Lobnikar. 2012. 'Integriteta vodij v gospodarstvu z vidika njihovih zaposlenih'. In *Kakovost, inovativnost, prihodnost: Zbornik 31. mednarodne konference o razvoju organizacijskih znanosti*, eds. Marko Ferjan, Mirjana Kljajić Borštnar, Miha Marič, Andreja Pucihar, Mojca Bernik, Boštjan Gomišček, Eva Jereb, Tomaž Kern, Jure Kovač, Gregor Lenart, Damjan Maletič, Matjaž Maletič, Gozdana Miglič, Aleš Novak, Vesna Novak, Vladislav Rajkovič, Uroš Rajkovič, Matjaž Roblek, Marjan Senegačnik, Branislav Šmitek, Polona Šprajc, Benjamin Urh, Marko Urh, Drago Vuk, Goran Vukovič, Borut Werber and Fakulteta za organizacijske vede (Kranj). Portorož: Fakulteta za organizacijske vede, pp. 1233–40.

Tavčar, Mitja I. 2000. *Kulture, etika in olika managementa*. Kranj: Moderna organizacija.

Tavčar, Mitja I. 2008. *Management in organizacija: Celostno snovanje politike organizacije*. Koper: Fakulteta za management.

Tourish, Dennis and Naheed Tourish. 2010. 'Spirituality at work, and its implications for leadership and followership: a post-structuralist perspective'. *Leadership* 6(2): 207–24.

Tracey, J. Bruce and Timothy R Hinkin. 1994. 'Transformational leaders in the hospitality industry'. *Cornell Hotel and Restaurant Administration Quarterly* 35(2): 18–24.

Trevino, Linda Klebe, Laura Pincus Hartman and Michael Brown. 2000. 'Moral person and moral manager: how executives develop a reputation for ethical leadership'. *California Management Review* 42(4): 128–42.

Trompenaars, Fons. 2009. 'Back-seat drivers'. *People Management* 15(10): 26–8.

Trompenaars, Fons and Ed Voerman. 2009. 'Power to the people'. *Engineering and Technology Magazine* 4(6). Available from: http://eandt.theiet.org/magazine/2009/06/power-people.cfm; accessed 30 May 2016.

Trompenaars, Fons and Ed Voerman. 2010. *Servant-Leadership across Cultures*. Oxford: Infinite Ideas.

Trompenaars, Fons and Peter Woolliams. 2009. 'Rising from the credit crunch: a new model for future sustainability'. *Adaptive Options: When Change Is Not Enough* 4(1): 4–7.

Turner, Nick, Julian Barling, Olga Epitropaki, Vicky Butcher and Caroline Milner. 2002. 'Transformational leadership and moral reasoning'. *Journal of Applied Psychology* 87(2): 304–11.

Vaill, Peter B. 1998. *The Power of Servant Leadership – Foreword*. San Francisco: Berrett-Koehler Publishers, Inc.

Vicchio, Stephen J. 1997. 'Ethics and police integrity'. *FBI Law Enforcement Bulletin* 66(7): 8–12.

Vidaver-Cohen, Deborah, Lora L. Reed and Scott R. Colwell. 2010. *Executive Servant Leadership: A New Scale to test if Leaders Dare to Care*. Academy of Management Annual Meeting Proceedings Montreal, pp. 1–6.

Waddock, Sandra. 2006. 'Forging a path for ethics and business in society'. *Academy of Management Learning and Education* 5(3): 334–45.

Waddock, Sandra. 2007. 'Leadership integrity in a fractured knowledge world'. *Academy of Management Learning and Education* 6(4): 543–57.

Waddock, A. Sandra, Charles Bodwell and Samuel B. Graves. 2002. 'Responsibility: the new business imperative'. *Academy of Management Executive* 16(2): 132–48.

Waldman, David A. and Donald Siegel. 2008. 'Defining the socially responsible leader'. *The Leadership Quarterly* 19(1): 117–31.

Walsh, Andrew. 2008. 'Servant-leadership through engagement'. In *Servant-Leadership: Bringing the Spirit of Work to Work*, eds. Ralph Lewis and John Noble. Gloucestershire: Management Books 2000 Ltd, pp. 84–97.

Washington, Rynetta R., Charlotte D. Sutton and Hubert S. Field. 2006. 'Individual differences in servant leadership: the roles of values and personality'. *Leadership and Organization Development Journal* 27(8): 700–16.

Watson, Charles E. 1991. 'Managing with integrity: social responsibilities of business as seen by America's CEOs'. *Business Horizons* 34(4): 99–109.

Wayne, J. Sandy, Lynn M. Shore and Robert C. Liden. 1997. 'Perceived organizational support and leader-member exchange: a social exchange perspective'. *Academy of Management Journal* 40(1): 82–111.

Weber, Max. 2009. *The Essential Weber: A Reader*, ed. Sam Whimster. London: Routledge.

Webster's Encyclopedic Unabridged Dictionary of the English Language. 1996. New York: Gramercy Books.

Whetstone, J. Thomas. 2001. 'How virtue fits within business ethics'. *Journal of Business Ethics* 33(2): 101–14.

Whetstone, J. Thomas. 2002. 'Personalism and moral leadership: the servant leader with a transforming vision'. *Business Ethics: A European Review* 11(4): 385–92.

Winston, Bruce E. 2010. 'The place for qualitative research methods in the study of servant leadership'. In *Servant Leadership: Developments in Theory and Research*, eds. Dirk van Dierendonck and Kathleen Patterson. New York: Palgrave Macmillan, pp. 180–91.

Woiceshyn, Jaana. 2011. 'A model for ethical decision making in business: reasoning, intuition, and rational moral principles'. *Journal of Business Ethics* 104(3): 311–23.

Wong, Paul T.P. and Don Page. 2003. 'Servant Leadership Profile – Revised'. Available from: www.twu.ca/academics/graduate/leadership/servant-leadership/servant-leadership-self-profile.pdf; accessed 30 May 2016.

Wood, Donna J. 1991. 'Corporate social performance revisited'. *Academy of Management Review* 16(4): 691–718.

Worden, Skip. 2003. 'The role of integrity as a mediator in strategic leadership: a recipe for reputational capital'. *Journal of Business Ethics* 46(1): 31–44.

Yammarino, Francis J., Shelley, D. Dionne, Jae Uk Chun and Fred Dansereau. 2005. 'Leadership and levels of analysis: a state-of-the-science review'. *The Leadership Quarterly* 16(6): 879–919.

Yukl, Gary. 2002. *Leadership in Organizations*, 5th edn. New Jersey: Prentice-Hall International.

Zupančič, Boštjan. M. 1993. *Kratka zgodovina etike – Predgovor*. Ljubljana: Znanstveno in publicistično središče.

Žalec, Bojan. 2006. *Odvisne racionalne živali: Zakaj potrebujemo vrline – Spremna beseda*. Ljubljana: Študentska založba.

Index

For Product Safety Concerns and Information please contact our EU
representative GPSR@taylorandfrancis.com
Taylor & Francis Verlag GmbH, Kaufingerstraße 24, 80331 München, Germany

www.ingramcontent.com/pod-product-compliance
Ingram Content Group UK Ltd.
Pitfield, Milton Keynes, MK11 3LW, UK
UKHW020955180425
457613UK00019B/691

* 9 7 8 0 3 6 7 5 9 6 0 6 4 *